The Great Fear of 1789

The Great Fear of 1789

Rural Panic in Revolutionary France

GEORGES LEFEBVRE

Introduction by George Rudé

Translated from the French by Joan White

PANTHEON BOOKS

A DIVISION OF RANDOM HOUSE, NEW YORK

Library of Congress Cataloging in Publication Data

Lefebvre, Georges, 1874–1959.
The Great Fear of 1789.

  Translation of La grande peur de 1789.
  Includes bibliographical references.
  1. France—History—Revolution, 1789. 2. France—History—Revolution—Causes and character. 3. France—Economic conditions. 4. Peasantry—France. 5. Panics. I. Title.
DC163.L413   1973   944.04   72–12379
ISBN 0–394–48494–4

Manufactured in the United States of America
by Halliday Lithograph, West Hanover, Massachusetts

First American Edition

9 8 7 6 5 4 3 2

Z49815

Contents

vi

Table of Maps

Translator's note : The quotations from Arthur Young are from his *Travels in France & Italy during the years 1787, 1788, and 1789*, with an Introduction by Thomas Okey, Everyman's Library, London, 1915.

The maps for this edition were drawn by Paul White.

Introduction

Georges Lefebvre's *La Grande Peur de 1789* – *The Great Fear of 1789* – was published in 1932; it marks the culmination of a long stage in his evolution as an historian of the French peasantry and of protest 'from below'. This stage began with Lefebvre's early interest in the distribution of food supplies: his first major work on the French Revolution was his study of *les subsistances* in the district of Bergues, near Dunkirk, the first volume of which goes back to 1914. This was followed, ten years later, by his massive doctoral dissertation, *Les paysans du Nord* (1924), which led to a number of shorter studies on the peasant problem, including *Questions agraires au temps de la Terreur* and 'La Révolution française et les paysans', both published in 1932. Meanwhile, he had begun to interest himself in crowd psychology and had, over a number of years, been reading the writings of the French sociologists, Le Bon, Durkheim and Maurice Halbwachs. The outcome was a paper on the behaviour of the revolutionary crowd, 'Les foules révolutionnaires', which he first gave as a lecture to the Centre de Synthèse in Paris in 1932, the same year *The Great Fear* appeared and summed up, as it were, the results of two decades of scholarly research.

So *The Great Fear* is a work of mature scholarship and reflection and is, in many respects, the most original of the many works Lefebvre wrote in his long career as a professional historian. It is, moreover, a classic of the French Revolution whose publication in English is long overdue. Like the author's longer study of the peasants in the department of the Nord, it has been long neglected outside France – except, perhaps, in Italy where a translation appeared in 1953. [Not that the French themselves have, in this respect, so much to boast about. *Les paysans du Nord*, first published

in a few hundred copies at the author's own expense in 1924, was only
republished in French (without notes) in Italy in 1959.]

  The Great Fear is not a large volume, but within its pages it unravels a
situation of immense complexity. France, in the spring and summer of
1789, was being convulsed by the onset of the Revolution, by that phase of
it that Taine, a shrewd though unsympathetic recorder, described as
'*l'anarchie spontanée*'. It was a period of deep economic depression both in
the towns and countryside. The harvest had failed and the price of food
was soaring. Unemployed workers, displaced by the crisis in industry,
were everywhere in search of jobs. Villagers flocked into the towns,
thousands of them to Paris, to beg for charity or work. Vagrants and
beggars, always a source of concern to the small rural proprietor, choked
the roads and threatened reprisals against householders who refused to
give them shelter or a crust of bread. Hungry men and women invaded
forests and fields and stripped them of firewood or grain before the harvest
was ripe to be gathered. There was a widespread belief that the rich were
deliberately withholding their supplies of corn from the markets, and food
riots broke out in the winter and continued through July and August.
Meanwhile, a political crisis had come to compound the economic one.
The government, yielding to aristocratic rebellion, had agreed to convene
the Estates General; and so, among the people, a 'great hope' had been
born that at last something was to be done to relieve the hardships and
sufferings of the poor. But when the rulers defeated these early hopes by
their intrigues and resistance to the *tiers'* demands at Versailles, hope
turned to deep hostility and suspicion and the conviction grew that the
Court party and aristocracy were plotting to disperse the Third Estate by
force of arms, to overawe Paris and to send an army of 'brigands' and
foreigners to subdue the provinces. And to lend substance to this belief in
an 'aristocratic plot' came news of the fall of the Bastille and the dis-
bandment of royal troops and unemployed from Paris, followed by further
rumours as bands of soldiers and workless men took to the roads and
trudged back to their country homes.

  So France became gripped by an almost universal fear, shared by
authorities and citizens alike, the fear of 'brigands' recruited as agents of
the aristocracy (or, as some believed, of the Third Estate). 'Fear bred fear',
writes Lefebvre; and fear in turn gave a great stimulus to the revolution in
the countryside. Citizens began to arm in self-defence; municipal revolu-
tions took place in a large number of towns; and agrarian revolts, challen-

ging the right to exact tithes or seigneurial dues, which had already begun in the winter and spring, acquired fresh life in the latter part of July. They broke out over widely scattered regions: in the Normandy Bocage (woodlands), in Franche-Comté, Alsace, the Mâconnais, Bresse, Hainault and Cambrésis. They were directed against carefully selected targets, stopped short of the cities, and sought out the seigneurial châteaux and the hated manorial rolls. Whole villages, sometimes led by their *syndics*, or local officials, went on the march and hundreds of châteaux went up in flames – often, the marchers claimed, by the direct order of the King himself. But there was no indiscriminate destruction and only three landlords are known to have been killed. There were few criminals among the marchers, they were single-minded and knew perfectly well what they were doing; and as one magistrate said of the two dozen men whom he later sentenced to prison or execution: 'They seem to have gathered by common consent with the intention of destroying châteaux and houses, and freeing themselves from their rents by burning their charters.'

So there was a generalized fear, a municipal revolution, the arming of the people; and there were food riots and widely scattered peasant revolts. The Great Fear was related to and grew out of all these; but, Lefebvre insists, earlier historians have confused the issue by submerging the one in the others and have failed to see that the Great Fear had an identity of its own. Moreover, its relations with these other movements varied from one region to the next. Above all, it must not be confused with the generalized fear that spread, almost without discrimination, all over France. It was no longer a fear that the 'brigands' were on the march; now there was a 'total certainty' that they were actually at the door and were ready to break in. It was no longer a case of scattered pockets of fear spread far and wide over the length and breadth of the country; panic had now become focused within certain well-defined regions and, within each of its circuits of operation, it escalated, by a process of chain-reaction and contagion, from one town or village to the next. It had, adds Lefebvre, precise boundaries of both time and place: it began on 20 July in the West and ended on 6 August on the Spanish border in the South; and it was limited to half-a-dozen regions and by-passed some of the main areas of peasant revolt: Brittany, for example, was virtually untouched, as were Alsace, the Mâconnais, the Landes and Basque country, and the Normandy *Bocage* and the most rebellious regions in the North, Hainault and Cambrésis, were hardly touched at all. Why this was so he does not tell us very precisely, though he attributes the exemption of Brittany largely to the cool-headedness of the local authorities who refused to spread rumours and kept arms from getting into the wrong hands.

Earlier historians of the Great Fear, Lefebvre argues further, got their perspectives wrong because they failed to trace it back to its points of departure. There was no longer, as with the generalized fear with which it overlapped, a single starting-point in Paris. Now there were half-a-dozen of them, as many as there were identifiable 'currents' of the Great Fear. So at Nantes, where the first great wave of fear began on 20 July, it sprang from a rumour that a detachment of dragoons was marching on the city in the wake of the panic caused by Necker's dismissal a week before. In the East, it rose directly from the peasant revolt in the Franche-Comté. In the Clermontois, near the centre, it sprang from a fight between poachers and gamekeepers; at Ruffec, in the South-West, from a fear of beggars and vagrants on the eve of the harvest; and so on. Once launched in this way, Lefebvre continues, the Fear was transmitted by a great variety of means: by the authorities themselves, both lay and military; by well-intentioned individuals who might be peasants or priests or nobles; by postal couriers who carried it, often with remarkable speed, from one posting station to the next. The immediate reaction was almost everywhere the same: to spread a general alarm and a call to arms by the sounding of the tocsin. And from these 'original' panics (as Lefebvre calls them), there sprang 'warning' panics and from these in turn 'relay' panics, all stages in the progression of rumour and defensive reaction that carried the Fear for fifty to a hundred miles or more beyond its initial point of departure. Lefebvre sums up the progression of each of his half-dozen currents as follows: 'The Great Fear of Les Mauges and Poitou started in Nantes on the 20th; that of Maine, in the east of the province, on the 20th or 21st; the Fear in the Franche-Comté which set the entire East and South-East in a panic on the 22nd; in southern Champagne it began on the 24th; in the Clermontois and the Soissonnais on the 26th; it crossed the South-West from a starting-point in Ruffec [north of Angoulême] on the 28th; it reached Barjols in Provence on 4 August and Lourdes, at the foot of the Pyrenees, on the 6th of the same month.' And, to complicate matters further, some Fears were geographical extensions of other Fears and some cities and districts served as meeting-points for Fears that reached them from different directions. Thus Dijon was a junction for the Champagne Fear from the North and the Mâconnais Fear from the East; the Maine and Ruffec Fears, coming respectively from north and south, met at Loches, south of Tours; Toulouse was caught in a pincer movement from north and west; while Millau, near Montpellier in the South, had the distinction of attracting 'the greatest number of currents' in the whole of France.

And from all this bewildering confusion of myth and rumour, defensive reaction and orderly and disorderly activity, Lefebvre draws the conclusion that the Great Fear was not just an interesting psychological phenomenon, underlining the idiocy and irrationality of human behaviour. On the contrary: he points to the important historical consequences to which it gave birth. It forced the towns and newly created militias to organize themselves in a more efficient and positive manner; it linked the towns and villages and thus laid the basis for the Federation of the future; and, above all, it stoked up class hatred of the nobility, which in turn, gave an impetus to the progress of the Revolution in the provinces. In one region only it precipitated, instead of being precipitated by, a *jacquerie* or peasant revolt. This was the Dauphiné, where the attack on the châteaux and manorial rolls flowed directly from the arming of the peasants to meet the 'brigands' whom the Great Fear had conjured up but who never appeared.

So rumour, panic and fear, for all their irrationality and for all the reflections they cast on the frailty of human behaviour, are presented as a new and significant dimension in the historical process. This is the first and the most important lesson we learn from this book. As Lefebvre himself puts it: 'What matters in seeking an explanation for the Great Fear is not so much the actual truth as what the people thought the aristocracy could and would do'; and it was not so much what had happened as what the townsmen and peasants believed to have happened that stirred them into feverish activity. The experience, of course, has by no means been limited to revolutionary France in the summer of 1789. The fear of brigands – though never quite assuming the proportions of the Great Fear itself – revived in the French countryside and provincial towns in the summer of 1790 and again after Louis XVI's flight to Varennes in June 1791; and it was similar fears – of both brigands and Prussian troops – that preceded the prison-massacres of September 1792; and there were further rumours of prison-plots, causing similar fears and defensive reactions (though on a far smaller scale) in the summer of 1794 and in October 1795 in Paris. So, fear and rumour were potent springs of collective behaviour that marked the whole course of the French Revolution. But not the

Revolution alone. There had been earlier panics of a similar nature in the days of the Camisards of Calvinist Languedoc towards the end of Louis XIV's reign; there were the grain riots, or *guerre des farines*, of 1775; and there was to be the cholera epidemic of 1832; and, more striking still, the succession of panics attending the Revolution of 1848. In British history, as Lefebvre himself points out, there was something similar to the Great Fear of 1789 in the little-known episode of the terrors and panics of the 'Irish Night' that followed James II's abdication, when it was widely believed that the Irish Catholic troops had landed in the West of England to assassinate the new King's Protestant subjects. There were the rumours concerning English Catholics, assuming almost panic proportions in London and the West Country, at the time of the Gordon Riots of 1780. And in the 'Swing' riots in the English southern counties in 1830 rumour again played a potent role in stimulating the labourers to revolt. [Here there were also some remarkable similarities with the French peasant revolt of 1789: the same faith in the King as protector; the exaction of payment for services rendered; the appeal to traditional 'justice'; and rumours that mysterious 'strangers' were riding around in gigs.]

So far, however, historians have done comparatively little to explore such phenomena and to apply to their investigations the methods of Georges Lefebvre. In the first twenty years after this book's original appearance it would be hard to find any sign that, beyond a small group of dedicated Revolutionary scholars, it had had any influence at all. There have been some, though all too few, developments since. In 1951 and 1952, René Baehrel, a Frenchman, wrote two pieces on epidemics and terror in which rumours of the poisoning of wells and contamination of food by the rich stirred up violent expressions of class hatred among the poor. In 1958, a similar theme was handled by Louis Chevalier and a team of French and English scholars who studied the cholera epidemic in England, France and Russia in 1832. The same year (1958), Michel Vovelle published an article on the food riots that broke out in the Beauce in successive waves in 1792; and, before this, I had myself published the first of two pieces on the French grain riots, which invaded Paris and Versailles and spread through half-a-dozen adjoining provinces in the early summer of 1775. Here again, there were remarkable similarities with the peasant rebellion and small consumers' movement of 1789: a similar pattern of rumour, carried (in this case) from village to village and market to market; the same absence of any concerted plan or organization as of any 'conspiracy' hatched from outside; the same conviction that the King was on the rioters' side and approved what they were doing to bring down the price of bread and flour. And it was by asking similar questions and by applying similar methods to a broadly similar situation that Eric Hobsbawm and I attempted to throw new light on the English farm labourers' rebellion of 1830.*

But such work is, of course, only a beginning in exploring a territory that to all intents and purposes still lies largely unexplored. So, broadly, the challenge offered by this book to historians and social scientists is one that still has to be taken up. If they do so, they will find it is not enough to rely on the old traditional methods of either history or the social sciences – and least of all on the arid abstractions of the 'structuralists' or the antiquated crowd-psychology of Le Bon and his followers, which dismiss rioters without discrimination as 'mobs' and see 'conspiracy' round every corner. Statistical methods certainly have their place; and the much-abused computer may, in such cases, serve as an excellent tool for classifying, correlating, enumerating and bringing order to material which, if voluminous enough, may easily get out of hand. Moreover, the techniques of the geographer may be indispensable for plotting the topography of a complex movement and might, even in the present instance, have helped to answer more convincingly such questions as to why the Great Fear struck some districts and not others. So the historian of similar movements requires such help as he can get from his colleagues in the other social sciences. But, equally, there can be no substitute for the intense industry and patient zeal of the professional historian, which enables him (as Lefebvre does here) to chart in precise detail the course of a movement by noting the days, and even the hours, of its appearance: by such means alone can the old bogey of rampaging 'mobs' and ubiquitous 'conspiracies' be laid to rest, or at least be reduced to proper historical proportions. Let

* R. Baehrel, 'Épidémie et terreur: histoire et sociologie', *Annales historiques de la Révolution française*, XXIII, 1951; 'La haine de classes en temps d'épidémie', *Annales*, VII, 1952. L. Chevalier *et al.*, *Le choléra. La première épidémie du XIXᵉ siècle*, La Roche-sur-Yon, 1958. M. Vovelle, 'Les taxations populaires de février–mars et novembre–décembre 1792 dans la Beauce et sur ses confins', *Mémoirs et documents*, no. XIII, Paris, 1958. G. Rudé, 'La taxation populaire de mai 1775 à Paris et dans la région parisienne', *Annales historique de la Révolution française*, no. 143, April–June 1956, 139–79; 'La taxation populaire de mai 1775 en Picardie, en Normandie et dans le Beauvaisis', ibid., no. 165, July–September 1961, 305–26. E. J. Hobsbawm and G. Rudé, *Captain Swing*, London and New York, 1969.

us therefore hope that the appearance of this book in an English-language edition will encourage English-speaking historians to learn its lessons and apply similar methods of inquiry to episodes in their national history that have been neglected in the past.

George Rudé
Montreal, 1972

Foreword

The Great Fear of 1789 is an astonishing event whose outer form has often been described, but whose inner motives have never been the subject of a thorough investigation. To its disconcerted contemporaries it was a total mystery, and those who insisted on finding some sort of explanation for it had to fall back on the idea of a conspiracy, which they attributed either to the aristocracy or to the revolutionaries, depending on their own political opinions. Since the revolutionary party had most to gain from the event, the theory of a plot hatched by the Third Estate has proved the longest-lived and indeed still has its partisans. Taine, who had a sense for social history, discerned some of the events which caused the panics, but he used them only to explain the popular uprisings.

Historians of considerable merit have studied the Great Fear – M. Conard for the Dauphiné, Miss Pickford for Touraine and Provence, M. Chaudron for southern Champagne and M. Dubreuil for Évreux – but they have described the progress and the effects of the panic rather than its origins, and indeed in most areas it came into the province from outside; to trace the current of panic right back to its starting point would entail a different study entirely and could only distract the writer from the chosen subject of his monograph.

Existing studies are therefore incomplete, though of course as far as they go they are most methodically prepared. Unfortunately there are still all too few of them. It might be claimed – not inappropriately perhaps – that the time is not yet ripe for a comprehensive study, but it is surely not unwise to take one's bearings, for indicating the problems to be solved and suggesting their possible solutions must necessarily encourage further research in this field.

There were too many gaps in the available source material for me to restrict my research to the very few studies and documents that have been published. This present work contains a certain amount of new information that has come to light through my researches in the Archives Nationales, the archives at the War Ministry and the Foreign Office and the various local archives in the many *départements* and *communes* I have visited over the last few years: I have also found much material in the Bibliothèque Nationale and various provincial libraries. These archives are not always properly catalogued and the documents are often scattered; the Bibliothèque Nationale is far from possessing every available local history: moreover, though my research has been lengthy, it has even so been limited and there must surely be a wealth of information still to be discovered. I hope however that my contribution in this field will be of value and I am glad to be able to offer my thanks to all the archivists and librarians as well as their colleagues who have willingly helped me in my work; I also wish to thank the many people who have passed documents on to me for my information and am most particularly grateful to the following: Commandant Klippfel in Metz; M. Caron, archivist at the Archives Nationales; M. Porée, archivist for the Yonne *département*; M. Duhem, archivist for the Aube; M. Morel, archivist for the Ain; M. Hubert, archivist for the Seine-et-Marne; M. Évrard, librarian at the Institut de Géographie, Paris University; M. Dubois, Emeritus Professor at Confrançon (Ain); M. Jacob, the Lycée Janson-de-Sailly; M. Lesourd, the Roanne *lycée*; M. Millot, the Sarreguemines *lycée*; M. Mauve, the École Normale in Moulins. I much regret that it has not been possible in this edition to provide a critical apparatus or a detailed bibliography, but I hope one day to be able to publish the documents I have collected, together with the appropriate commentaries.

In the course of my researches, I began by reconstructing the currents of the Great Fear, indicating its secondary causes as I went along; I finished by going right back to their starting points and I then endeavoured to reveal their general causes. At this point, however, I wanted to produce a synthesis, not write a detailed textbook, and so in the account which follows I have travelled in the reverse direction. To reach the origins of the Great Fear, I have had to go back to the early days of 1789, but in looking yet again at the events of this period, I have tried to view them from the popular standpoint and I have assumed a knowledge of parliamentary history and contemporary events in Paris. It will surely seem right and proper that in seeking to explain the Great Fear I should try to set myself amongst those who experienced it the most fully.

Glossary

ateliers de charité	Workshops set up by the state to provide work for the unemployed.
bailliage	Administrative area comparable to the medieval bailliwick.
cahiers de doléance	The list of grievances drawn up by each of the three orders for presentation to the Estates-General.
fermiers-généraux	A group of financiers who in return for a special lease or bail (*ferme*) collected the indirect taxes and the income from the royal domains and royal monopolies. The *directeur des fermes* was the local agent concerned with this system of tax collection and the *bureaux des fermes* were the offices responsible for its administration.
intendant	An official in charge of one of the thirty-four *généralités* into which France was divided in 1789.
justice prévôtale	Military courts set up to deal summarily with local offences.
laboureur	A wealthy farmer, usually a figure of some importance in the village community and not to be confused with the *petits propriétaires* (small-holders), *métayers* (share-croppers) or *journaliers* (day-labourers).
maréchaussée	Mounted constabulary used to police the countryside.
procureur du roi	Special prosecutor attached to all the more important judicial bodies, sometimes translated as 'public prosecutor'.
procureur-syndic	The *procureur*'s deputy, a government official usually appointed by the local municipality.
sénéchaussée	A judicial area, possibly best rendered by 'magistracy'.
sub-délégué	Usually the local government agent.

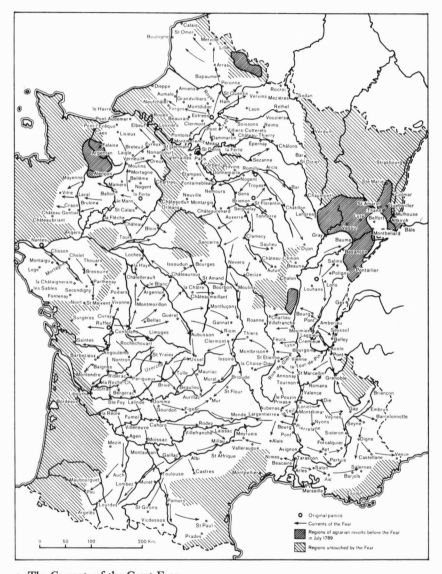

I. The Currents of the Great Fear

Part I
The Countryside in 1789

Hunger

'The people,' writes Taine in his *Ancien Régime*, 'are like a man walking in a pond with water up to his mouth: the slightest dip in the ground, the slightest ripple, makes him lose his footing – he sinks and chokes.' His description of the common people may be summary, but his conclusion is nevertheless valid. On the eve of the Revolution, hunger was the great enemy for the majority of Frenchmen.

No one has disputed the fact that in the towns, the workers, the urban *canaille*, lived in appalling poverty. In Paris and every other major city, their agitation at the slightest increase in bread prices caused grave concern to the authorities. The better-off earned from thirty to forty sous; when bread cost more than two sous a pound, there was unrest in those gloomy slums where they lived and which still survive in some French cities. As well as tradespeople and craftsmen, there was a vast floating population of unskilled workers and porters, a reserve army doomed to unemployment and swollen at the slightest crisis by crowds of vagrants and out-of-work labourers from the country.

What has been disputed is Taine's judgement on the countryside, where most outbreaks of the Great Fear started. Even his closest admirers have raised objections: that there were already many small landowners in 1789, that the peasants were by no means as poor as they made out and that the *cahiers de doléance** drawn up for the Estates-General were not to be trusted. 'A pretended poverty,' it was said recently, 'and behind the outer rags, a peaceful life, often comfortable, sometimes even affluent.' In point of fact, the studies of the *cahiers* which have been going on since 1900 have proved their accuracy, and detailed researches into the condition of the rural population now show Taine to be perfectly correct.

It is true that in 1789 the peasants owned a sizeable proportion of the land, possibly as much as a third. But this proportion varied considerably

* See Glossary on page 3 for specialized terminology not translated.

from region to region and even from parish to parish. In the Limousin, around Sens and in the south of maritime Flanders, it was about a half; only just over a quarter in the Cambrésis and just under around Toulouse. It was often less than a tenth or even a twentieth around the big towns – around Versailles, for instance – and in the forest, moorland and marshy regions.

As the country areas were much more densely populated than they are today, there were many families who owned nothing, not even their cottages or their gardens: this was the case for the Cambrésis and around Tulle where one in five owned nothing; it was one in four in the Orléannais; the proportion rose to two-fifths in the Normandy Bocage and to three-quarters in certain parts of Flanders and around Versailles where there was a rapidly increasing rural proletariat. As for the peasant landowners, their holding was usually extremely small; out of every hundred, 58 in the Limousin and 76 in the Laon area owned no more than five arpents, which makes less than two hectares; in what was to become the Nord *département*, 75 owned less that a hectare. This was not enough to feed a family.

The agrarian crisis would have been acute indeed if the farming system had not been far more favourable to the peasants than anywhere else in Europe. There were few priests, nobles or bourgeois who troubled to exploit their lands themselves. Unlike the country gentlemen of central and eastern Europe who could call on vast numbers of serfs for forced labour, the French upper classes leased out their land like English landlords; but whilst in England farming was carried out on a large-scale basis, here in France there were farms of every size, from estates comprising several hundred hectares to small-holdings, share-holdings and tiny tenancies only a few poles in area; most of these were farmed by poor share-croppers; many plots were even rented out individually so that journeymen could lease one small patch of field or meadow and small landowners could find a means to round off their property. In this way, the number of those who had nothing to farm was reduced, often to a considerable extent. But even if the problem was lessened, it was by no means completely solved, for the great majority of these farms were not able to support a family either: in the North, 60 to 70 out of every 100 held less than one hectare and 20 to 25 had less than five.

The situation grew worse and worse because the population increased steadily except in a few areas like inland Brittany which was ravaged by epidemics. Between 1770 and 1790, France seems to have acquired an additional two million inhabitants. 'The number of our children plunges us into despair,' the villagers of La Caure in the Châlons *bailliage* wrote in their *cahiers de doléance*, 'we do not have the means to feed or clothe them; many of us have eight and nine children.' The number of peasants who held no land, neither by freehold nor leasehold, thus increased and as from this time onwards land owned by commoners was frequently divided among the heirs at the death of the owner, rural holdings were split up into smaller and smaller units. In Lorraine, the *cahiers* often indicate that the *laboureurs*, i.e. peasants working an average-sized farm, were growing fewer in number. At the end of the *ancien régime*, people everywhere were searching for land; the poor took over the common land, overran forests, open country and the borders of marshland; they complained about the privileged classes who used bailiffs and foremen to farm their land; they demanded the sale or even the free distribution of the king's estates and sometimes of the clergy's property too; there was a very strong movement against the existence of the great estates, for their division into small lots would have provided work for many families.

All men who had no land of their own needed work; all those who did not have enough land to support them needed additional income. Where could this be found? Those with either initiative or luck became merchants or craftsmen. In some villages and more especially in the small towns, there were millers, inn-keepers and tavern-keepers, egg merchants, seedsmen or corn-chandlers; there were distillers in the South and the Centre, brewers in the North; tanners were less common, but cart-wrights, harness-makers, farriers and clog-makers more frequent. Building works provided employment for some, as did quarries, brickworks and tileries. But the vast majority was reduced to seeking for work on the great estates: the *cahiers* of seven parishes in the Vic *bailliage* in Lorraine show that there were 82 labourers for every 100 head of population; there were 64 in every 100 in the *bailliage* of Troyes. Except at harvest-time and grape-gathering, there was no readily available work; in winter, only a few beaters were taken on and almost every labourer was out of work. Wages were therefore very low and lagged very far behind food prices which rose constantly in the years before the Revolution. It was only when the harvest was actually ready that they could try to force the masters' hand; then there were frequent clashes, especially around Paris, and these provide an explanation for certain incidents of the Great Fear. In the North, agricultural workers earned at best twelve to fifteen sous and their food, but often it was less than ten and in the winter it might be only five or six. Those who owned a little land managed as best they could in the good years, especially if they were able to fix up their children with jobs as ploughboys, shepherds or farm servants, but ordinary labourers were doomed to perpetual poverty, as witnessed by many a moving passage in the *cahiers*. 'Sire king,' cried the peasants of Champniers in Angoulême, 'if only you knew what was happening in France and what great misery and poverty your humble people suffer!'

Luckily, in certain areas rural industry offered an extra means of supplementing income. Merchants had been quick to take advantage of this large labour force willing to work for ludicrous wages. Almost all the spinning and a large part of the weaving and knitted goods industries had been moved into the villages of Flanders, Picardy, Champagne, Maine, Brittany, Normandy and Languedoc. The peasants were provided with raw materials and sometimes with equipment as well; the man sat weaving in his cottage whilst his wife and children ceaselessly spun; when it was time to work in the fields, he left his loom. The metallurgical and glass industries were still country-based because they could thrive only alongside the forests which fed their furnaces and provided work for a whole army of woodcutters and charcoal burners. There was in addition a steady movement towards the towns if for any reason an industry could not or would not move outside: a whole contingent of seasonal workers came into Nantes and left again every spring; in Troyes, in October 1788, there must have been over ten thousand unemployed, but six thousand of these were people from elsewhere who moved on as soon as work grew short. Of course, industrial wages were just as low as any others. In the North, skilled workers earned twenty-five to forty sous, without food; assistants and labourers fifteen to twenty; the *mulquinier* who wove batiste could earn twenty sous at the most; the spinner no more than eight or twelve. In 1790, a town council in Flanders declared: 'It is certain that a man who earns only twenty sous a day cannot feed a large family; he who has only fifteen sous a day is poor indeed.'

Right up to the end of the *ancien régime*, collective rights were a great boon to the poor peasants; they could glean as well as gather the stubble which was left standing high when sickles were used for harvesting and this was used for repairing roofs and covering the stable floor; the right of *vaine pâture* allowed them to send their cattle into the fields left fallow and also into the open fields after the second crop, often even after the first; in addition, many villages had the use of wide areas of common pasture. In the second half of the eighteenth century, however, these 'rights' had suffered considerably at the hands of privileged landowners and large-scale farmers enjoying government support. The countryside resisted as best it could. In *Les Paysans*, Balzac described the silent, never-ending wars the peasants waged against the usurpers and their men without acknowledging that the poor could not exist once they had lost their rights and their land.

All things considered, the greater part of the peasants managed to eat reasonably well in normal times only in fertile and hard-working provinces. This was progress indeed. . . . There were many more who were not so lucky and even the most fortunate were always at the mercy of the slightest mishap. And crises occurred all too frequently.

First of all, the future depended on the harvest. Even if it was a good year, there would be no lack of problems. Since they threshed with flails, corn became available only gradually, as the winter went on. Meanwhile, the sheaves often had to be kept in stacks since there were no barns. Dangers abounded. Meteors, field-mice, fire. They had to live on the 'old corn' till the last sheaf was threshed. If the harvest was bad, then the future looked black indeed, for the granaries would be empty next year and there would be a long and agonizing shortage till the new harvest was ready. This is why peasants and townsfolk alike grew angry when they saw merchants taking away the grain to sell it elsewhere: there was never enough old grain in reserve. They looked with equal disapproval on such agricultural innovations as the extending of meadows and orchards, the introduction of oil seeds or madder; the big landowners made good profits, but it meant less land for corn.

Wind and weather were not the only hazards the peasant had to fear. There were wars which brought increased taxes and laid the frontier lands open to requisitioning, to forced labour for transport and road works as well as to the violence of the soldiery and general devastation. Then again, the progress of industry, whilst it kept a considerable number of people in wages, at the same time left them at the mercy of trade fluctuations. France had become an exporting country, and war or famine in some distant territory, or some increase in customs dues or a new prohibition could plunge French workers into unemployment.

As it happened, all these individual calamities occurred simultaneously in the months immediately preceding the Revolution. In 1788 the harvest was appalling. Turkey had just declared war on the Austro-Russian coalition; Sweden intervened on her behalf; Prussia indicated her intention of following suit with the support of England and Holland and at her instigation Poland sought to throw off the Russian yoke. As a result, the Baltic and the eastern Mediterranean became unsafe for shipping and the markets of central and eastern Europe gradually closed. A final blow came when Spain forbade the import of French cloth and fashion itself became involved: lawn came into favour and silk went out of fashion, compromising the prosperity of the Lyons silk manufacture.

It is a sad and even pitiful fact that the policies of the crown contributed very largely to the aggravation of the crisis which played so important a part in the fall of the *ancien régime*. The edict of 1787 had removed all form of control from the corn trade; until then, all producers had been obliged to take their corn to market, but after the edict, they were allowed to sell direct to consumers; corn could be sent anywhere by land or by sea and it could even be exported with no restrictions whatsoever. The intention had been to encourage agriculture by thus guaranteeing profitable returns. But when the harvest failed in 1788, granaries were found to be empty and prices shot irresistibly upwards; they did not reach their height till July 1789; in that month, bread in Paris cost four and a half sous a pound and was even dearer in some areas: around Caux, it was six sous a pound.

During the same period, the government's lack of foresight caused a crisis in unemployment. In 1786, France and England had signed a trade agreement which made considerable reductions in the customs dues imposed on manufactured products imported into France. The idea was basically sound: it was considered vital to adopt the English 'mechanical systems' and it was felt that the only way to impose these on French industrialists was to force some form of competition. In the circumstances, it would have been wiser to introduce this plan gradually and preserve some suitable protection for national products during the adaptation period. This sudden opening of French frontiers to English industry (whose superiority was quite overwhelming) caused terrible distress. In 1785 there were 5,672 looms working in Amiens and Abbeville; in 1789, 3,668 of these were silent and this, it was estimated, threw thirty-six thousand people out of work; in the knitted goods industry, seven thousand looms out of eight thousand had no work. It was the same everywhere, in other industries as well.

If things had been normal, the crisis might possibly have been short-lived. As it was, export restrictions complicated matters considerably and at the same time the cost of living rose steeply: the crisis proved insurmountable.

2

The Wanderers

Begging was a natural consequence of hunger. It was the scourge of the
countryside. Was there any other course open to the disabled, the old,
the orphaned and the widowed, let alone the sick? Relief organizations,
scarce enough in the towns, were almost completely lacking in the country
and in any case there was no help for the unemployed: begging was their
only way out. At least one-tenth of the rural population did nothing but
beg from one year's end to the other, trudging from farm to farm in
search of a crust of bread or a ha'porth of charity. In the North, in 1790,
about a fifth of the population was so engaged. When prices rose, it was
even worse because regular workers got no rise in wages and could no
longer afford to feed their families. Not everyone was hostile to beggars.
Some *cahiers* went so far as to protest against their imprisonment: those
who had prepared them were probably small farmers who had gone
begging themselves in former times and who knew only too well that
begging lay in wait for them once again when they had eaten their last
sack of corn and sold their last pathetic possessions. The poorer the
village, the stronger the feeling of brotherly compassion. At the end of
November 1789, the inhabitants of Nantiat in the Limousin decided to
share out the needy poor among the better-off villagers who would feed
them 'and so provide for them until it be otherwise enacted'. But in
general the farmers, the 'coqs de village', the 'matadors' as they called
them in the North, were unwilling to help and complained bitterly in
their *cahiers*. There was a good reason for their anger against the tithe-
collectors, for part of the tithe was supposed to go towards feeding the
poor: but even after they had paid their proper share, there was still a
constant stream of beggars at the door. Helping the poor of the parish was
one thing – an official distribution of relief kept them and their needs well
in hand. But many of the poor and needy left their own villages and
wandered off for miles around. Such excursions made the situation worse.

Those who were strong enough took to the roads; strange and alarming faces appeared at the door: and fear came close behind.

The genuine beggar was joined by the professional mendicant. Exasperated farmers were quick to accuse them of laziness and one cannot truly say that they were totally mistaken. No one was ashamed to beg. Fathers of large families had no qualms about sending their children out 'to earn their bread'. It was a trade like any other. If the bread they were given was too hard, then it would do to feed the cattle. In the taxation rolls appear the names of 'landowners' and these are sometimes qualified by the description 'beggar'. It was traditional for the abbeys to distribute alms on certain special days. The Honfleur *cahier* says: 'Distribution day is a feast day; a man can lay down his spade and his axe and fall into a slothful slumber.' In this way, the clergy carried on the Christian tradition which considers piously perpetuated poverty a respectable state and even an evidence of sanctity. The mendicant friars confirmed this opinion. During the Great Fear, several alarms were caused by vagrants disguised as Brothers of Mercy, the fraternity authorized to beg on behalf of Christians reduced to slavery by the Barbary corsairs.

The general feeling of anxiety aroused by these beggars must have been increased by the movements of the working population. The people as a whole were a great deal more unstable than we sometimes realize. 'As far as they are concerned, nothing matters,' commented the Rouen Chamber of Commerce in 1754, 'so long as they earn a living.' Apart from the genuine journeyman who travelled the roads as part of his craft, there were always plenty of men moving around looking for work. Out of the 10,200 unemployed who were supposed to be in Troyes in October 1788, it appears that 6,000 had in fact already moved away, as we have noted earlier; some must have gone back to their villages, but many were probably wandering from town to town looking for someone to give them a job. The works in progress on the Canal du Centre, the Picardy canal and the Cherbourg dyke automatically attracted many unemployed and so did the *ateliers de charité* in Montmartre. But not everyone could be taken on and so meanwhile they begged. This was why the principal towns, and Paris in particular, saw their floating populations grow so inordinately in 1789. Discontent and the spirit of adventure also helped to swell the numbers. Farm servants often left their jobs without warning; farmers complained bitterly, but never seemed to appreciate that they treated their servants harshly or that despair and humiliation naturally breed instability. Others ran away to avoid military service. There was in addition the usual migrant population which ebbed and flowed with the seasons. Paris had a small army of building workers from the Limousin; there were Auvergnats in considerable number practically everywhere: the Saintonge tanners took on a good number every year and quite a few went over the mountains into Spain where they worked with migrants from the French side of the Pyrenees. A steady flow of workers regularly left Savoy: the local population in Lorraine complained bitterly of their numbers. It was especially at harvest-time and grape-gathering that these migrations were the greatest: down from the mountains and into the plains flowed the great mass of unemployed; from Basse-Bourgogne and Lorraine thousands of workers spread through Brie and the Valois; men from Breisgau and German Lorraine crossed into Alsace; they streamed from the Bocage to the Caen plain, from Artois to the maritime plain of Flanders, from the Causses and the Montagne Noire to Bas-Languedoc.

A fair number of pedlars travelled around the countryside. Many of them were genuinely honest traders who performed a most useful service since retail shops were very scarce in the villages; a typical pedlar was Girolamo Nozeda. During the Great Fear, he will be found in Charlelieu where he had been regularly hawking jewellery for a good twenty years. However, most of the others inspired little confidence. Every year a host of shabby hawkers came from the Normandy Bocage and travelled as far afield as Picardy and Holland selling the horsehair sieves their wives made at home; others peddled bits of copperware and ironmongery from Tinchebray and Villedieu; in Argenteuil, the *cahiers* complained about the men selling rabbit-skins; in the Boulonnais, they had seen more than enough of mountebanks and bear-leaders, not to mention travelling tinsmiths. The prior-priest of Villemoyenne wrote to the elected assembly at Bar-sur-Seine that they must have a care to 'put a stop to the incursions of this great gang of people who trail about with a pack on their backs and crowds of children – and their mothers – who are never away from our doors and even manage to get inside our houses. We priests are much pained to see these hussies who roam around with a variety of sturdy rogues, all packmen in the prime of life; they spend their time carousing in our local taverns; we know full well that they sleep with whoever takes their fancy, though for a certainty not a one of them is married.'

All these travellers, even if they were not beggars in the proper meaning of the word, would even so stop at a farmhouse and ask for food and a bed for the night. They were not turned away, any more than genuine beggars were. This was not through charity or good nature: the farmer cursed furiously behind their backs. 'Begging slowly and subtly undermines us all and brings us to destruction,' says the *cahier* for Villamblain, near Patay. But the farmers were afraid. Afraid of a direct attack, naturally, but even more afraid of anonymous vengeance, trees and fences mysteriously cut down, cattle mutilated and, worst of all, fire. Moreover, even if the farmer paid his tithe without argument, he had certainly not finished with the wandering poor. These vagabonds were not necessarily bad, but they often had only a modicum of respect for other people's property. What about the fruit on the trees? If it hung over the road, surely any passer-by could take it? And what was wrong with taking a few grapes if you were thirsty? Carters were not very scrupulous either; the Brie *cahiers* were most agitated about the men who drove the charcoal waggons from Thiérache to Paris: they drove their carts straight through ploughed fields, broke down fences to take short cuts and grazed their horses in the local meadows. Once they had started, vagabonds might go far, carried along by some sudden whim or the spur of hunger. When their numbers increased – as in 1789, for example – they tended to move around in bands and thus emboldened slid slowly into brigandage. The housewife would see them suddenly appear when the men had gone to the fields or to market; if they thought her charity meagre, they would help themselves to what they wanted, demand more money, move into the barn and settle down. Finally, they would start begging by night, waking the frightened farm with a dreadful start. 'About a dozen arrived in the early hours of Thursday morning,' wrote an Aumale landowner on 25 March. 'We have much to fear during the month of August'; and on 30 July, 'We cannot go to bed unafraid; we are much troubled by the night-time beggars, not to mention those who come in the daytime in great numbers.'

When the harvest time drew near, fear walked abroad. The corn was cut at night though it was barely ripe. Even before it was gathered into sheaves, bands of gleaners travelling from parish to parish hastened into the fields in defiance of the law. As early as 19 June, the *commission intermédiaire* in the Soissonais wrote to the Baron de Besenval asking him to send dragoons 'to ensure the safe gathering of the harvest'; on 11 July similar requests from the Calais town council were sent to Paris by the Comte de Sommyèvre, the military commander in Artois, and on the 16th he added: 'Requests for troops to guard the harvest are coming to me from all parts of Picardy.' On the 24th, a person living near Chartres wrote: 'The general temper of the populace at the moment is so highly charged that considering its present pressing needs it may well feel itself authorized to ease its poverty as soon as the harvest starts. They may seek more than the gleanings, their usual part – driven to the last extremity by high prices and shortages, they may well say: Make amends for our past misery; let us share and share alike when things are short; fill our bellies. . . . An eruption from the people could be as bad as a hail storm. Dire necessity considers neither what is right nor what is reasonable.' The administrators by no means dismissed these fears as groundless. 'You will see how important it is to make advance provision for measures which could avert a disaster terrible to envisage and which might end in incalculable ills,' Esmangart, the *intendant* for Lille, wrote to the war minister as early as 18 June. 'The whole question revolves around the awful fear that the harvest might be pillaged either before it is properly ready or else once it has been gathered. . . . It is all too certain that attacks of this sort have been planned in many cantons and all the local farmers are in a terrible state of fear – indeed we must prepare to meet this dread eventuality whilst yet pretending to believe that it does not exist.' But in spite of these precautions, reports did reach the towns, Paris in particular, and were instantly believed. Every day in July, there were reports of corn cut whilst still unripe or damaged harvests. During the Great Fear, exploits such as these were blamed on to the brigands.

Internal security was not helped by successful contrabandism across the local customs lines, for example on the Picardy-Artois borders, all around the *villes d'octrois*, especially Paris, and most particularly on the frontiers of those provinces where a heavy salt tax was imposed (*pays de grande gabelle*). For instance, salt was sold at 2 *livres* a *minot* in Brittany whilst in Maine, right alongside, it cost 58 *livres*. Temptation and rewards were too great – the poor could not resist dealing in contraband salt; a weaver or a mason from Maine who normally earned ten or twelve sous a day could take a load on his back and earn twenty to thirty *livres* a journey; women were equally eager to start smuggling; 3,670 were arrested around Laval in 1780. It was the same story in the Les Mauges area on the frontier between Anjou and Poitou. In 1788 the trade in contraband salt turned into a civil war: it was Mandrin's brigands all over again. A certain René Hamart, known as Catinat, formed a gang which started with ten men and swiftly grew to fifty-four. They attacked the local *gabelous* (salt-tax collectors). The peasants were naturally inclined to be full of forbearance for the occasional amateur smuggler, but professionals alarmed them. 'In the morning,' says one *cahier*, 'the smuggler rises from the straw where he has spent the night – usually without the farmer's knowledge – and he pays for his lodging by offering his contraband at some low price; he tempts the farmer or threatens him; if the fancy takes him, he will seize everything he can without a glimmer of pity for his hosts, especially if he comes from a distant parish, taking food, furniture, the farm money and often, quite shamelessly, the church's money too. And all too often, he kills in a fit of rage.' In an effort to restrict possible damage, the *fermiers-généraux* maintained a small army which was hated and feared even more than the smugglers. The *gabelous*, ill-paid and recruited from practically anywhere, were as bad as their worst opponents and committed even greater excesses with perfect impunity. 'By day and by night, in twos or small groups, but never alone, the *gabelou* descends on the farm, kills the barking dog, lets his horse loose in the fodder, in the second growth and even in the ripe corn. Everyone trembles at his approach; he threatens the men, strikes the women, smashes the furniture, opens everything, kicks over the chests and cupboards and finally departs, always loaded with stolen booty if some unlucky candidate for jail has not fallen into his hands.'

It is not surprising that such a crowd of beggars, hungry vagrants and amateur smugglers should have produced a few genuine criminals here and there. The judiciary itself must bear part of the blame; its workhouses were schools for crime where the poor rubbed shoulders daily with hardened criminals; one of its most frequent punishments was dismissal from the area of the court's competence, and those so banished naturally joined the vagrant section of the population. In Maine, horse-stealing – which had been the despair of Normandy and Flanders in the middle ages – was still prevalent. In Picardy and the Cambrésis, the *sommeurs* made extortion a popular pastime: one morning, a farmer would find nailed to his door a pack of matches and a 'summons' ordering him to leave a certain amount of money at some special spot – on pain of destruction by fire; if he called in the authorities, they would be able to find nothing: but the farm would burn down just the same. Most criminals preferred to work in gangs. Cartouche's was still very famous and in 1783 a similar gang was broken up at Orgères at the head of the Loir, but it re-formed and even during the Directory was still being talked about all over France; bandits of this type were operating even before the end of the *ancien régime* and regularly 'warmed their victims' feet' to make them tell where their savings were hidden. In the Vivarais, the insurrection against the authorities known as the Masques' uprising was soon put down, but small bands reappeared from time to time though their crimes were mostly of a minor variety. During Holy Week in 1789, a lawyer called Barrot was beaten up in Villefort, his house broken into and his papers burnt; this was exactly the sort of activity typical of the Masques, but these bandits went a step further: on 27 March, some parish consuls who were going to Villeneuve-de-Berg to elect deputies for the Estates-General were robbed and murdered. During this same spring, many other gangs of wandering beggars took to brigandage in various parts of the country. In March, forty masked men were seen in Dampierre near Paris; at the end of April, fifteen armed men attacked farmers at night in the Étampes area, demanding money, smashing doors and windows and threatening to burn the farms down. Troops were sent to deal with a gang of twelve or so armed men around Bellême, Mortagne and Nogent-le-Rotrou.

Even when things were normal it was difficult to keep proper control. The *maréchaussée* with its three or four thousand horsemen was far from adequate in numbers and many villages kept no official crop-watchers because they would have had to pay them; and even if they did decide to appoint guards, there was no guarantee that it would be worth the money – it was a job with too many inbuilt risks for anyone to do it with proper enthusiasm. The guards who worked for the lord of the manor were more efficient, but they were mainly concerned with poachers; since they were supposed to keep the peasants out of the woods, they were looked on as enemies rather than protectors. From time to time there would be a general round-up; statutes were enacted in 1764 and 1766 condemning persistent beggars to be branded and sent to the galleys, though others were merely sent to prison. Occasionally, an example was made: on 15 March 1781, the Paris *parlement* condemned four Picards to be beaten and sent to the galleys 'for stealing corn from the fields and during the harvest'. This intermittent severity was not particularly intimidating. Once the workhouses were full, the gates were opened and the whole thing began again. All that the king had achieved – and indeed this was no mean achievement – was to clear the brigands away from the highways. In any case, in times of crisis the police force found itself overwhelmed. 'For quite some time,' said the *cahier* of Saint-Viatre in Sologne, 'the laws have been ignored; beggars are appearing once again in the area.' 'My brigades,' wrote de Sainte-Suzanne, the *prévot-général* of the *maréchaussée* on 29 April 1789, concerning the brigand movements around Étampes, 'have been operating in this area since the end of last November, doing the job of twice or three times their number, trying to maintain order and keep peace in the market place so that the farmers could export their grain in safety; [they] are not sufficient in number or in strength to keep numbers of bandits out of the capital; [they] cannot be everywhere at once'.

If the peasant had been left to his own devices, he could have defended himself quite well: his fear was by no means a sign of cowardice. Rough, tough and violent, too often inclined to draw his knife, jealous for his possessions and little inclined to care about others, he would gladly have shot down anyone threatening him. If the police were better organized, commented the *cahier* of Mairé-Levescault in the *sénéchaussée* of Civray, 'we should not be obliged to spend the night armed to the teeth guarding our own property'. The public authorities were full of misgivings: firearms could equally well be used against the king's men or might fall into the hands of the brigands and, even more to the point, if a peasant had a gun he would use it for hunting, less for pleasure than for getting rid of the game which ravaged his crops. So towards the end of the *ancien régime*, the peasants were systematically disarmed at the request of their seigneurs, starting with Hainault and the Cambrésis in 1762 and 1771, Flanders and Artois in 1777; between 1785 and 1787 various provinces were disarmed at the behest of the nobles – Normandy (the Duc d'Harcourt), Guyenne (the Comte de Mouchy and the Comte d'Esparbes). On the night of 26–27 January 1789, the Chevalier d'Hangest called in the *maréchaussée* to invade the village of Rumigny in the Thiérache and seek for arms; the Attorney-General of the Paris *parlement* ordered similar expeditions during the night of 22–23 June in the Chartres area; at the same time, villages around the forest of Fontainebleau were systematically searched.

Though a general feeling of uneasiness prevailed, it would be wrong to think that this was everywhere equally intense. Some areas were particularly sensitive – for example the flat open country bounded by bocage, plateau or mountains. In the Auxois, they said sourly that nothing good ever came out from the Morvan. There was equal tension in the contrabanding country and on the forest outskirts, for the woods were full of woodcutters, charcoal-burners, smiths and glass-blowers who lived in a half-wild state, much feared and little known; here too all sorts of suspicious characters had their hideouts. This was typical of the forests of Perche around Laigle and Conches, of Montmirail in the Haut-Maine, the Braconne near Angoulême and the famous Barade forest to the east of Périgueux. In 1789, these forests covered a much wider area and were far more populated than they are today. There were no longer any chance encounters with the devil, fairies or Merlin the Enchanter, but there were plenty of wolves and evil-looking men; the fear of 1789 often crept out of their sombre depths.

Just because crime was rife in France in the spring of 1789, one must not think that the entire country was in a state of disorder. Crimes there were, but few of them were mentioned in the archive documents. The ones they listed were mainly threats, harassments and extortions. Taine's picture of the period is frankly over-painted. An artist rather than a historian, he liked to etch deep and had a predilection for the strong oppositions of light and shade which are a special feature of wood engraving. However, even though his description lacks the objective value sought by the historian, it is still true from the subjective point of view, so to speak, for this is the way the peasants saw their situation in 1789. They had no way of getting accurate information and were so ignorant and untutored that they were quite incapable of sifting out the truth from the rumours which trickled through to their villages, constantly exaggerated and distorted. Popular memory doubtless served to add credence, for the fireside tale preserves past memories far better than one imagines. For centuries, the countryside had been ravaged by armed men, half-soldiers, half-brigands, who came from God knows where and fought for God knows what. There were tales of villages burnt to the ground, women raped, men tortured and murdered, all the horrors of war so accurately portrayed in the engravings of Jacques Callot.

Lorraine and Alsace remembered the Swedes all too clearly from the Thirty Years War; in the North, anybody who disturbed the peace was called a *mazarin*, probably in memory of the French campaigns directly prior to the Treaty of the Pyrenees. In Picardy and Normandy, they still feared the *carabots*, active as early as the fifteenth century, and in central France and the Midi, the traditional bogeys probably went as far back as the Hundred Years War: in the Vivarais, one of the Masques' extortion notes was signed 'in the name of the English'. Nearer in time, people in 1789 spoke fearfully of Cartouche and Mandrin; they called the contrabanders *mandrins*. Today it seems surprising that at the end of July 1789 everyone was so ready to believe in 'the brigands', but the word occurs continually in contemporary documents. Even the government used it freely to describe both the hordes of beggars and the gangs of petty criminals, those who stole the corn as well as those who rebelled against the seigneurs; indeed the Convention took over the word and applied it to the Vendée rebels. And what was more natural than that contemporaries should have seen these brigands as an instrument of civil war, used by the privileged classes to crush the Third Estate? For a long time, there had been little difference between the soldier and the brigand, and people were still far from clear which was which. After all, did not the recruiting officers usually start their business with the rag, tag and bobtail of society, just as they had done when the Écorcheurs and the Great Companies ravaged France? Fear, that terrible spectre, the child of hunger, awakened memories best forgotten; it was not the only cause of the Great Fear, but it was the one which went deepest and which most stirred the hearts of the people.

3

The Riots

When things were short, hunger too started riots and in their train came a new or a greater fear. The people were never willing to admit that the forces of nature alone might be responsible for their poverty and distress. Why had they not stored away corn during the years of plenty? Quite simply because the rich, farmers as well as landowners, with the complicity of the merchants and the full cooperation of the king's ministers and other royal officials (who were always favourable to men of position and influence), had exported the surplus and sold it abroad for vast profits. When they told the peasant that bread costs must be high so as to encourage farmers to grow more corn and that this would in the end stop shortages and make things better for everyone, what could he do but shrug his shoulders? If the general interest demanded a sacrifice, why did he seem to be the only person making one? As far as he was concerned, this was a poverty-increasing policy which could only serve to swell other men's profits. Was progress possible only at the expense of the poor? In the eighteenth century, people were not slow to say so and even today there are plenty of people who still think so, but dare not admit it. But the poor would find it hard to believe: in 1789, they said again and again that they could not possibly die of hunger. If the government saw fit to let the price of bread rise, then all they had to do was raise wages too – or else make the rich feed the poor. Otherwise they would help themselves and have their revenge.

Necker, restored to power at the end of August 1788, hastened to suspend exports, make bulk purchases abroad and offer import subsidies. But the mischief had already been done. There was no famine, but it was too late to check rising prices. Moreover, everyone believed that the ban on exports was being evaded and that corn was being sold abroad as usual. That they exaggerated the gravity of the situation is certain; but that they were totally mistaken is not true at all. The corn trade was carried on at that time in a way that was bound to arouse suspicion and stir up hatred. Every day, heavy carts loaded with corn and flour travelled the roads; the farmer took his grain to market, the corn-chandler travelled from one market to another, the miller sought for corn to grind or else carried flour back to his customers, the baker looked for supplies and stocks bought by the king, the provinces and the towns moved slowly along the roads of France in never-ending lines. How could anyone die of hunger when so much corn was on the move? They were taking it away from the people to hoard it up in shops, or else they were moving it abroad to bring it straight back into France again and so earn the import subsidy promised by the government. How could they resist the temptation to lay hands on the corn when it was constantly trailed back and forth before their hungry, desperate eyes? There was only one way to allay the people's lack of confidence: they must draw up the strictest possible rules to govern the movement of corn. Already in November 1788, Necker had introduced the regulation requiring all corn to be sold in the market and in April 1789 he at last ordered proper crop returns and requisitioning. But even if the Artois Estates and some of the *intendants* (from Soissons and Châlons, for instance) forbade farmers and merchants to take their corn outside the boundaries of their jurisdiction, most administrators were much more interested in encouraging crop production and ignored most of the powers invested in them by the central government: they preferred each local town to buy corn and resell it above market price; like Necker, they sought to gain time without restricting the freedom of commercial enterprise too greatly. Disturbances were clearly inevitable.

The towns were more at risk than any other area and indeed there was continual rioting in the main population centres of France in March and April 1789. All statistics have some geographical and historical value and the following details relating to what would become the Nord *département* are therefore not without significance, though this region was not the most distressed area: a riot in Cambrai on 13 March, in Hondschoote on the 22nd, in Hazebrouck and Valenciennes on the 30th, in Bergues on 6 April, in Dunkirk on the 11th, Lille on the 29th, Douai on the 30th, Cambrai again on 6 and 7 May, Valenciennes, Armentières, Hazebrouck and Estaires some time during the month, Armentières towards the middle of the month, Dunkirk on 6 and 20 June, Valenciennes on the 30th. Some of these riots caused a great stir, like the one in Orléans on 24 and 25 April, but the demonstrations in the Faubourg Saint-Antoine on the 27th and 28th of the same month were especially alarming. On such occasions, what usually happened was that a few of the rioters were arrested at random and they were either hanged or sent to the galleys with very few formalities and of course as an example to all the others. This is in fact what followed the riots in Paris, Sète, Cambrai and Bagnols. On 24 May, the king was sufficiently alarmed to give the *justice prévôtale* the duty of repressing these disturbances. There was a short period of calm from the end of May and through June because there was a general expectation that the Estates-General would find some way out of the problem. Then in July, the whole movement burst into new life, in Rouen for instance on 12 and 13 July, in Sens on the 13th, Amiens on the 13th and 14th and during the night of the 15th–16th. Soldiers and *maréchaussée*, scattered uselessly about the town, rushed from one market place to another, usually arriving too late or in any case without being able to do anything useful. The rioters were busy stealing corn from the markets, the merchants and the *magasins publics* or else they were sharing it out at a price they fixed themselves. More than once, the police came to terms with the rioters: the soldiers shared the feelings of the crowd and were not happy with their strong-arm role. The intendant of Alençon wrote on 2 April that the *maréchaussée* were much in agreement with the local people and were anxious to see lower bread prices, 'they probably do not do all they can to prevent these seditious outbursts'; in Bellême, their sergeant even 'upheld the people's spirits by the warmth of his words'. 'I cannot hide,' said M. de Sommyèvre, the military commander in Picardy on 16 July, 'that the soldiers show little willingness or resolve.'

Contrary to usual beliefs, the countryside was no less agitated than the towns. Probably the large landowners and wealthy farmers wanted to maintain freedom of action and sell for high prices. Most of the peasants, though, were in full agreement with the urban population. Small farmers and share-croppers were soon short of corn and the day-labourers were even worse off than the urban population because the village councils were unwilling or unable to help them; the farmer refused to let them have any corn on the grounds that he was obliged to sell it in the local market, but the authorities here were reluctant to grant admittance to any person not actually a local resident. There was only one course left to them – to stop the waggons in transit and seize the sacks of corn and flour, paying either the appropriate price or nothing at all. The police could do nothing to stop them: only really large convoys were granted an escort and very often this was unable to offer adequate protection. After a riot at the end of September 1788, the *syndic* of Avoise near La Flèche wrote that they had sought for half a league around and not even for a hundred louis could they find a man who would drive a waggon loaded with corn. 'The people are so disturbed that they would kill for a mere bushel. Ordinary folk dare not leave their houses of a night-time.'

Between town and country, the market formed a formidable link which nothing should have broken. In spite of the 1787 decree allowing corn to be sold where it was grown and even before Necker revoked it, farmers went on selling corn in the market either through genuine fear or force of habit, though they nevertheless sold to merchants who came directly to the farms. And if the town clung to its market because it was the basic source of its food supplies and even more so because its livelihood was based on the buying and spending of its customers, the peasant clung to it no less firmly because it was after all his main source of entertainment. Arthur Young ridiculed the yokel who walked miles to go and sell a couple of chickens and waxed indignant when he saw him waste both his time and the small amount of money his goods brought him; he could not appreciate the psychological factor in these transactions. The market was also the event of greatest importance for all local consumers: principally, they bought their supplies of corn for the week or the month, took it to be ground, then cooked it themselves or else gave their dough to the bakers who cooked it for them. In a few big towns, in Paris particularly, people had taken to buying bread daily from the baker, but everywhere else the only people who bought daily were the poor who never had any money in hand for advance provisions. All over France the country labourers flocked to market; when riots broke out, they were not slow to join in and if the authorities tried to make them keep clear, they spread the disturbance further. Then they went back to their villages in a state of wild excitement and as they told the tale of what had happened, spread revolt among their fellows and fear among the farmers. 'It would be to our advantage,' the farmers of La Chapelle-Bénouville in the Arques *bailliage* wrote in their parish *cahier*, 'to put a stop to the rumours, excitements and seditious chatter on the part of the lower orders in the market place where the *laboureurs* are exposed to insult and forced to sell their corn at prices of the buyers' choosing'; 'otherwise,' added the Croixdalle farmers, 'we shall be forced to give up farming'.

But in spite of this apparent solidarity, town and country had many points of conflict. The bourgeois feared the greedy, ravenous country-folk who so gladly lent a hand to the urban rabble and they were afraid that once they had stolen the corn they would turn to the houses of the rich. On 22 April, the municipality of Bergerac announced to its colleagues in Périgueux that the peasants were preparing to come into town to fix the price of food-stuffs; on 24 June, Bar-sur-Seine took steps to 'ensure the safety of the shops in town and to avoid the conflagrations threatened by people from outside who claim that there is not sufficient bread in the markets'; on 13 July 'the country-folk' in Sens attacked and captured the corn store; on the 18th, in Amiens, the peasants came in a body to demand a share in the lower prices granted to urban consumers on the 14th; on the 21st riots were started in Lille by the arrival of bands of peasants who wanted to force the canons of Saint Pierre to distribute a third of its tithes to the poor; at Montdidier on the 25th, the militia were careful to disarm any peasants travelling to market carrying cudgels. The towns had much to fear from the countryside.

The reverse was no less true. The farmers constantly heard that the townspeople were threatening to come and take the corn by force if it was not brought to market. They knew that the town councils were trying to force the *intendants* to give permission for crop returns and requisitioning. They were even more alarmed by a series of sudden and apparently spontaneous expeditions which came out from the towns and went from farm to farm buying corn – or, more accurately, forcing the farmers to sell their stocks. During the disturbances in La Ferté-Bernard at the beginning of April, rioters spread all over the surrounding districts; in Agde, too, on the 17th, the insurgents 'broke up into groups and went off to disturb the labours of the country-folk'; on 1 March, the Alençon *intendant* reported that since the *laboureurs* had announced that they would no longer come to market now that corn prices had been fixed, 'the people say straight out that if the farmers do not bring their corn to market, then they will go and take it from the farms'.

In turn, though the peasants were eager to ransack the larger farms, they were not anxious to see the granaries totally emptied for these were their only reserves and they were much alarmed at the prospect of visits from urban rioters whose ready violence would affect every single inhabitant of the village, however humble. In its turn, the town terrified the country.

The big towns frightened the smaller towns because they announced that they would come and buy in their smaller markets and to that end they would send commissioners under armed escort. After 14 July, Paris spread much unhappiness and fear through Pontoise, Étampes and Provins by threatening to come and buy supplies.

Normally, the arbitration of the *intendant* and the intervention of the police force removed these threats and settled any conflict as well as possible but when the authority of the royal administration was completely paralysed, fear became universal.

Revolt engendered by hunger might readily take on a political or social form. Political because it was directed against the municipality, the *intendant* and his deputy, and against the government. In the first place, the king was very strongly suspected not only of supporting food-hoarders but also of secretly sharing in their activities so as to fill the treasury. The operations of the Malisset company to which the government of Louis XV had entrusted the victualling of Paris gave a firm basis to the idea of a 'famine pact'. It is pure legend that government ministers sought to meet the needs of the state by speculating in corn, but there is nothing more possible than that many highly-placed people took an interest in the Malisset company, expecting it to bring high returns, just as they schemed amongst themselves in the hope of being 'carried along' by a *fermier-général*, or that company agents speculated on their own account from the safe protection of their privileges. More than this, it is very possible that Louis XV himself invested in this particular enterprise with money from his own private funds. In 1792, the *intendant* of the civil list, M. de Septeuil, was to speculate on the falling exchange rate on behalf of Louis XVI by buying goods abroad. When Necker imported corn from other countries, all those who were entrusted with his orders or who agreed to hold stocks of state-purchased corn in the provinces immediately aroused suspicion. So too did the municipalities and the dealers who became their agents. The conviction that there was some malpractice was not restricted to the people, whose so-called stupidity aroused Taine's scorn. In Paris, the bookseller Hardy noted in December 1788 that the *parlement* had discussed food-hoarding without actually taking action against it and commented: 'The plan originated at too high a level for the magistrates to deal with it discreetly and sensibly.' Perrot, secretary to the Duc de Beuvron, the military commander in Normandy, wrote on 28 June: 'No one can rid me of the conviction that the *intendant* and the town council [of Caen] are the principal agents in this monopoly business.' On 26 September 1788, the mayor of Le Mans, Négrier de la Ferrière, accused the *maréchaussée* of taking bribes from monopolists. It is only too likely that remarks of this nature, almost criminal in their careless triviality, were common in upper-class society; overheard and retained by servants, passed around and constantly distorted, they could only serve to inflame existing passions. 'If they have no bread, then let them eat cake': there is no proof that the queen ever said these words, but it is very likely that some courtier may have found such a sally irresistible, without ever meaning it to be taken seriously. Foulon is not the only person who is supposed to have suggested that the people had better eat grass. At Lons-le-Saulnier, two members of the *parlement* were accused of having wanted to 'make the people eat grass'; at Sainte-Maure in Touraine, Turquet, *procureur du roi* for the municipality, and his son were charged with insulting remarks: 'that these beggarly peasants should be forced to eat grass and roots to stay alive, that they should feed their children on stone-dust gruel and that they should never eat their fill of barley-bread'. In Orléans in the year II, an old alderman was arrested for having said in 1789 (or so they claimed) that 'if all the little girls died, there would be plenty of bread', a remark exaggerated into 'all children should be thrown into the river because bread is too dear'. Many people whose quality, functions or more or less incorrectly reported comments laid them open to public censure were riot victims both before and after 14 July: in Besançon in March, several parliamentary councillors were robbed or had to flee for their lives; Bertier, the *intendant* for Paris, and his son-in-law Foulon were murdered in Paris on 22 July; so were Pellicier in Bar-le-Duc and Girard in Tours – both were merchants; the mayor of Cherbourg, who was also the *sub-délégué* and lieutenant to the *bailliage*, had his house sacked and owed his life to his speedy flight. Food riots disrupted the life of administrative, judicial and even governmental personnel.

One reason for the prevailing poverty was that it cost the poor so very much just to keep alive. There were loud and constant complaints everywhere about taxes; the *cahiers* bear eloquent witness. Direct taxes – *taille*, capitation and *vingtième* – grew and grew; in 1787, Brienne took advantage of the first meeting of the provincial assemblies he had set up to try and impose an increase in the *vingtième*. It was the indirect taxes which seemed particularly impossible to bear: in the *pays de grande gabelle*, the cost of obligatory salt amounted to 18 sous a pound; excise duties weighed hard on many goods, drinks in particular; tolls and market dues made no exception for corn. Royal taxes were joined by local taxes. It has always been maintained that the franchise enjoyed by provinces and towns brought considerable advantages to the people. Certainly, in parts of France which still retained their provincial estates, royal taxes were lower; the provincial oligarchy resisted the demands of the central power as hard as it could because any increase in taxes might reduce rents (*fermages*). But the local budget was managed in such a way that its full weight fell on the people through a system of indirect taxes which Taine considered most unfair – milling dues, the Provençal *piquet*, taxes on wine and beer. In towns, the municipalities did the same and drew their revenue from city tolls which increased the cost of living. Food riots were necessarily directed against taxes; the people refused to pay them, demanded the abolition of tolls, refused absolutely to deal with the agents of the *fermiers-généraux*. There being no public funds, the disturbances had the indirect consequence of depriving the king of his means of government and of further upsetting the administrative machinery.

The movement also had a disturbing effect on the structure of society. Royal taxes would have been less heavy if the privileged classes had paid their fair share. They would have been smaller still if the nobles had not encouraged the king to increase his personal expenditure. It would have been less unbearable if these same privileged people had not made additional levies on the peasant's income by the imposition of the tithe and feudal dues. When the tithe and the *champart* coincided (which to be quite truthful did not always happen) then the peasant lost a sixth or a fifth of his harvest. Tithe-collectors and seigneurs thus had a ready-made corner in the grain market and were attacked for the same reasons as the merchants. In reply to charges of this nature, they could claim that their barns were merely storehouses for their own surplus produce, but the peasants knew that many of them were only waiting for a substantial rise in prices. The administration realized this too and in moments of crisis would suggest discreetly that some stocks might be released to ease the market situation. In addition, the seigneur had the milling monopoly and he farmed out its taxes. The miller who ran the common mill indulged in a wealth of small demands to increase his own profits: he cheated over weight, charged special rates and above all took payment in kind, as did his master with the *champart* and the feudal dues; an outrageous paradox –

the dearer the grain, the heavier the feudal dues. And on top of this, there were the pigeons and the lord's game, all of which fed themselves at the expense of the peasants; around Versailles and Paris the king's official hunt and the princes' hunting parties drove people to despair: then of course, all the nobility had the right to hunt, it was their especial privilege and they abused it a thousand times. The peasant had redress only if he indulged in expensive processes of law of doubtful outcome.

These were only two of the feudal dues which directly reduced the peasant's meagre income. There were of course many others and to delve into their depths lies beyond our scope. Suffice to say that in moments of crisis they seemed worse than ever, all the more so since by the end of the *ancien régime* the seigneurs themselves were impoverished by the rise in the cost of living and the increased luxury of court life and they tended to insist even more strongly on their swift payment. Unable to manage their affairs themselves, they farmed them out and their new administrators proved even more rapacious. New registers were drawn up; rights long fallen into disuse were revived; arrears, often of considerable size, were demanded, though these ordinarily became invalid after thirty years. In several provinces, the larger landowners were granted enclosure rights and deprived the peasant of *vaine pâture*, without however ceasing to graze their own beasts on their vassals' lands. The king had granted a distribution of the common lands and they took one third. They endeavoured to suppress common rights in the forests for these had become extremely productive since the developments in iron-working and glass-making had made the price of wood rise steeply.

Desperate with hunger, the peasant was an inevitable threat to the aristocracy. The bourgeoisie itself was by no means secure. Their share of taxes, too, remained unpaid; they held a good number of seigneuries; they provided the lords of the manor with judges and *intendants*; as tax-farmers, they took over the collection of feudal dues. Great landowners, wealthy farmers and corn merchants all profited just as much as tithe-collectors and seigneurs from the king's agricultural policy which restricted the *droits collectifs*, so dear to the peasant, and which by its insistence on commercial freedom increased the price of food. As the people had no wish to die of hunger, they saw no reason why the rich, whoever they might be, should not put their hands in their pockets on behalf of the poor. Lawyers, *rentiers*, merchants, farmers and, in Alsace,

Jews were threatened just as much as priests and nobles. They too had reason to be afraid.

Town and country burst into open revolt, each stricken with a terrible fear of the other, and in the same way the peasant mobs existed in mutual terror. Those who revolted rarely accepted a refusal to join their band and were usually prepared to use force if necessary; they insisted that neighbouring villages follow them and threatened to loot or even to set fire to their houses if they refused to go with them; on the way, they stopped anywhere they fancied to eat and drink: there was no one however poor who would not share what he had with his rebel brothers, even though it vexed him greatly to do so. In Wassigny in the Thiérache, at the height of the May uprisings, the mob met with resistance. When their arrival was announced, the local peasants – who were themselves far from innocent in matters of resistance to authority – took up arms and fought to keep them out of the village; shots were exchanged; some were wounded, others taken prisoner. Every revolt presented the peasant with a double emotion: he wanted to follow suit, but at the same time the prospect of using force terrified him. The people was afraid of its own violence.

But the ancient monarchic and feudal structure had survived many similar crises and the reigns of greatest glory had not been short of jacqueries. King and nobles had always managed to lead the simple good-natured peasant back to his chains. Now in 1789 there came a piece of news so extraordinary that excitement knew no bounds: Louis XVI himself, in an unparalleled desire to save the peasant from his age-old oppression, had summoned the Estates-General.

4

The Beginnings of the Revolution
and the First Peasant Revolts

For a long time, men of reason had been suggesting that the king's finances should be reorganized. The distribution of the tax load was a challenge to justice and common sense: to justice because the richer a man, the less taxes he paid; and to common sense because the government's desire to encourage agricultural prosperity threw a heavy burden on to the peasant and made it impossible for him to save money, and without savings, there could be no development capital, hence no agricultural improvements. Few controllers-general lost much sleep over problems like these, though there was one which they were forced to take into consideration. They had to find enough money to meet national expenditure. This increased constantly. As the royal power extended its competence, it had to develop its bureaucratic apparatus, its *maréchaussée* and its police force. In addition, since prices went on rising, the budget grew ever larger. Finally, Louis XVI had taken part in the American war and it had cost him dear. Even if all his ministers had been thrifty, they would still have been forced to spend more and more. Unfortunately for the régime, contemporary Frenchmen could not accept this; they complained about the wasteful extravagance of the court, the increasing number of civil servants and the greed of the aristocracy. Clearly, Louis XVI could have made some savings: the court consumed unbelievable amounts of money; there were countless sinecures; as for the army, the officers alone cost as much as their entire regiment. It would however have been impossible to make any valid reduction in expenditure without an open quarrel with the aristocracy; it would have taken nothing less than a royal revolution. The ministers who wanted to try this failed miserably. Others borrowed or contrived a few petty taxes. Finally, in 1787, credit being exhausted, Calonne decided that the only way out of the impasse was a new tax giving a considerable return. It was obvious to anybody that he could get little out of the already over-burdened people. Calonne was no fool, far from it, and he suggested that the new 'territorial subvention' should be paid by the privileged classes as well. A fine reform indeed. . . . Though the greater burden would fall on the rich, the poor would still have to pay part of it; the distribution of the tax would none the less be absurd and only the treasury would benefit. The privileged orders were summoned for consultation in the form of an Assembly of Notables (but nominated by the king): they had every opportunity to defend 'the public good' and the result was Calonne's dismissal. When his successor Brienne reopened the project, the *parlements* offered the most insurmountable resistance. They demanded the calling of the Estates-General which was, they claimed, the only body authorized to vote new taxes. Finally the king gave in: the Estates-General was summoned for the first time since 1614. A similar conflict was in progress with the *assemblées provinciales* created by Brienne. They were provincial only in name, since they were in fact established on the basis of *généralités* (the area within the competence of the *intendant*) and their main flaw lay in the fact that the king had been responsible for appointing them. The aristocracy everywhere demanded the re-establishment of the old Provincial Estates elected by the three orders in the same way as the Estates-General. In the Dauphiné, they held an impromptu meeting in July 1788. The king capitulated and authorized the election of the old-style Provincial Estates in the Dauphiné, the Franche-Comté, Provence and several other provinces. Thus, noted Chateaubriand, 'the strongest blows against the ancient constitution of the state were struck by *gentilshommes*. The patricians started the revolution: the plebeians finished it.'

This totally aristocratic origin of the revolution which so many writers have been careful to leave unexplored explains the violent reaction of the Third Estate and gave rise to the idea of a plot hatched against them by the privileged classes, an idea without which the Great Fear would be difficult to understand. What did the aristocracy want, anyway? To win back control of the state. Its struggle with Louis XVI represented the last stage in a series of battles between the nobility and the monarchy which had started with the Capets. The aristocracy was a violent critic of despotism, it was said, and wanted to force the king to promulgate a constitution so that henceforward no laws could be made or taxes imposed without the consent of the Estates-General. This is true. But they nevertheless intended that the Estates-General should stay divided into three, each order having one voice, the clergy and the nobility being thus assured of a majority. Some even claimed that each order should have the right of veto, in case there should be a coalition of clergy and Third Estate against the nobility, although the composition of the Third was intended to be such that they would never have used this veto. The idea was for the deputies to be elected by the Provincial Estates in which the Third was represented only by *commissaires* of privileged municipalities whose members bought their places and were often newly-created nobles – or else aspired to be nobles very soon. The higher clergy and the Breton nobility never appeared at Versailles because the king had refused to agree to this demand; for the same reason, the Provençal nobles took no part in the election. If the king had listened to them, the deputies of the Third Estate would in the main have been chosen by the aristocracy in the same way that members of the House of Commons in England were basically nominated by men of privilege.

Much has been made of the offers of clergy and nobility to make contributions to the national expenditure from this time onwards. But let us not exaggerate: a very small section of these two orders was genuinely disposed to do so, but another minority took great exception to paying taxes like commoners; in Alençon, the privileged orders refused to write in their *cahiers* the required renunciation of financial exemptions and this is by no means the only instance. Others merely promised to help wipe out the debt and get rid of the deficit, or else specified that they would set their own contributions separately. In any case, the most generous, those who agreed purely and simply to pay their taxes like anyone else, went no further than this. The idea of a nation in which every citizen had exactly the same rights horrified them; they wanted to retain their honorific prerogatives, keep their rank and, with even greater reason, preserve the feudal servitudes. Masters of the state, they would have instituted a formidable aristocratic reaction. Many traces of this state of mind can be found in letters written at the end of the *ancien régime*. To a person living in Jarnac whose relation was apparently responsible for a movement against the use of the communal bakehouse oven, M. de Rohan-Chabot wrote in 1767: 'Your father-in-law was born a vassal of my father, yet not even vassal, for such a title is the right of the nobility, rather is he tenant and villein on my estate of Jarnac. Without the authority of the king, our common master, he cannot evade the slightest duty imposed upon him since time immemorial by the ancient possessors of the land which his fathers have cleared and farmed. He should know that I give way in little, and, since I am strong in my purpose, no good will come to him nor to those who join him.' 'The villages,' said the chief of the chancellery of the Duc de Deux-Ponts in Ribauvillé in 1786, 'are the natural enemies of their seigneurs in Alsace. . . . It is in our interest to feed them, but it would be dangerous to fatten them.' The newly-ennobled were no less recalcitrant. Mme Duperré de l'Isle, wife of the lieutenant at the *bailliage présidial* of Caen, wrote reprovingly to Camus on 9 July 1789: 'The Third Estate is everything, it is twenty-three millions against one; what madness! Whom do they include in their count? All the hired servants, workers, beggars, criminals in prison cells, youths, women and children? Take away this rabble and see what is left of their twenty-three millions. . . . Everything is in its place, every-thing as it should be, nothing wild, nothing base; three powers with the same rights and the same authority. Is there a true Frenchman living who does not weep to see this wild fury which seeks to sweep away our worthy laws?' And on 3 August: 'The ignorant and misled do not repre-sent the whole nation; their numbers are great but they lack both weight and substance.'

On the other hand, the upper bourgeoisie – men of finance, business, men living 'nobly' on their income – were not opposed to conciliation. In the Dauphiné, where on the whole the aristocracy seemed disposed to accept the principle of voting by head as well as civil equality, bourgeois and seigneurs made common cause and drew up the provincial *cahiers* themselves without consulting the rural communities. If this sort of agreement had been more widespread, the nobility would have kept its honorific prerogatives, its property and indeed a pre-eminent position in the state. But there were few *bailliages* like Bourg and Longwy where they agreed to draw up a common *cahier* with the other two orders. In Châteauroux, they refused completely.

The bourgeoisie – mainly the lawyers and, coming close behind, the merchants and craftsmen – returned blow for blow and a class conflict of extreme violence broke out all over the kingdom. At the end of 1788, an ever-increasing number of petitions asked the king to grant the Third the same number of deputies as the other two orders combined (*double-ment*) as well as voting by head. When this *doublement* was granted, the struggle was transferred to the Provincial Estates. On 6 January 1789, the nobles of the Franche-Comté rebelled against Louis's decision: they were nicknamed 'protestants'. Similar opposition came from the *gentilshommes* of Bas-Poitou meeting in Fontenay-le-Comte on 17 February in answer to the appeal of M. de la Lézardière. There was a particularly violent clash in Aix where the great voice of Mirabeau inveighed against the aristocracy which had disowned him and, more especially, in Brittany where on 8 January the nobles had rejected all reform for the Provincial Estates and had sworn 'never to form part of any administration other than that of the Estates, elected and instituted according to the present constitution'; on 27 January, civil war broke out in the streets of Rennes; the young bourgeois of the city had formed a federal pact and their brothers in Nantes and Saint-Malo set off to join them; on 17 April, the local *gentilshommes* in Saint-Brieuc swore yet again never to attend the Estates-General.

Until that moment, the people had been calm, especially in the countryside; the quarrels between the king, the privileged classes and the bourgeoisie did not touch them directly and besides, for most of the time they heard little of what was going on. But when the king decided on 29 January 1789 that the deputies for the Third Estate should be elected in each *bailliage* by delegates of the urban and rural communities, things took quite a different turn. The villagers had to form electoral assemblies; there was a very wide suffrage: all Frenchmen over twenty-five listed on the taxation rolls were allowed to take part. They were then invited not only to elect their representatives but also to draw up the *cahiers de doléance*: the king wished to hear the true voice of his people so that he might know their sufferings, their needs and their desires, presumably so that he could redress all wrongs. The novelty of the affair was truly astonishing. The king, the church's anointed, the lieutenant of God was all-powerful. Goodbye poverty and pain! But as hope sprang in the people's breasts, so did hatred for the nobility: in the sure certainty of royal support, the peasants, invited to speak their minds, reiterated with growing bitterness their present miseries and from the depths of their memory the stifled remembrance of past injustices.

Here and there the *cahiers* reveal unbounded confidence in the king and a fervent hatred of the seigneur. 'Thank God, we have no nobles in this parish,' said the *cahier* of Villaine-la-Juhel in Maine. 'They have four seigneurs, bloodsuckers all,' declared the peasants of Aillevans in the Franche-Comté. 'The Bretons are treated like slaves by the nobles and the gentlemen of the upper clergy,' commented the people of Pont-l'Abbé in the Quimper *bailliage*. But to consult the *cahiers* alone gives a very imperfect impression of the excitement aroused by the calling of the Estates-General. Most of the time, the peasants did not write down what they truly thought: and indeed they had every reason to be careful in this respect, for did not the seigneur himself usually choose the judge who would lead the assembly? Many peasants who were entitled to attend never came. And a great many more, servants in regular employment but living in their father's house, found themselves ineligible. Other documents are far more informative on the people's hopes and fears. On 12 July, Arthur Young met a poor woman as he travelled on foot along the Islettes coast; she described her poverty to him: 'It was said . . . that something was to be done by some great folks for such poor ones, but she did not know who nor how, but God send us better, *car les tailles et les droits nous écrasent*.' The rumour spread around Paris that the king was to allow free hunting on his game preserves; in Alsace, they said that no one needed to pay taxes till the deputies were elected: on 20 May, the *commission intermédiaire* had to deny this information officially. On 7 July, Imbert Colomès, the mayor of Lyons, ascribed the insurrection that had just shaken the town to the fact that 'all import duties were to be abolished by the Estates-General. . . . Inn-keepers took advantage of the occasion to put it about to the people that all customs dues were to be abolished and that meanwhile, in consideration of the meeting of the three orders (27 June), three days' free import of goods into Paris had been decreed by the king and that the same was to happen in Lyons.' 'What is really tiresome,' wrote Desmé de Dubuisson, lieutenant-general of the Saumur *bailliage* during the elections, 'is that these assemblies that have been summoned have generally believed themselves invested with some sovereign authority and that when they came to an end, the peasants went home with the idea that henceforward they were free from tithes, hunting prohibitions and the payment of feudal dues.' The same cries of alarm were heard in Provence after the March disturbances: 'The lower classes of the people,' announced a member of the Aix *parlement*, 'are convinced that when the Estates-General sat to bring about the regeneration of the kingdom we would see a period of total and absolute change, not only in present procedures, but also in conditions and income.' M. de Caraman commented as early as 28 March: 'The people have been told that the king wishes every man to be equal, that he wants neither bishops nor lords; no more rank; no more tithes or seigneurial rights. And so these poor misguided people believe they are exercising their rights and obeying the king.' And at the other end of the kingdom, the *sub-délégué* for Ploërmel uttered a cry of alarm on 4 July 1789: 'Tempers are so high that the threats I hear make me and all other sensible folk greatly fear the riots and disturbances which will surely follow the tithe-gathering this year. . . . All the peasants around here and in my area generally are preparing to refuse their quota of sheaves to the tithe-collectors and say quite openly that there will be no collection without bloodshed on the senseless grounds that as the request for the abolition of these tithes was included in the *cahiers* of this *sénéchaussée*, such an abolition has now come into effect.' In simplest terms, when the king appealed for the abolition of these heavy dues, the peasants believed that they would indeed be abolished and for this reason decided that there was no point in paying any further taxes. Well before 14 July, the privileged classes were faced with a strong community of resistance from the lower orders. When rioters attacked the seigneur of Chatou, a master locksmith was ordered to state 'if he belonged to the Third Estate' and as he replied that he did not, evidently meaning that he did not wish to take part in the riot, he was told: 'You say that you don't belong to the Third Estate; then we'll show it to you.' The election of the parish delegates had a further consequence in that rural communities now found themselves with leaders whose attendance at the *bailliage* assemblies had brought them into contact with bourgeois revolutionaries, a contact they were eager to maintain. Proud of their importance, and more especially if they were young, they played a large part in the agrarian uprisings. Moreover, when famine was general, the simple fact of gathering the peasants into electoral assemblies could only create natural hotbeds of revolt.

In the spring of 1789, risings caused by famine conditions were matched by a series of revolts against tax-gathering and more particularly against the privileged classes. The disturbances in Provence were typical of events all over the country. The prime cause was famine: as early as 14 March, there were riots in Manosque when the local people stoned and insulted the bishop of Senez who was accused of encouraging hoarding. However, it was the occasion of the electoral assemblies which provided the right opportunities. Marseille and Toulon gave the signal on 23 March. There was nothing too serious in Marseille, but in Toulon there was an out-and-out revolt, which can hardly be surprising when one considers that the workers at the arsenal had not been paid for two months. The revolt moved further afield, reaching Solliès on the 24th and Hyères on the 26th; in La Seyne, the electoral assembly was sent home. On the 24th, there was also a riot in Aix at the very doors of the assembly when the first consul rashly defied the crowds gathered outside and refused to bring down the price of bread. On the 26th and for several days afterwards the revolt travelled via the south and west to the centre of the province: Peynier, Saint-Maximin, Brignoles; then to the north: Barjols, Salernes, Aups; it even reached Pertuis beyond the Durance. The wave of rioting rolled as far as Riez where the bishop was attacked in his palace; there were outbreaks in Soleilhas to the east of Castellane. The storm was short but violent. Troops arrived at the beginning of April and now it was the people's turn to be afraid.

Everywhere, there was a general hunt for corn: the public granaries, merchants' shops, and the storehouses and barns of religious establishments and private persons were ruthlessly pillaged. The local councils were forced to lower the prices of bread and meat, abolish customs dues and the notorious *piquet* relating to milling dues. Here and there, the movement took a political form: in Marseille on 21 March posters had invited the workers who were excluded from the electoral assemblies to come and protest: 'It is right and proper that our opinion be heard; if you have courage, show it now.' Since the electoral assembly was closed in Peynier, malcontents demanded the appointment of another one so that they could vote too 'even though most of them were workers from the soap factories with no property'; it was the administration they were after: in Barjols, the consuls and the judge were forced to be 'town servants'; the people were the masters, they declared, 'and will see to law and order'; in Saint-Maximin, new consuls and law-officers were appointed; the members of the Aix *parlement* were threatened. Above all, the rebels attacked the privileged orders. Apart from incidents in Salernes, local priests were not troubled; but nobody was especially concerned with protecting bishops and religious establishments in general, much less the nobles and their property; the Ursulines were held to ransom in Barjols; in Toulon, the bishop's palace was ransacked; the mob forced the bishop of Riez to hand over his papers; the châteaux of Solliès and Besse were ravaged; the communal mills were destroyed in Pertuis; almost everywhere lawyers and agents appointed by the seigneurs were forced to hand over their archives, pay back the fines they had collected, and formally disclaim all their masters' rights; some nobles fled or were beaten up. In Aups, M. de Montferrat was murdered on 26 March because, it was claimed, he tried to resist. Once the disorders had died down, local tolls and the *piquet* were restored, at least in principle; but tithes and feudal dues never recovered from the attacks launched against them. 'They refuse to pay tithes and seigneurial dues,' announced Caraman as early as 27 March; on 16 August, the canons of Saint-Victor de Marseille confirmed that the peasants had stood firm on this point: 'Since the popular uprising at the end of March last, tithes and other feudal dues are held to be merely voluntary obligations to be discarded at will . . . ; most shepherds refused point blank to pay their tithe [on lambs]; as to the communal ovens, most people in the country have got around this by baking their bread in private ovens.' The rising began to take on a truly agrarian form: *vaine pâture* became a reality once again; herds of cattle and sheep invaded the seigneur's lands and sometimes those of other people too. Neither the bourgeoisie nor the rich peasants were spared; the mob wanted to be fed and very often paid as well. This was what they wanted in La Seyne on the 27th, saying that they had abandoned their work and could not be expected to take all this trouble for nothing.

There can be no mistake about the nature of these disturbances. Taine claimed they were the work of brigands. This is acceptable, but only if we make sure that 'brigands' is used in its eighteenth-century sense: that is, they were mobs of rioters disturbing the forces of law and order. But this is not what Taine meant. In the eighteenth century, the 'brigands' were not highway robbers or escaped galley slaves: the brigands were the lower orders of both town and country driven to attack the *ancien régime* by sheer hunger and a profound conviction that the king was on their side.

In the Dauphiné, trouble had been brewing for quite some time: as early as 13 February, the president de Vaulx had warned Necker that various cantons were refusing to pay their feudal dues. It is probable that the disturbances in Provence found a ready echo here and this is possibly why there were sudden uprisings on 18 April in three villages to the east of Gap in the Avance valley. The population of Avançon did not trouble to conceal from their seigneur M. d'Espraux, councillor in the Aix *parlement*, that they considered themselves well and truly freed by the Estates-General from all the dues they had hitherto paid; at this point, M. d'Espraux suggested that he should authorize the redemption of the dues, but with no success; wisely, he sent all his deeds and titles for safe-keeping in Grenoble. It was as well that he did, because in April his vassals, spurred on by famine and hunger, decided to seize the corn they had paid to him in 1788 and the affair instantly turned into an agrarian revolt of what one might call classic proportions, so often did the same type of revolt break out in exactly the same way right up to 1792. Things would begin to stir on a Sunday: throughout the whole period, this day, like feast days in honour of local saints and *baladoires*, was always a most critical day; the peasants would go to mass, then, having nothing else to do, would drift along to the local café: there was nothing like this for starting a riot. On Monday the 20th, the Avançon villagers formed an armed band and marched to Saint-Étienne, persuading the people there to go along with them to the Château de Valserres. D'Espraux was not at home. His house was invaded and searched from top to bottom, though on his own admission nothing was either damaged or stolen. The terrified servants offered drinks to the mob. They were forced to promise that by the 26th they would get their master to produce a formal renunciation of his rights, otherwise a new raid was threatened. The *maréchaussée* appeared. The villagers were totally unperturbed: they turned out the seigneur's share-cropper tenants and threatened to drive their cattle into the growing corn. The cavalry was called out. Everybody fled into the woods. When the local magistrates took a hand, the rebels had second thoughts and began talking about making amends. But d'Espraux said that he could not collect his rents: no bailiff could have served writs without a full escort.

Two villages further to the north (Passage on 13 April and Paladru on 13 May) decided without any sort of violence to pay no more money to their seigneurs if they did not hand over a proper deed of concession relating to lands held on lease. These decisions were printed and handed round. On 28 June, those living in the barony of Thodure issued similar claims. According to the president d'Ornacieux, the movement spread further: 'There is daily talk of attacking the nobility, or setting fire to their châteaux in order to burn all their title deeds. . . . In those cantons where unrest has been less sensational, the inhabitants meet daily to pass resolutions that they will pay no more rent or other seigneurial dues, but fix a moderate price for the redemption of these, and lower the rate of the *lods*; endless hostile projects of this sort spring from that spirit of equality and independence which prevails in men's minds today.' At the beginning of June, we learn that there was a rumour going around Crémieu to the effect 'that we must burn and pillage the châteaux'.

It was not long before a third insurrection flared up at the other end of the kingdom, in Hainault, the Cambrésis and Picardy. The electoral assemblies in the villages here had been extremely tumultuous; in Saint-Amand on 30 April, the day appointed for the general assembly of the *prévoté*, peasants had come from all over the district to lay siege to the abbey. In Cambrai, bread riots raged throughout 6 and 7 May and subsequently spread to the lowlands all around the town. As in Provence, the peasants went looking for corn in the large farms and in the abbeys of Vaucelles, Walincourt, Honnecourt, Mont-Saint-Martin and Oisy-le-Verger. M de Bécelaer, seigneur of Walincourt, was also forced to hand over some of his stocks. The riots spread into the Thiérache via Le Catelet, Bohain and Le Nouvion, reaching as far as Rozoy, then on into the Vermandois and right up to the outskirts of Saint-Quentin; parties of peasants from two to five hundred strong forced those who still had corn to hand it over at prices of their own choosing. There were similar extortions in the neighbourhood of La Fère and in June there was apparently a plot to break into the Carthusian monastery at Noyon. In this area, both bourgeoisie and rich peasants were treated in the same way as the privileged orders; the latter were alarmed to find their feudal rights challenged; around Oisy-le-Verger a dozen villages wiped out all the game in the region and announced that they would pay no more dues. At the beginning of July, when tithe-collecting rights went up for sale as usual in Flanders, disturbances broke out all around Lille: the canons of Saint-Pierre were attacked and forced to promise that they would hand part of the proceeds to the poor.

There was soon a fourth area of constant rioting in the Paris and Versailles region; many of the disturbances were caused by the ravages of the royal game: there was in fact much to endure, thanks to the general freedom of the royal hunt and the vast extent of the royal forests. The *sub-délégué* for Enghien acknowledged that it was famine that had thrown 'a sort of despair into the peasant's soul and that this was the cause of the trouble'. It had started in 1788 in the Prince de Conti's game preserves between Pontoise and L'Isle-Adam; during the early months of 1789, gangs of peasants broke into them and determinedly hunted the game. The lands of the Austrian ambassador, the Comte de Mercy-Argenteau, got the same treatment from Pierrelaye, Herblay and Conflans in the early months of 1789; Gennevilliers attacked the preserves of the Duc d'Orléans; on 28 March, two gamekeepers working for the Prince de Condé were shot dead; in May, the trouble spread to Fontainebleau and in June the queen's private preserves at Saint-Cloud were invaded. The woods themselves were laid waste; on 11 June, Besenval reported considerable damage to the lands of the Abbey of Saint-Denis near Vaujours and Villepinte; 'many of the richest farmers hereabouts now own four-horse vehicles which once belonged to the abbey and which they bought for ludicrously low prices from the local inhabitants'. In this area, there were very few acts of real violence; the main incident occurred in Chatou where on 11 May the villagers forced the authorities to reopen a public path which crossed the château grounds and which had been shut off by the seigneur.

In other provinces, there was not so strong a relationship between hunger riots and the anti-seigneurial movement; it was the latter which occurred most frequently. 'Agitation has spread from the towns to the countryside,' said the weekly *feuille* in the Franche-Comté on 5 January 1789, 'many cantons have decreed that all subsidies and payments shall cease until matters have altered. We are on the verge of a general uprising.' 'The hatred of the country-people for their lords is everywhere at a great height,' wrote the seigneur of Tahure in Champagne, on 7 June. 'Whole districts have organized gangs to hunt and kill the game in the Duc de Mailly's land in this province.' 'In many areas round here,' Imbert-Colomès wrote from Lyons on 7 July, 'many villages have refused to pay their tithes and the countryside is as disturbed as the towns.' At the beginning of June, the bishop of Uzès wrote to the king to beg him to order the peasants to allow the tithes to be collected as usual. At the end of May in Languedoc, the Marquis de Portalis complained of crowds gathering in Cournon-Terral and the seigneur of Bagnols tried to calm down his vassals by authorizing the redemption of feudal dues. The fears of the Ploërmel *sub-délégué* have already been noted; in July, the *intendant* for Rennes grew anxious in his turn; the Breton *parlement* had already given warning of growing bands of peasants in the bishopric of Nantes. In Maine, the parish of Montfort announced in May that they would no longer pay their rents: 'they have been paying them blindly for far too long and now have had enough'. In the same month, the Marquis d'Aguisy complained that there were a great many acts of violence in Poitou.

Contraband was on the increase, direct taxes were paid ever more slowly and here and there corn riots were accompanied by attacks on the tax offices: in Limoux they were destroyed during the riots of 3 and 4 May. At the beginning of June, the village of Biennet in the *jugerie* of Rivière-Verdun decided that they would pay no more taxes and informed the tax collector that they would kill him if he went on trying to collect them.

The pattern of the great peasant revolts was established as early as the beginning of spring; they were preceded by a long period of simmering agitation which spread unrest far and wide. A whole new cause of 'fear' had come to join the old ones: it was a splendid preparation for the idea of an 'aristocrats' plot' devised to return the peasant to his yoke and it was this which transformed the Great Fear into a national phenomenon.

5

The People in Arms and the
First Outbreaks of Fear

Growing anarchy soon left the authorities unable to cope. There seemed to be no proper appreciation of the dangers inherent in the riots, and efforts to put them down were sporadic and ineffectual; moreover, basic rivalries between the different legal bodies made their cooperation almost impossible. The fact that the disturbances were widespread left the army powerless; the troops were exhausted and too widely scattered to be much help. Lower-ranking officers and officers risen from the ranks were in general ill-disposed towards the nobility, for the 1781 and 1787 edicts tended to reserve senior commissions for the nobles, and the soldiers, usually drawn from the lower classes, were gradually warming to the people's cause. On 19 June, Besenval warned: 'Our excellent decision to try most cases by the military courts has turned out to be pointless, for the *prévôt* is hindered at every turn by the local judiciary who want to try the cases themselves. . . . These incidents are unprecedented; licence increases daily; there is a very real danger of famine and things may well reach a point where the troops will be unable to do more than defend themselves.' He could have added that before long, they would not even *want* to defend themselves.

In these circumstances, the town councils agreed with the bourgeoisie that they should provide their own defence forces. It has been suggested that the Great Fear was spread around deliberately so that the provinces would be forced to take up arms. We shall consider the possibility of this later, but for the moment we must note that from the spring and the beginning of summer onwards the general feeling of unrest, which arose from causes already discussed, provided the first reasons for general armament. Many towns had already been exempted from the *taille* because they provided their own local guard: they had their own citizens' militia. At the end of the *ancien régime*, these forces usually existed in name only and put in an appearance only as part of official ceremonies. The riots and the fear aroused by the unemployed and the hungry gave them a new lease of life. Where such forces were not already in existence, steps were often taken to organize them. As far back as April 1788, the municipality of Troyes had called out patrols to intimidate the workers; in Provence, the March troubles inspired most local towns to form their own militia; on 1 February the town of Gaillac decided in principle to raise a militia to combat 'the wildness of local ruffians'; in Poitou, the town of Mortagne organized a voluntary patrol against contrabandists; on 7 April, Étampes re-formed its bourgeois units; the same happened in Caen on 25 April, in Orléans on the 27th after the shops of a merchant called Rime had been sacked, and on the 29th Beaugency called out its volunteers. On 8 May, the market town of Neuilly-Saint-Front followed the example of its larger neighbours and ordered the formation of a town guard. On 24 June, Bar-sur-Aube decided to close the town gates at night and set up both guard and patrol. On 15 July, Amiens ordered the distribution of arms following a local disturbance and Sens, which had acted in a similar way on the 13th, shortly afterwards issued a decree appointing 'a military dictator'. As harvest time drew nearer, the rural communities demanded the right to bear arms and in Flanders a compulsory guard was mounted on the harvest from June onwards.

In the provinces, the authorities hesitated: Sommyèvre, the military commander in Artois and Picardy, was afraid to arm the people. In the towns, the militia was still composed exclusively of dependable bourgeois – or at least, they would be dependable providing that the political struggle did not align them with the National Assembly and against the royal authority; in 1788, however, Marseille had allowed younger men and citizens from the lower bourgeoisie to join the citizen bands, but their disorderly conduct led to the dissolution of the militia on 11 May 1789. The thorniest question was whether to arm the peasants. Generally speaking, the matter was left undecided. D'Agay, the *intendant* for Picardy, alarmed by previous orders, opposed Sommyèvre. In June the *bailliage* of Douai and on 3 July that of Lille issued orders that villages were to mount guard and sound the tocsin at the slightest sign of danger – a perfect way of spreading panic! Permission to bear arms was granted by various military commanders – d'Esparbès in Gascony and the Comet de Périgord in Languedoc; in Hainault, Esterhazy ordered all villages to mount guard on 12 May after the disturbances in the Cambrésis and asked the government to arm the general public. It comes as no surprise to find the Duc d'Orléans approving the precautions taken in his seigneurie of Mortagne.

It was not long before the disturbances brought the unexpected conjunction of nobles and bourgeois in an attempt to protect their property from the 'fourth estate'. In Caen during the month of April, they decided to arm conjointly; in Étampes at the end of the month, the nobles opted to serve in the militia. There was the same joint action in Provence – Caraman congratulated himself on 22 April: 'The peasants' attack being directed against everything which appeared dominant, the Third Estate was the worst treated since it was the nearest to them in station. This event turned the Third towards the nobles, though it was by nature strongly opposed to them, and their union against the common enemy which will continue indefinitely unless the nobility breaks it through misplaced arrogance will form one body from two classes which have hitherto never been united. This body will be composed of landowners and men of talent and we can be certain that the union will provide a basis for peace in the countryside.' The events in Versailles and Paris struck a hard blow at this union, but it managed to survive till 14 July: during the subsequent troubles it reappeared in the provinces far more frequently than is realized.

At the very first breath of trouble the town councils felt their grasp loosening on the powers they held through right of heredity, the corruptness of public office, the king's special appointment or at the very least his stated approval: the municipal revolution was about to begin. Every time there was a disturbance, the lower orders wanted to kick out the municipal officers. There had been a good example of this in Provence and the same thing had happened in Agde in April: 'The audacity of the rebels led them to want to turn us out of our jobs and to think they could appoint new consuls drawn for the most part from their own class.' Even more formidable was the discontent of the bourgeoisie who demanded reforms in the urban administration and wanted to spark it into new life by elections – which they hoped they would win. Without their help, the oligarchic municipality, ill-supported by the higher authorities, felt itself in great danger. In Châteaubriant, the electoral assembly had gone so far as to dismiss it from office. Here and there a few concessions were made: on 3 April, Autun appointed a supplies committee to collaborate with the town hall; in June, a permanent committee was set up in La

Ferté-Bernard; the king authorized the creation of an elective political committee in Tonnerre; the government was amazed to receive from Saint-André-de-Valborgne, a tiny town in the Cévennes, a petition seeking permission to set up 'a patriotic association' to pronounce judgement on disputes between local residents.

Of course, all these random precautions calmed no one; on the contrary, they seem even to have increased the general anxiety and indeed gave official sanction to the dangers which appeared to threaten.

Now when an assembly, an army or an entire population sits waiting for the arrival of some enemy, it would be very unusual if this enemy were not actually sighted at some time or other. It is the excitable individuals who respond to this sort of atmosphere, especially when placed in isolation or on guard duty, or when they feel particularly exposed or else when some responsibility suddenly lies heavy on their shoulders. A suspicious character, a cloud of dust, less than this even: a sound, a light, a shadow is enough to start an alarm. Auto-suggestion plays an even greater part and they imagine that they see or hear something. This is how whole armies fly into panics, usually at night, and this too lies at the origin of the panics which started the Great Fear. But in these conditions it would be extremely surprising if they had been confined exclusively to the second fortnight of July since the general agitation which led to the individual disturbances had developed steadily over a period of months. In fact, several incidents, which cannot be described fully or explained satisfactorily through lack of sufficiently detailed documentation, show that from May onwards there were many local 'fears' or outbreaks of panic.

Hardy, the Paris bookseller, wrote in his diary for 12 May 1789: 'Private letters from Montpellier announce that M. le Comte de Périgord, the king's commander for that town, had ordered everyone with the sole exception of priests and monks to take up arms for the common defence in view of the disturbing news that a number of brigands had landed near Cette in two boats apparently with the express intention of setting fire to the port.' This alarm, mentioned only in Hardy's diary, must relate to the uprising in Agde and if it seemed quite natural for the brigands to arrive by sea, this is probably because the people of Languedoc remembered very well those not too distant times when Barbary pirates roamed the Mediterranean. At the end of May, a rumour went around Beaucaire to the effect that while the fair was being held, the ruffians roaming the province were to descend on the town in a body and rob the merchants: this was probably the disturbances in Provence having their effect on the right bank of the Rhône. If we are to believe the author of the history of the town of Ribemont, the anarchy prevailing throughout Picardy which kept every person with money or property on tenterhooks seems to have started off a very typical outbreak of 'fear' at the end of June; a gang of soldiers broke into the Abbey of Saint Nicolas, forced the monks to give them drinks and then caused a great tumult. One of the monks managed to escape and rushed into town shouting: 'The brigands are here!' The whole town dashed out armed with sticks, pitchforks and scythes; they rushed to the abbey and saved the monks from the soldiers. At the time of the riots in Lyons on 1–2 July, the local people were sure they were being attacked by brigands; this is easily explained by the fact that, according to the correspondence of Imbert-Colomès, peasants from the surrounding districts were under the impression that all dues were to be suspended and rushed into town in full force, some to bring in their wine and others to buy whatever they lacked. They took part in a series of attacks on offices and the town gates. The bookseller Hardy wrote in his diary for 18 July, commenting on a letter written to his wife by a female relative in Lyons: 'All the young men in the town, some 3,000 of them, took up arms to stop the brigands coming in and to protect the lives of the citizens'; he added that there were three hundred dead and wounded, 'of whom very few were from Lyons itself; they could tell they were brigands because they still bore the marks of the branding irons and the lash. . . . They said there were four or five thousand of them laying waste all the towns around.' This way of presenting events will be encountered many times after the uprisings which followed 14 July; the municipalities tried to preserve the reputation of their citizens by insisting that they had nothing to do with the prevailing violence and that they were all the victims of ruffians from elsewhere; or alternatively, they argued that they were quite within their rights to carry arms since there were all sorts of suspicious-looking characters in the area, an argument intended to protect them should the authorities in Paris ask for an account of their activities; in either case, the stories went a long way towards convincing the least credulous that the brigands were not a myth.

Shortly afterwards there was a scare in Bourg where on 8 July the mayor and the first *syndic* told the Council in extraordinary session that 'panic has spread all through the town thanks to the news we learned yesterday that a band of about six hundred vagrants has come in from the duchy of Savoy, that they are thought to be moving towards Lyons and that it would be extremely dangerous if all or indeed any of them came into our town and committed acts of violence'. The news from Lyons had perhaps prepared the people of Bourg for some sort of panic, but the initial incident of which we know nothing must have taken place on the frontier with Savoy, and indeed a few weeks later something similar was to happen in the same area: M. Conard's study of the fear in the Dauphiné notes that during July everyone feared an invasion of Savoyards. We are here confronted with one of the first manifestations of the Great Fear: the panic probably started in the Pont de Beauvoisin area, travelling across the Dauphiné and Le Bugey as far as Bourg, moving from there to Trévoux where in July the guard was called out and the gates locked. Another very important fact is that for the first time a fear of foreigners is mentioned – unless of course the Montpellier rumour related to foreign pirates, which is quite possible. A few weeks later, there was talk of auxiliaries brought in by the *émigré* nobles; at the beginning of July, it is easy to see why the rumour specified Savoy: people thought of this particular area as a land of high inhospitable mountains, occupied by a rough and poverty-stricken population which every year sent ever-increasing bands of hungry, suspicious-looking immigrants into France; it was probably not the first time that rumours of a mass 'invasion' had gone around the Dauphiné and Le Bugey: Savoy too suffered from hordes of beggars and vagabonds, as one can well imagine, and between 1781 and 1784 there had been a systematic hunt for vagrants, with villagers searching the woods and inn-keepers denouncing strangers and people without passes. It is very probable that, having been flushed out of their usual haunts, these wanderers turned and headed for France.

It was fears like this, caused by incidents of the same type as well as others of a different nature, which combined to make the Great Fear. What constitutes the originality of the latter is the number of its constituent parts and even more (for after all this number was not so very great, as we shall see) their relative simultaneity and their extraordinary speed of propagation. Obviously, after 14 July, when riots of every sort were on the increase it was natural that, on the eve of the harvest, feelings of anxiety should run high and panics occur and multiply more freely than before. But the disproportion is such that it would be rewarding to find some additional explanation which would apply particularly to the second fortnight in July. A comparison with other periods might help, for the history of France has seen many other fears both before and after the revolution of 1789, and indeed so have other countries. Could there be some feature common to all which would throw light on the fear of 1789?

During the Camisard troubles in September 1703, a Protestant troop of a hundred and fifty men made their way into the Vabres diocese and from there moved into Castres, burning several churches and living off the land; they got as far as the borders of the Montagne Noire, then turned towards the diocese of Saint-Pons. This was the signal for a panic which gradually crossed the rye-fields, reached the Tarn in the north and Toulouse in the west and possibly went even further. Contemporary accounts show that its external features were exactly like those of the Great Fear: the tocsin would sound; each village would send a runner to warn their neighbours and ask for help; detachments of soldiers arriving to help the villages would be taken for enemies and messages would be sent saying that the incident feared had actually taken place. On 22 September, the Cordes militia set off towards Castres: 'When the inhabitants of Saint-Genest or La Poussié saw this great crowd of men passing by in some disorder and carrying arms, they became much afraid and shouted to Batigne's son from La Poussié who was working in the fields, telling him to hurry to Réalmont and say that some rebel fanatics had come and burnt down the church at Saint-Genest. It was between six and seven in the evening and this boy caused such a panic and confusion that everybody came out armed with halberds, pikes, spits and so on; they joined the militia in the market place; the consuls had logs piled up at the gates to stop anyone coming in: but nobody came.' The bishop of Castres fled, but the *sub-délégué* kept his head and brought out the militia; in Saint-Pons, the bishop ordered the populace to mount guard. On 29 September, the Maréchal de Montrevel wrote to the War Minister that calm was gradually being restored, but, he added: 'You can tell from all this how easy it is to stir up this province.' Why was the region so sensitive? Because they were convinced that the Protestants were armed not to defend themselves but to wipe out the Catholics and that they had an agreement with the foreign powers who had taken up arms against Louis XIV during the War of the Spanish Succession. This is why contemporary accounts saw this panic as the outcome of a plot and transformed its general features to make it fit into a legendary pattern; following this preconceived idea, there was an alarm; 'it was a false alarm, but even so it spread as far as Paris. The situation was explosive.' It was preserved in that form in popular memory; it was attributed to the machinations of William III, though he had been dead since 1702. In 1789, it had still not been forgotten and speaking on 1 August about the fear which had just disturbed the Limousin, Girondex, judge for the duchy of Ventadour, wrote from Neuvic: 'I am delighted to find that all this was a scare like the one started off by the Prince of Orange'; which incidentally suggests that the panic of 1703 must have gone well beyond the Dordogne. Similarly in Agen, Boudons de Saint-Amans noted in 1789 that the great fear was like 'la pâou des Higou-naous, the Huguenot fear of 1690' [*sic*].

In 1848, nearly a century and a half later, Paris proclaimed the Second Republic and instantly rumours flew around that the workers were fomenting riots: the blame was set fair and square on the *partageux*, those early communists who wanted fair shares for all and who, it was claimed, might invade the countryside and rob the peasant of his lands and his crops. In April there was an outbreak of fear in Champagne. Then came the street fighting in Paris in June: there was desperate anxiety everywhere. At the beginning of July, a panic swept through Calvados, Manche and Orne, right up to Seine-Inférieure. M. Chiselle has detailed documentation on this in his study on the latter *département*. It was 1789 all over again.

On 4 July at about eight o' clock in the morning, between Burcy and Vire, an old woman was walking to her field when she was alarmed to see two rather strange men at the roadside; one was lying down apparently exhausted and distressed, the other was walking up and down with a desperate expression on his face. The son of a local bailiff came by on horseback: she told him what she had seen; she said they looked frighten-ing, like brigands; he agreed, flew into a panic, clapped spurs to his horse and rode like the wind to Vire, shouting as he went that the brigands were coming: everyone who saw the two men pass along the road was con-vinced that they were dangerous. The rumour spread and grew with great speed; in Burcy, they said there were two brigands; in Presles, there were ten, three hundred in Vassy, six hundred in Vire; by the time the news got to Saint-Lô, Bayeux and Caen, there were supposed to be three thousand brigands gathered in the woods around Vire, looting, burning and killing. The local mayors who believed the rumours instantly called for help from every side: 'The national guard of Tinchebray,' wrote the mayor to his colleague in Domfront, 'with only five hundred guns, cannot hold out against the considerable forces poised to attack us and apparently increased hourly by every ruffian in the country. It is of the greatest urgency that the Domfront national guard arrive here with all speed by forced marches and with plenty of ammunition.' Less than seven hours later, the tocsin sounded for twenty-five leagues around. In Caen, the authorities delayed no longer. General Ordener, at the head of the local garrison and the national guard, set out for the attack, whilst more than thirty thousand men rushed to join him. As soon as they realized it was a false alert, they hastened to reassure the rest of Normandy which stood on the brink of mobilization. There was an inquiry and this is how we know exactly how the panic started: the two men were local people. The man with the desperate expression was insane; the other man was his father who was in charge of him. The disproportion between cause and effect was so great that at first the affair was thought to be some political manoeuvre. The party of law and order would have been delighted to put the blame on to the 'reds': hence the zeal and enthusiasm of the commission of inquiry. However, since the outbreak could only benefit the forces of reaction, the democrats blamed their opponents. At least, on 17 September Napias Piquet referred to the excitements of April during a speech in Champagne and commented on the peasants: 'They saw only too well that they had been deceived; they never set eyes on a single one of the desperate workers they were told were coming to rob and loot. *Agents provocateurs* who spend their time spreading rumours . . . dream up civil war.' For us, however, there can be no doubt. All these panics start with the fear of some enemy, the Paris revolutionary coming into 'the rich areas of the countryside to order everything to be held in common', and if 'decent folk' have a share of responsibility in the matter, it is because their fears of a democratic régime led them to use events in Paris for their own propaganda purposes and persuaded the provinces to accept the idea that they were threatened with looting and robbery. In such circumstances, the fears of an old woman were quite enough to start the hue and cry.

So in 1848 as in 1703, apart from the feeling of insecurity naturally aroused by the economic situation and prevailing political circumstances, there lay at the root of these panics the idea that one party or one social class was threatening the life and the property of the greater part of the nation, sometimes with the help of a foreign power. It is this fear, universal and everywhere the same, which gives local alarms (whose causes and importance may vary) their emotive value and their power of expansion. It was exactly the same in England when James II was deposed and everyone thought that hordes of wild fanatical Irish would invade the country to set him on the throne again: panic broke out everywhere during 'the Irish night'. The same happened in France in 1789; local alarms were absolutely inevitable and could be predicted from the start. But there were 'multiplying factors': the 'aristocrats' plot' feared by the Third Estate, and the unrest spread throughout the provinces by the July revolution.

Part II
The 'Aristocrats' Plot'

I

Paris and the Idea of Conspiracy

As soon as the three orders met in Versailles, they started arguing about voting by head and spent the next month and a half achieving nothing. Suspicion was quick to arise: if the nobles and the clergy persisted in their refusal to vote by head, then it was because they knew they could not win control of the Estates and wished for that reason to provoke its dissolution. The court was party to their plan: the queen and the princes were trying to force the king to dismiss Necker; a *coup de force* had been expected since 15 May. An informant whose reports to M. de Montmorin, the foreign minister, have been preserved, passed on some of the rumours circulating at the time: 'There is a general anxiety about the results of the Assembly,' he wrote on 15 May. 'Everyone is astonished to see troops arriving daily and taking up positions around Paris and the outskirts. Everyone notices with resentment that most of the troops are foreign.' On 21 May, 'many people fear the dissolution of the Estates-General'; on 3 June, 'rumour has it today that the Estates-General will not meet'; and on the 13th, 'the clergy, the nobility and the *parlement* have joined together to bring about the downfall of M. Necker'.

When the Third proclaimed itself the National Assembly on 17 June, no one thought that the privileged orders would give in: 'We expect the nobles to appear on horseback.' The temporary closing of the hall where the Third Estate was meeting led to the Tennis Court oath, and the subsequent royal session of 23 June showed that the king had decided to support the other two estates. In the event, Louis had to back down, but neither this nor the apparent union of the three orders could calm the prevailing excitement; it was suspected that those involved in the plot were playing for time, and thanks to their lack of enthusiasm and their attitude towards the Assembly, the majority of the nobles left everybody convinced that their submission was not sincere. On 2 July in Paris, 'everyone is talking about a *coup d'autorité* which the government has been organizing for several days with the assistance of M. le Maréchal de Broglie. . . . It is said that camps are being set up all around the town. Apparently a lot of foreign troops are being brought in, the bridges at Sèvres and Saint-Cloud are under guard.' Emigration was already a question of the moment. 'They say that the Comte d'Artois wants to leave for Spain if he cannot subdue the Estates.' From this to the idea that he would return with an army of foreign troops was but a simple step and it was one that was all too readily taken. A deputy representing the nobility of Marseilles was even more explicit on 9 June: 'Malicious tongues are saying that the arrival of these troops is a manoeuvre of the expiring aristocracy and the nobility . . . that the nobility plans to massacre the plebeians.'

There can be no doubt that many *gentilshommes* were not slow to utter threats. Montlosier tells that one day on the terrace at Versailles he heard a group of people, including the Comte d'Autichamp, speak with pleasurable anticipation of what joy it would give them to throw the whole Estates-General out of the window: 'They have tricked us once, but this time our knives are well and truly sharpened.' Others less violent made no secret of their hopes: 'We shan't hang you,' said M. de La Châtre kindly to the elder Thibaudeau, 'we shall just send you back to Poitiers.' As a matter of fact, the Third Estate endowed its adversaries with a skill and strength of purpose which they totally lacked; when the court stupidly dismissed Necker on 11 July, it had no preconcerted plan and in any case its preliminary preparations were by no means complete. But it had decided to act and if the people of Paris had not risen, the Assembly would have been doomed. The people made no mistake on this point, though what matters in seeking an explanation for the Great Fear is not so much the actual truth as what the people thought the aristocracy could and would do. After 14 July, everybody discussed with a wealth of detail the plan to 'clean up Paris' which the newspapers attributed to the Maréchal de Broglie. Gorsas's *Courrier* for 13 and 17 August was full of it: the town was to be attacked concentrically: bombarded from Montmartre, methodically occupied and sacked, the Palais-Royal being reserved for the Hussars; since the inhabitants of Franconville and Sannois had been warned – apparently – at eleven o'clock on the morning of 12 July 'that their safety could not be guaranteed if they took food into Paris during the night of Sunday to Monday', it was assumed 'that the plan to destroy us had been most definitely decided'. These are not the inventions of malicious journalists. All these writers were doing was summarizing the rumours which ran like wildfire round the capital from 13 and 14 July onwards: the secret correspondence published by M. Lescure relates them to 23 July. This indicates that the first panics started by the aristocracy's conspiracy broke out in Paris itself. Various official statements to this effect were recorded by the Electors at the time. At two o'clock in the morning during the night of 13-14 July, it was announced that fifteen thousand men had advanced into the Faubourg Saint-Antoine. During the morning of the 14th, there was panic everywhere; at seven o'clock, the Royal Allemand were supposed to be at the Trône *barrière*; soon afterwards they said that the Royal Allemand and the Royal Cravate were killing everybody in sight in the *faubourg*. Next, the army encamped at Saint-Denis was said to be advancing towards La Chapelle. At eight, then at ten o'clock the presence of hussars and dragoons was reported, still in Saint-Antoine. The night of 14-15 July was no less disturbed. The *Quinzaine mémorable* notes that 'rumour has it that M. le Prince de Condé really will enter Paris tonight at the head of forty thousand men, with the intention of massacring perhaps a hundred thousand souls'. Between midnight and one o'clock in the morning, says the *Annales parisiennes*, 'the hussars, who were probably only sentries on observation duty, brought the terror to its height by coming as far as the customs barriers, and crowds of terrified people came at least a dozen times to warn the town hall of an armed attack'. In the Rue Saint-Jacques, Hardy saw five or six thousand *gardes-françaises* hurrying to repel them. On the 15th, at eleven o'clock in the morning, the Assembly of Electors was once more plunged into consternation by the arrival of a postilion who had been sent on a reconnaissance by his district: he claimed that he had seen troops in Saint-Denis preparing for an attack.

The victory of the people brought little reassurance. On the 15th, after midnight, various people came to the Electors to complain that 'the king's actions are not sincere: they conceal a trap devised by our enemies to make us lay down our arms and be more vulnerable to attack'. The rumours got worse. Very early on, it was believed that the meeting hall of the Estates-General had been mined and when the château de Quincey near Vesoul blew up – more of this later – there could no longer be any doubts. On the night of 2-3 August, an official search was made of the cellars beneath the stables belonging to the Comte d'Artois which, it was said, were the starting point for a network of tunnels. As the *gardes-françaises* had declared for the people, they believed that the aristocrats would seek revenge against them, and on 18 and 19 July rumour said that they had been poisoned; one of them was suddenly struck with violent stomach pains in the street, thought he was dying and precipitated a riot. Such events account for the people's lack of trust, the arrest of suspects, the murders of Foulon and Bertier and the difficulties involved in saving Besenval. This is why the Assembly and the Committee of Electors thought it absolutely essential to restore some sort of order by setting up a committee of investigation to take charge of political surveillance.

Further proof of the existence of a plot seemed to appear in the fact that emigration was now well established. The Comte d'Artois, the Prince de Condé and his family, the Polignacs, the Comte de Vaudreuil, the Prince de Lambesc and the Maréchal de Broglie had fled, no one knew where. The Comte d'Artois was said to be in Spain or else Turin. From the provinces came news which showed that emigration was a desperate need for many; everywhere, arrests were being made of members of the upper clergy and the old *parlements*, of the nobility and of deputies who were supposed to be returning to their constituencies in search of new powers. They were suspected of seeking to get out of the country and this suspicion was not necessarily ill-founded, for many of them had indeed been found very near the frontier, near Pontarlier for example. On 31 July, letters came from Saint-Brieuc saying that many Breton gentlemen had fled to the Channel Islands or to England. Was there any reason to suppose that once there, the *émigrés* would stay put and do nothing? 'They imagine,' explained a deputy from the nobility to the Marquise de Créquy, 'that princes cannot allow themselves to be exiled from a kingdom which is their native land and their heritage without plotting a revenge for which they would gladly sacrifice everything. They think they are capable of bringing foreign troops into France, of intriguing with the nobility to wipe out Paris and everything pertaining to the Estates-General.' Every scrap of gold in the kingdom was being taken abroad by the *émigrés*; they would use it to pay mercenaries. They could do this easily – who could doubt it? Did not the king have in his service foreign regiments who were the very ones most feared and hated? Was not the history of France littered with the memories of *reiters* and *lansquenets* and other mercenaries who had fought in France in the service of the aristocracy? It was the same in other countries, probably worse: Europe was full of vagrants ready to do anything for money. If we are to believe the *Quinzaine mémorable*, there was talk on 8 July of 'sixty thousand foreign brigands who are said to come from Italy, England and Germany to increase the general disorders and upset the operations of the Estates-General'. This could be a distant echo of the rumours from Montpellier and Bourg mentioned in an earlier chapter.

One thing is certain: the *émigrés* found ready listeners abroad. It was obvious that England would have a keen interest in French affairs. Any excess which cast a shadow on a national victory was instantly attributed to the knights of St George. Montmorin's agent commented on 1 July: 'Everyone says that England is spending money very freely and paying a considerable number of agents to foment trouble.' People were equally certain that Pitt had agents acting with certain aristocrats for the destruction of the navy and the capture of the war ports. Rumour had it that a British squadron was cruising at the entrance to the Channel and that Brest was to be thrown open to it. The affair caused an enormous outcry at the end of July because the English ambassador, the Duke of Dorset, took the opportunity to make an official protest to Montmorin who passed his letter to the Assembly on the following day. But the rumour must be of much earlier date, for Dorset stated that at the beginning of May, certain conspirators – whom he unfortunately does not name – had tried to get in touch with him with a view to an attack on Brest and that he had warned the Court immediately: perhaps someone had been indiscreet. It is possible though that the warning could have come from Brest itself, for local people did not have much confidence in the naval authorities. In any case, not many people rejected the story out of hand. The bourgeoisie, like the people, had very distinct memories of history learned at school: hadn't the princes once upon a time handed Le Havre to the English and Paris to the Spaniards?

Finally, was it possible that the rest of the European aristocracy and the royal despots would sit back and do nothing whilst the revolution swept on towards victory? The French themselves were convinced from the very first that other people would follow their example, and during August there were many false reports claiming that there had been popular risings abroad. It was in every monarch's best interest to help the *émigrés* and provide them with the means to return the rebels to their servitude. Family ties must not be forgotten either: Spain and the Two

Sicilies belonged to the Bourbons; the king of Sardinia was father-in-law to Louis XVI's two brothers; the Emperor and the Elector of Cologne were brothers of the Queen of France. All these arguments are echoed in a denunciation sent to the Committee of Electors on 26 July by a lawyer in the Paris *parlement*, de Mailly, son of the lieutenant-general of the *bailliage* of Laon. He said that his information came from a deputy from his province whose informants were very closely linked to certain people at court and who had already warned him when Necker was dismissed that a coup was being prepared and that he himself was in great personal danger. 'He assured me . . . that the aristocratic party was very far from considering itself crushed; that it was secretly concocting a plot no less heinous than the first; that it was hoping to gather its forces for a new attack on Paris, to buy foreign troops for money, to bring them here at night-time by roundabout ways and through the woods, to make the most of the excessive security measures used by people in the capital and to wipe out with blood the shame of its original defeat; that it was with this plan in mind that M. le Comte d'Artois, M. le prince de Condé, M. le prince de Lambesc and M. le Maréchal de Breuil were to join forces.' From July 1789 onwards, the collusion of the aristocracy and the foreign powers which hung so heavily over the history of the French revolution was considered as absolutely certain.

So during the second fortnight in July, there occurred a sudden synthesis between the innumerable causes of insecurity and the 'aristocrats' plot' and this was the determining cause of the Great Fear.

As to famine and high prices, one had known for a long time what to expect. Since everybody believed that food-hoarding was rife and ascribed it to the government, its agents, the tithe-collectors and the nobility, when the political and social conflict grew worse, it did not take long to decide that the conspirators must be planning to destroy the Third Estate by means of famine. On 3 February, the bookseller Hardy noted that 'some people were heard to say that the princes had been hoarding corn with the express purpose of overthrowing M. Necker. . . ; others were convinced that the Director-General of Finance himself was the chief and the ringleader of all the hoarders, with the king's consent, and that he encouraged and supported this enterprise with everything in his power so as to procure money for his Majesty more promptly and in larger amounts and also so as to ensure payment of the revenue of the Hôtel de Ville'. On 6 July, Hardy returned to this topic: it is regarded as 'quite certain' that the government is responsible for hoarding the corn supplies and that the same thing will happen with the next harvest in order to procure the money they will need 'in case the efforts of the Third Estate should come to nothing'. The *Vérités bonnes à dire* soon took an opposing attitude and ascribed these machinations to the enemies 'of the restorer of the nation': should they succeed in overthrowing him, 'the aim of this cabal was to deceive people about the magnitude and the reality of their loss by throwing open the granaries they had kept closed and by lowering the price of bread at the same time. Past centuries can offer no example of a conspiracy so black as the one this dying aristocracy has hatched against humanity.' But the people went further still: they accused the aristocracy of wishing to avenge themselves by allowing them to die of hunger and, though the bourgeoisie was slightly more reasonable in this matter, it still suspected that hoarding might have been a pretext for stirring up the riots which were now convulsing the country and which could compromise the success of the revolution by encouraging the spread of anarchy.

The same ideas also seemed apposite when it was said that some scoundrels were reaping the corn whilst it was still green and that the harvest would be ruined. The *Révolutions de Paris* mocked the credulity of the general public but convinced no one, more especially since the danger was far from imaginary and the authorities themselves, as we have seen, were ready to believe in it. A deputy from the Provençal nobility wrote on 28 July: 'No one knows who is responsible for this infamous idea of cutting down the unripe corn; the people can only believe it to be a plot hatched by the dying aristocracy, the nobles and the clergy who want to avenge themselves on the capital for its violent attack on them by reducing it to famine conditions by ruining the harvest; others fear that the brigands are soldiers in disguise trying to trap and destroy the Paris militia. In any case, the damage is considered the work of the ministerial and aristocratic cabal.'

France stood on the threshold of the Great Fear: the rumour went around that the much-dreaded vagrants had taken service with the aristocracy. It was common knowledge that many had already fled to Paris: they were working in the *ateliers de charité*, especially in Montmartre, and they roamed freely around the streets and the Palais-Royal; that there were also large numbers of wanderers all around Paris was also common knowledge, for the government had made official statements to this effect and indeed had used their presence to justify the troop concentrations which so threatened the Assembly. Today we know that these vagrants were only unemployed workers and peasants driven to despair by hunger, but everybody else, the king as well as the bourgeoisie, neither of whom had any more understanding of these poor devils than Taine himself, called them 'brigands' as though they were professional bandits. That one could easily hire them to foment riots goes without saying and each side, the privileged orders as well as the Third Estate, accused the other of unscrupulously trying to do so. When the Saint-Antoine riots broke out, those responsible were relentlessly pursued; the bourgeoisie saw it as the work of the court faction; the court attributed it to the Duc d'Orléans. When riots broke out on 12 July, everything that happened was blamed on 'the aristocrats' plot' and the plotters were accused of trying to employ the brigands in the attack they were planning against Paris. Once again Hardy had something to say: on 17 July he wrote about 'the dastardly plot which planned to bring into Paris on the night of 14–15 July fifteen or thirty thousand men supported by brigands'. In the days that followed, those who expected to see the princes return in triumph with foreign brigands in their pay naturally thought that local brigands would be taken on too. When Mailly announced that foreign troops were to advance secretly 'through the woods', he not only prepared the country to welcome without question the news that the Comte d'Artois was returning at the head of an army, as was announced so often during the Great Fear; he also condemned all those who were to take his accusations as gospel truth to accept the poor devils lurking in the forests as the tools of the aristocracy. In the National Assembly on the 23rd, the president read out letters received 'from various towns asking for help in dispersing the brigands who were rampaging all over the countryside and disturbing the peace on the grounds that they had no corn': this was a stunning confirmation of popular suspicions.

And so in Paris and Versailles the mainspring of the Great Fear was formed. It would be wrong to suppose that the provinces would never have reached the same conclusion of their own accord. But all eyes were fixed on the Assembly and on the capital; every word that came out of Paris was eagerly absorbed. So the rumours travelling around the city had great importance everywhere. Sooner or later, everything spread across the kingdom. What we have to find out now is how.

2

How the News was Spread

The main towns on the post roads – Lille, Lyons and Marseilles, for instance – got news every day, or at least three to six times a week: the post left Paris for Strasbourg six times a week, for Nantes five times, for Bordeaux four times and for Toulouse three times. At the end of the *ancien régime*, letters went by mail coach or post-chaise along the main roads. Elsewhere they were loaded on to a horse, the *mallier*, accompanied by a postman and a postilion. The post-chaise could travel at an average speed of ten to twelve kilometres an hour which meant that Orléans, Sens, Beauvais, Chartres and Évreux were about ten hours from Paris; Amiens, Rouen and Auxerre were fourteen, Châlons fifteen, Valenciennes, Tours and Caen twenty, Nevers twenty-two. It took twenty-seven hours to reach Moulins, Poitiers, Rennes, Cherbourg or Nancy; twenty-nine for Dijon; thirty-two for Calais and forty-one for Mâcon. Two full days were spent on the road for Lyons (49 hours), Bordeaux (53 hours) and Brest (60 hours); three days for Avignon (77 hours), Marseille (90 hours) and Toulouse; four days for Toulon and towns in the Pyrenees. In the main centres of commerce, merchants paid for a postal service of their own, possibly for greater speed and frequency: Le Havre heard the events of 14 July through such a postal service on the 17th, at three in the morning.

Apart from this, news could travel quickly only if sent by special postilions or couriers riding at full gallop. This is how news of the meeting of the Three Orders got to Lyons in thirty-six hours, the courier riding at a speed of thirteen and a half kilometres an hour, including stops to change horses; Lons-le-Saulnier heard that the Bastille had fallen thirty-five hours later thanks to a similar journey, and a messenger riding at the same speed could have reached Brest in fifty-four hours. Naturally, the time taken varied; the courier would ride more slowly at night-time. In 1791, a messenger coming from Meaux to announce the king's flight left Châlons on 21 June at ten o' clock in the evening and did not reach Bar-le-Duc till eight in the morning on the 22nd, having apparently travelled at just over eight kilometres an hour. Yet leaving Bar at half-past nine, he got to Toul at two in the afternoon, which makes fourteen and a half kilometres an hour. This means of sending news was of course extremely expensive and was used only in special circumstances. Merchants in Lyons clubbed together to send their colleagues at the fair at Beaucaire news of the events in Paris during 14–15 July, asking them to pass the news on in the same way to their colleagues in Montpellier. This is probably how the elder Cambon got the news on the 21st; Béziers also heard it on the 21st, but Nîmes heard on the 20th at eight o'clock in the evening. The government also had official couriers, but the public seems to have benefited from this service only once during the first months of the Estates-General; when Louis XVI visited the Assembly on 15 July, the government hastened to despatch the news, hoping thereby to forestall any disturbances. Langeron, the commander in the Franche-Comté, got the news in Besançon through the government service at six o'clock in the evening of the 17th, Rennes had it that same day at eleven in the morning; Dijon, Poitiers and Limoges also heard it on the 17th, probably from the same source.

News reached the smaller towns more slowly still. The post travelled to Bourg via Mâcon. On 20 July, it was noted that the post for Saturday the 18th had not arrived on Monday as it usually did: the lieutenant of the *maréchaussée* offered to have the letters brought over on the Saturday in future. At Villefranche-sur-Saône, news of the events in Paris came through Lyons. Le Puy usually had to wait six or seven days for post to come from the capital. Villedieu's letter on the events of 15 July reached Verdun and Saint-Dié only on the 19th; Louhans heard on the 21st, Perpignan and Foix only on the 28th. So in times of great anxiety, people turned for help to local volunteers – Machecoul, for instance, sent two reliable citizens to Nantes to get what news they could; they covered the forty-six kilometres in nine hours; since they obviously must have spent at least an hour in Nantes, they seem to have travelled every bit as fast as the special couriers. Private citizens used their servants and in the main it was by this means that the Great Fear travelled around the country.

In May and June, the only news that came by post was contained in letters. The Paris newspapers were very slow to give information on the meetings of the Assembly: the *Gazette de France* published nothing about them and Garat's first article on the subject in the *Journal de Paris* appeared on 20 May. It is true that papers of a distinctly political character were published, but in the early days the government tried to suppress them and their numbers did not increase until July. The Paris papers did not have a wide circulation in the provinces. Young was constantly amazed by this and never stopped complaining. In Château-Thierry there was not a single newspaper to be had; it was the same from Strasbourg to Besançon; in the capital of the Franche-Comté, only the *Gazette de France* could be bought; in Dijon, 'there was one gloomy café in the main square and one single paper passing from hand to hand – an hour to wait before it came around'; in Moulins, 'it would have been easier to get an elephant than a newspaper'. In Poitiers on 6 July, the town council decided in view of the circumstances to buy 'a collection of the best articles on the Estates-General'. This cost them a great deal of money. The deputy of Guérande warned his constituents against such an expenditure and told them on 10 July that Barère's *Point du jour* cost six *livres* a month in Versailles and that in the provinces transport costs could bring the price up to fifteen or eighteen *livres*. As to the provincial newspapers, they seemed very reluctant to print what had already appeared in their Paris counterparts. The *Affiches de Poitou* did not mention the Estates-General before 11 June; on 16 July, they had got no further than the session of 10 June. As in the days before the revolution, news came mainly through private letters and conversations with travellers. Saint-Pierre-le-Moûtier heard about the events of 15 July through 'a multitude' of private letters; news of the taking of the Bastille reached Charleville and Sedan through a goldsmith from Paris on the 17th; Châteauroux too heard the news from travellers; in Vitteaux in the Auxois a local tailor travelled without stopping for two days and nights to tell his fellow citizens.

At the time of the elections, the *bailliage* assemblies, anxious to keep an eye on their elected representatives and aware that only fragmentary and much-delayed intelligence would come from Versailles, had taken precautions and instructed their deputies to keep them fully informed. Indeed, some assemblies had made a special point of this in their *cahiers*, Toul and Bourg, for instance. Often, the electors chose a permanent correspondence committee from amongst themselves, nobles and clergy as well as Third Estate, on the grounds that the deputies might have to consult their constituents on points not considered in the *cahiers*. In fact, these committees were supposed to keep in touch with their deputies by correspondence and pass on to the public everything they heard. It is true that some of them never managed this: the town council of Saint-Jean-d'Angély complained bitterly that they heard nothing from the members of their committee. In general, however, they fulfilled their functions with remarkable zeal. The provincial committees responded to the same concerns as their counterparts in Paris where the district committees and the Assembly of Electors did not consider themselves dismissed after the elections and went on meeting from time to time. Things were best organized in Brittany and indeed this should cause no surprise, for in 1787 and 1788 the nobility and the members of the *parlement*, at odds with the royal power, had everywhere created correspondence committees which also acted in a parallel capacity as action committees charged with moulding public opinion and organizing resistance, as described by A. Cochin: the Third Estate had only to follow their example, though it never achieved the same degree of perfection and did not manage to set up committees in every constituency. Nevertheless, it was active and enterprising in many towns, kept a close eye on the municipality or else tried to supplant it; it achieved this in Tréguier; Saint-Brieuc was less successful but even so gained a considerable ascendancy. In Provence, where the struggle with the aristocracy had been very violent, the Third had a central body at its disposition: the Commissaires des Communes who sat in Aix. Where no correspondence committee existed, the deputies wrote to the municipality of the chief town in the *bailliage*, or to the magistrates or to some trustworthy person: in Bourg, du Plantier, the lieutenant of the *bailliage*, offered his services. Sometimes the public did not place too much confidence in these voluntary correspondents. In Toul, the electors, stirred to action by François de Neufchâteau, their acting deputy, complained to Maillot that they were not receiving their information directly and said that he should not send his letters to a municipality whose official status they had sought to suppress through their *cahier*. They were better pleased when the deputies wrote to the Chambre littéraire, as in Angers, or the Club des Terreaux in Lyons. These semi-official accounts were accompanied by others of almost equal importance. The elder Thibaudeau, a deputy from Poitou, spent his time in Paris in transports of fear and seems never to have uttered a word; his son, the future member of the Convention, never missed a session: 'I took notes,' he said, 'and on these I based the correspondence I sent to one of my friends in Poitiers so that he could read it to a meeting of young patriots.'

Usually letters from the deputies were read out to the population from the town hall or in the main square. They aroused the most unusual curiosity and their arrival was awaited with great impatience. In Clermont, people came in crowds to the Place d'Espagne to see the post arrive and then hurried as fast as they could to the town hall; in Besançon, when Langeron received the government's despatch on 17 July, he was amazed to find crowds of people gathered at the town hall; in Dôle, Mme de Mailly reported that on Sunday the 19th 'the post arrived very late; there were about eleven hundred people waiting in the Grande Rue; there was a great deal of excitement'. On 10 July, the municipality of Brest wrote to its deputies: 'We are being driven out of our minds by a public eager for news and only too willing to suspect us of hiding the letters you send us.' In Rennes, 'so many people gather when the post arrives,' wrote the *intendant* on 13 July, 'that even though the room can hold more than three thousand, it is still not big enough and we are forced to give it extra supports in case it collapses under the weight and the constant movement of those who gather there, many of whom, we note, are soldiers.' When the municipality was slow to pass on the news, people came and demanded to hear it: in Laon on 30 June, when there was a meeting of guild deputies, many people insisted on being brought up to date with events in Versailles and the mayor was forced to read out the letters he had received. Sometimes they allowed anyone who wanted to make copies. It would have been better to have had them printed: the committees in Rennes, Brest, Nantes and Angers did this and their collected letters are extremely valuable; unfortunately, they were rather slow to go into print and the first number of the *Correspondance de Nantes* is dated 24 June.

In July, the authorities began to grow alarmed. In Poitiers, the *intendant* refused to allow one of the electors, a M. Laurence, to read his brother's letters publicly in the Parc de Boissac. In Tartas on the 23rd, the seneschal's lieutenant officially forbade a lawyer called Chanton to read the daily news aloud in public 'in view of the unfortunate situation in which the kingdom finds itself, this reading not being proper and being unlikely to produce any effect other than that of exciting people and encouraging them to follow the unfortunate example of insurrection and possibly lead them into rebellion'. But Chanton took no notice. In

Longwy on 9 August, the *procureur du roi* also protested against a public reading of letters from the deputy Claude that had taken place on 23 July: this correspondence was 'wrong' because it was addressed to the electors who 'were nothing' and not to him, the *procureur du roi*, or some other magistrate. Too late: the decisive events had already taken place when the *procureur*'s resistance started.

It was a great deal more difficult to carry the news into the countryside. 'I do not think it possible,' said Maillot, the delegate for Toul, 'to get any information to them; the best we can do is let them know that the information is at the town hall where they can come and either read it or copy it; a group of villages or a *prévôté* could elect a local councillor to come to Toul and take a copy, or, what might be even more expedient, ask a magistrate or some other trustworthy person living in Toul to send such a copy all around the area.' It is highly unlikely that the peasants would have been willing to spend so much money. But more than once, hand-written bulletins were passed around the countryside; quite a few travelled around Brittany. The curé of Gagnac in Quercy wrote on 26 October: 'All we see is a wretched bulletin which is sent by one of the local deputies and which tells us precious little.' The peasants still got their information by word of mouth, with all the inconveniences that go with this: the news was waiting for them in the market place; a very important part in all this must have been played by those parish delegates to the *bailliage* assemblies who were still in contact with their urban counterparts. When important events were announced in this way, it was possible to go to the neighbouring town and make an official request for full details: on 26 July, several villages sent messengers to the municipality of Brive to make just such a request for information.

If one excludes information on the debates in the Assembly, described in general terms in the delegates' correspondence, all news until the month of August was transmitted by word of mouth. One must also bear in mind that many *bailliages* had no communications from their appointed agents and that at the most critical moment the latter either stopped writing or else found that their letters were being intercepted. The writer of a private letter would most often set down information that was sheer hearsay. The Marquis de Roux had passed on the contents of a letter written from Versailles on 13 July to someone living in Poitiers: Mirabeau and Bailly have fled; the people are rioting in Paris and 'have gone in a great crowd to Versailles determined to stop at nothing. Their way was barred by a cordon of thirty-five thousand men under the command of the Maréchal de Broglie and armed with artillery. They have been fighting since morning. We can hear guns and cannons firing. There has been a dreadful slaughter about a league from Paris, especially between foreign officers and French guards, mostly deserters.' This was written on 13 July and by whom? None other than the Abbé Guyot, Barentin's secretary. No wonder that the people exaggerated the strength of the royal army and thought that Paris had been put to fire and sword. Finally, one must not forget that the letters themselves were read by only a very small number of people.

The account of a meeting of local people held in Charlieu in the Forez on 28 July 1789 shows clearly how the news went around. Rigollet the inn-keeper announced that he had let a room to a merchant who had given him a lot of information on the brigands. He was sent for. He was a travelling jeweller named Girolamo Nozeda, known in Charlieu for the last twenty years. He said that he had come from Luzy by way of Toulon-sur-Arroux, Charolles and La Clayette; that all the people there were 'in arms'; that in Charolles they had arrested a brigand carrying seven hundred and forty *louis*, which was perfectly true; that he knew from hearsay that in Bourbon-Lancy eighty other brigands had come and forced the population to pay them money, which was false; 'that everywhere people talk of nothing but brigands'. At this point, everybody burst out talking. A merchant living in Charlieu said that 'when he was in Digoin a week ago he noticed the bourgeoisie mounting guard to defend themselves; that a Charolles man had been attacked and robbed on his way back from selling cattle in Villefranche; that brigands had fired a pistol at him and shattered his horse's leg and had stolen a hundred *louis* from him'. Other people present told a few more 'tales of brigands', in particular that Saint-Étienne had been attacked by six hundred men and that the garrison and the militia had beaten them off.

Government despotism was not the only thing responsible for this situation; it was also caused by the material and the moral state of the country. The vast majority of the French people depended entirely on oral tradition for the dissemination of news. What would most of them have done with a newspaper in any case? They could not read and between five and six million of them could not even speak French.

But for the government and the aristocracy, this means of transmission was a great deal more dangerous than freedom of the press. It goes without saying that it favoured the spread of false reports, the distortion and exaggeration of fact, the growth of legends. Even the most level-headed could not help believing what they heard because they had no way of finding out the truth. In the empty silence of the provinces, every word had the most extraordinary resonance and was taken as gospel. In due course, the rumour would reach the ears of a journalist who would imbue it with new strength by putting it into print. The *Quinzaine mémorable* announced that Mme de Polignac had been murdered in Essones; the *Vérités bonnes à dire* said that the people of Clermont-Ferrand had massacred an entire regiment; the *Correspondance de Nantes* claimed that the Maréchal de Mailly had been beheaded in his country home.

Indeed, what was the Great Fear if not one gigantic rumour? The object of this book is to explain what made it so very convincing.

3

The Reaction
to the 'Plot' in the Provinces
I: The Towns

In the provinces, the news from Versailles and Paris found ready listeners fully prepared to accept the 'aristocrats' plot'. Naturally, people in the main towns reasoned like their counterparts in Paris and their suspicions were just as swiftly roused. A publication condemned on 20 May by the Châtelet of Orléans accused 'the princes, linked in a common bond with the nobility, the clergy and all the *parlements*' of having 'bought up all the corn in the kingdom; their abominable intentions are to prevent the meeting of the Estates-General by spreading famine throughout France and to make part of the people die of hunger and the rest rise up against the king'. In the small towns, the power of the nobles was even more perceptible; they could be observed at closer quarters; here, they displayed in full both the inflated opinion they held of their own superiority and their stubborn desire to hold aloof from the rest of the world by clinging to their honorific prerogatives. It was difficult to believe that they would resign their privileges with no attempt at resistance. Here as in Versailles, many aristocratic remarks roused mistrust among the bourgeois, just as middle-class comments irritated the *gentilhomme*. In Lons-le-Saulnier, a councillor in the *parlement* was supposed to have said: 'If we could hang half the inhabitants, we could spare the rest'; in Sarreguemines on 3 July a lieutenant in the Flemish *chasseurs* exclaimed: 'The Third Estate are a pack of *jean-foutres*; I could kill a dozen of them on my own and then hang Necker'; on the 9th, Young was in Châlons and fell into conversation with an officer who was taking his regiment to Paris; he knew that the Assembly was to be brought to heel and rejoiced openly: 'It was necessary – the *tiers état* were running mad – and wanted some wholesale correction.' The notion of a plot was already in bud or possibly even half-developed by the time information which confirmed and strengthened it arrived from Paris.

However, in its early stages it was supposed to be the brain-child of the deputies in the Assembly. On 15 June, Montmorin's informant wrote: 'I am informed on good authority that many deputies to the Estates-General and especially priests render an exact account of their doings, that they keep up dangerous correspondence and that they seek to rouse the people against the nobility and the upper clergy; it should be possible to stop this process and I think it would be wise to do so. It is true that some deputations have taken the precaution of sending couriers but private individuals use the ordinary post to avoid the extra expense.' In fact, when the court began to prepare for the *coup d'état*, letters from deputies were intercepted, at least for some time: there are gaps during the month of July in the correspondence which has survived; in Bourg, no letters arrived between 28 June and 26 July and the deputy Populus attributed this to postal censorship. But it was rather late in the day and on 13 July the *intendant* for Rennes complained discreetly: 'It is much to be desired that the provinces receive only soothing bulletins likely to maintain a proper calm; up to now, we have seen the contrary and all that has come from Versailles has been extremely contentious; we have received letters dictated by the utmost imprudence, letters packed with the most disturbing errors, letters which have been read aloud to the gathered multitudes by the town hall in Rennes.' What errors? After 14 July, the defeated aristocracy claimed that the deputies had acted together to rouse the people to revolt and this statement had an instant success. Just as the Third Estate was convinced in 1789 that a plot was being hatched against it, a whole body of literature in the nineteenth century and even today insists that the plot was of plebeian origin. This matter is important, for disturbances in the towns went a long way towards preparing for the Great Fear and indeed there is a considerable body of opinion which attributes the Great Fear itself to the manoeuvres of the conspirators.

In actual fact, none of the letters which have been preserved urged insurrection; possibly all compromising documents have been destroyed, but it would be surprising indeed to find that not a single one had escaped or that no mention had been made of them; in any case, one cannot accept as truth a gratuitous hypothesis which is at variance with the character, ideas and political tactics of the deputies of the Third Estate. These were sound bourgeois citizens, often middle-aged, who feared street disturbances both for themselves and the class they represented, for such excesses could only compromise their cause. They expected to win a peaceful victory by exploiting the government's financial difficulties and by making the most of public opinion, just as the *parlements* had done so successfully during the previous year. Never till 14 July did they advocate taking up arms for the defence of the people. Their letters were most moderate in tone, though they grew more heated as the struggle intensified. For instance, Maupetit, the deputy for Laval, criticized 'the ridiculous claims in most of the *cahiers*' and 'the intransigence of the Bretons'; 'you cannot imagine the vehemence and passion of the inhabitants of that province'. Sometimes it is the constituents themselves who commend firmness and audacity to their deputies. Speaking of voting by order, the municipality of Brest wrote on 1 June: 'You will appreciate how strongly this means of voting lends support to the aristocracy which has for so long pressed heavily on the Third Estate and you will doubtless oppose with every ounce of strength the spread of the aristocracy's powers'; and on the 24th: 'All our compatriots wish the assembly to pass a resolution which will make public the names of all those who desert our good cause to pay court to the privileged orders.' One of the deputies so exhorted, Legendre, was not at all pleased to find that the correspondence committee had communicated such a large part of his letters to the general public: 'the facts they contain are and will go on being perfectly accurate, but the comments which accompany them, no less true in themselves, are sometimes expressed with a liberty which should be passed on to the public only with great circumspection and after you have thoroughly sifted through the material I send you in a rough, unpolished shape, not having time to look it over, sort it out or get it into proper order myself.' Legendre was afraid of being compromised: the recommendation he wrote would exclude any idea of his being engaged in a secret or seditious correspondence.

But moderate as they were, these deputies from the Third Estate were firmly resolved not to give in on the question of voting by head, and precisely because they were counting on support from public opinion, they felt it vital to explain the importance of this to their constituents. 'Such correspondence between deputies and constituents in every province in the country,' wrote Maillot, the deputy for Toul, on

3 June, 'will mould the mind of the public, which in turn will force the hand of the government.' They therefore insisted that the upper clergy and the nobility had allied themselves in order to maintain their dominant position: 'We need this support,' Maillot went on, 'in the present circumstance in which all the powers of heaven and earth, by which I mean the prelates and the nobles, are allied together and conspire to perpetuate the servitude and oppression of the common people.' On 22 May, Maupetit himself agreed that 'there could be no certainty of anything stable if the division of the three orders was approved'. Bazoche, the deputy for Bar-le-Duc, announced on 3 June that the Third would shortly set itself up as a National Assembly, adding: 'This is doubtless a desperate measure, but if we adopt the method of voting by order, then we shackle ourselves in chains for ever, we submit ourselves to the eternal oppressions of the aristocracy, we accept our ancient bondage.' Were these fatal mistakes? In the eyes of an *intendant* they certainly were and so too they appeared to all counter-revolutionaries: but for the Third Estate, they were self-evident truths. Were the words they chose intemperate and hasty? Remember – they were fighting words. One thing is certain: they were the very words needed to bring the 'aristocrats' plot' to its full and final expression and that is what matters here. Where was the machiavellism in this? The deputies wrote exactly what they thought; and basically they were right.

The drama heightened in the days after 20 June: threatened with dissolution or worse, the deputies of the Third Estate wrote to their constituents asking for support in some concrete form. There was no question of using force: they simply asked their electors to write to the Assembly sending addresses which would then be made public and eventually reach the eyes of the king. These addresses arrived in great numbers, though we do not know exactly how many. Three hundred of them have been studied and divided into four groups: the first, which alludes to the royal session of 23 June and offers support for the decree of 17 June instituting the Third Estate as the National Assembly, covers the period 25 June to 7 July; the second, from 29 June to 13 July, refers to the meeting of the Three Orders and expresses satisfaction; the third, from 15 to 20 July, voices the strong emotions aroused by the dismissal of Necker and the threat of a military coup; the fourth, roused by the fall of the Bastille and the royal surrender, starts on 18 July and goes on till 10 August or even longer: it brought congratulations and thanks from the provinces to the Assembly, the people of Paris and Louis XVI.

These documents which mainly but not solely emanated from cities and small towns reveal a far more widespread concern than the petitions sent to the king at the end of 1788 to plead for *doublement* and voting by head, a plea which had been organized by the municipalities. Sometimes, it is true, the latter endeavoured to maintain their monopoly in this field. In Angers, for instance, the town hall refused to call a meeting of the local citizens, evidently because it was afraid of finding its authority challenged and diminished: it made itself entirely responsible for the address prepared on 8 July; but on the 7th, the banned meeting had been held notwithstanding and during a new session on the 16th the people declared that the address drawn up by the local councillors had no significance and that theirs was the only legal document. Almost always, the municipality tried to widen the field by inviting a few notables of their own choice to join them, but only thirty-six resolutions were issued by local bodies so formed. Fourteen come from impromptu meetings of *bailliage* electors, a hundred and forty-four from the local 'three orders', a hundred and six from 'citizens': all together, 250 out of 300 express the opinion of the greater majority of the inhabitants. In most towns, great crowds came to sign. In Lons-le-Saunier on 19 July, 3,260 people gathered and 1,842 put their names to the address. The fact that small towns and villages were often content to repeat the words of addresses already prepared by such big towns as Grenoble and Lyons in no way indicates that they were not personally and directly involved in their final preparation.

Their involvement was heightened by the sensational news of the closing of the Third Estate's meeting hall on the 20th and the subsequent royal session on the 23rd. The government sent to the *intendants* copies of both the king's speech and the two declarations he had had read; with them went instructions that they should be read aloud in public and posted up in every parish: the local authorities took fright at this. The *intendant* in Moulins deferred the matter; in Meulan, the *procureur du roi* complained about the distribution of printed matter and advised against its use, in case it increased the prevailing agitation; in Granville, one of the posters was torn down. Reaction was especially strong in Brittany and addresses from this province expressed a violence stronger than was usual in the Assembly. The people of Pontivy 'have learnt with the greatest consternation that the royal authority used force of arms to disperse the National Assembly by forbidding them entrance to the temple of our country' (28 June); Dinan declared that 'this could only have happened through some criminal plot or deliberate trick against His Majesty'; in Lannion they went further still; on 27 June, the municipality, the nobles, bourgeois and common people, 'after the silent expression of their grief and consternation, pronounce traitors to their country those cowardly impostors who for their own vile purposes seek to betray religion and the justice of a kindly king'.

The meeting of the orders was joyfully welcomed and relieved the tension. The anger at the news which followed seemed all the greater on this account. From Thiaucourt in Lorraine on 7 July came the fear 'that presence of troops between Paris and Versailles will restrict the freedom of the Assembly'. All documents bear witness to the 'general excitement and consternation' at the news of Necker's dismissal. As in Paris, it was felt that the uniting of the orders had been nothing more than a ploy – 'a pretended union of aristocrats and patriots was the foul means' used to lull the suspicions of the nation, proclaimed Pont-à-Mousson on 27 July.

Reaction was instant and vigorous and this time no one could blame the deputies or the Paris newspapers. Certainly, there was surprise and excitement in the Assembly. 'When I was writing to you last Saturday [11 July],' confessed Malès, the deputy for Brive, 'I was very far from thinking about the dangers which threatened us; the manoeuvres of the abuse-protecting cabal and the frequent meetings of the Polignac faction had made me fear some new set-backs, but I could never have imagined so black a plot as the one which has burst upon us with such surprise. M. Necker disappears on Saturday evening – and we hear nothing about it till Sunday morning, when we learn that he has been forced to flee abroad. The same day the rumour goes around that we ourselves are by no means safe! The people look on us as so many victims destined for the cells or the scaffold.' The deputies faced the danger bravely, but there was no need for them to stick their heads directly into the lion's jaws: it is quite possible that some of them went to Paris deliberately to plan armed resistance with local patriots, but to send a call to arms through the post or by private courier was another matter entirely. In any event, things happened so quickly that there was hardly time to write (Malès's letter is dated the 18th) and in addition the despatch of letters was suspended. 'Perhaps this is just as well,' wrote Populus, the deputy for Bourg, 'they would have carried terror and despair into the provinces'; Populus for one was not likely to take a share in the vigorous actions of his fellow patriots! It was not till the 15th, after the king's visit to the Assembly and the resolution of the crisis, that the deputies were able to send instructions to their friends. Between the news of Necker's dismissal and that of 15 July, the provinces were left to their own devices for two or three days. Even so, a good number of towns took precautionary measures to resist a possible *coup d'état* and come to the aid of the Assembly. This is a vital fact which must be made plain. It is usual to date the 'municipal' revolution from the moment when the news of the capture of the Bastille reached the provinces, but in fact their demonstrations in favour of Necker, though less effective than those of their counterparts in Paris, nevertheless took place simultaneously and without any possibility of prompting from the capital.

First, a third series of addresses were sent off to Versailles. This time, there was no doubting their revolutionary tone. In Lyons on the 17th, the Assembly of the Three Orders, summoned on the 16th, declared that the ministers and councillors of the king 'of whatever rank, condition or function they might be' were solely responsible for misfortunes present and to come; if the Estates were dissolved, they would cease to collect taxes. On the 20th, the citizens of Nîmes declared scoundrels and traitors to their country 'all agents of despotism and all supporters of the aristocracy, all generals, officers and soldiers, foreigners or otherwise, who would dare to turn against Frenchmen the arms they have received expressly for the defence of the state'; they enjoined all men of Nîmes 'now in the army to disobey the atrocious order to shed the blood of their fellow citizens should any such order be given'. Smaller towns were no less violent: the inhabitants of Orgelet in the Jura declared on the 19th that they were 'ready to set off at the first signal' for the defence of the Assembly, 'to sacrifice their peace, their possessions, everything down to the last drop of blood' and to wreak on the guilty 'a terrible vengeance . . . on their persons and their goods'.

It is of course by their acts and not by their paper threats that men must be judged. The first act was to strip the local authorities of every means of helping the central government: in Nantes, Bourg and Château-Gontier they seized all the public funds; in general, they took over the powder magazines or the arsenal; in Lyons, they wanted to dismiss the entire garrison, but the soldiers declared their loyalty to the nation. In Le Havre on the 16th, the people refused absolutely to permit any flour or grain to be sent to Paris 'in case these provisions were given to the troops apparently still encamped around the city'; on the 15th, in response to a rumour that hussars were sailing from Honfleur to requisition corn, the garrison was driven out of the port and a ship thought to be loaded with soldiers was fired on and forced to withdraw out to sea. Elsewhere, militia were formed and suspect municipalities either had to accept ancillary committees or else resigned and were replaced by new councils who took over control of local affairs, as in Montauban, Lyons, Bourg and Laval. On the 19th, the villagers of Machecoul's various parishes elected an executive bureau and decreed the organization of a militia 'ready to take up arms whenever circumstances should require'; in Château-Gontier, a militia was organized on the 14th 'with the aim of rushing to the aid of our oppressed nation'. The first steps were taken to draw up federal pacts: Château-Gontier wrote to its brothers in Angers, Laval and Craon to determine 'the time when the said inhabitants of Château-Gontier would join them and go to the aid of the deputies in session at Versailles and help in the defence of the nation'; in Machecoul, they instantly elected committees to work conjointly with 'their brothers in Nantes'; the committee in Bourg had an appeal printed and sent around the different parishes asking them to send their contingent of supporters at the very first signal.

The most serious incidents occurred in Rennes and Dijon. In Rennes the military commander, Langeron, doubled the guard and sent to Vitré and Fougères for reinforcements when he learnt that Necker had been dismissed. On the next day, the 16th, the local people assembled and formed their own militia, seized public funds and suspended the payment of taxes. A great number of soldiers joined them; the armouries were ransacked and finally the cannons were seized. When the news arrived from Paris on the 17th, Langeron surrendered: he promised neither to move the garrison nor to call for reinforcements and said that he would pardon the soldiers; on the 19th, the arsenal was invaded and the troops went over to the people; Langeron left the town. It was even worse in Dijon: on the 15th, when the news of Necker's dismissal arrived, the crowd seized the château and the armouries, set up a militia and as a final touch imprisoned the military commander, M. de Gouvernet, confining all nobles and priests to their homes. Elsewhere, in Besançon for example, the news of 15 July arrived just in time to prevent disturbances: the young men of the town 'announced that during the night they would destroy all the members of the *parlement*'.

Of course, prudence often won the day and if one forgets this, the electrifying influence of the taking of the Bastille is somewhat weakened. When Young heard in Nancy on the 15th that the popular Necker had been dismissed, he remarked that the effect of this news was 'considerable', but when he asked what people intended to do about it, he was told: 'We must wait to see what is done at Paris.' The citizens of Abbeville also waited to see how things were going to turn out before they announced to those in Paris that they had shared their anxieties and 'would like to have shared in their daring patriotism'. In Châtillon-sur-Seine, the *procureur syndic* gathered the inhabitants together on the 21st to bring them up to date with the news and declared ingenuously: 'Whilst the success of the Estates-General remained uncertain . . . we, the officers of the town council, have feared to tell you of the alarms which have shaken it and which you would have shared all too eagerly. Instead, we have restricted ourselves to the most ardent wishes for the preservation of our country.' After the first excitements, the committees in charge often took a backward step. Château-Gontier quickly denied the seizure of public funds and the too-explicit terms of their resolutions when they heard that the king and the Assembly were reconciled; in Bourg, as soon as the agrarian disturbances started, they sent hasty messages to the rural communities saying that their support was no longer needed and they should endeavour to keep calm. In some places, there was even some resistance, even after the news of the Bastille had arrived: on the 22nd, in L'Isle-Bouchard in Touraine, Charles Prévots de Saint-Cyr, cavalry captain and mayor of Villaine, came to invite the parish deputies to adopt two draft addresses he had prepared for the king and the Assembly and also to form a militia, apparently assuring the people that he had received 'orders' from the Third Estate; the citizens of the parish of Saint-Gilles refused to hear him and denounced him to Versailles. These were exceptions, however, and the movement must be considered a truly national one.

It had preceded the taking of the Bastille, but it ensured the success of this event and guaranteed its extension into other spheres. Once the king had given his assent to the victory of the Third, the enemies of the people became his enemies and the partisans of counter-revolution were legally open to attack. As in Paris, they were considered dangerous and ready to return in force. They might, it was thought, take over one of the provinces and make it their base for an attack on the capital, especially if they managed to persuade the king to join them; if this were to happen, then it would be much easier for the *émigrés* and the foreign troops to enter the country. There was every reason to take care. One of the members of the Machecoul committee spoke in similar terms to the assembled villagers on 22 July: 'We must not be deceived by this apparent peace and tranquillity; we must not be dazzled by this brief restoration of law and order. A diabolical cabal has sworn to ruin France: its close proximity to the throne makes it even more dangerous. By all means be joyful, but remember at all times that if we let the enemies of the people triumph for one single moment, we shall never see the regeneration of France; let us always be on our guard against the triple autocracy of ministers, nobility and clergy.'

Now masters of the situation, the deputies began to grow bolder. Some did no more than give approval to measures already taken: Populus, the deputy for Bourg, was typical of these. But others, concerned both with the overthrow of the aristocracy and the maintenance of order, offered advice and suggested two ways of achieving this: sending loyal addresses to the Assembly and forming local militia. Barnave addressed his supporters in Grenoble to this end on the 15th: 'So what is to be done? two things: hundreds of addresses must go to the National Assembly, and a bourgeois militia must be ready to march. . . . The rich are the most concerned for the general good. The greater part of the Paris militia is drawn from solid bourgeois citizens and for this reason it is as efficient in the maintenance of public order as it is tireless in the struggle against tyranny. We must not lose a single moment in circulating these ideas throughout the province. . . . I count on the energy of your town whose job it is to see this accomplished. The same movement will exist in every province, but it is here that it has been planned.' And Boullé, deputy for Pontivy, in response to a letter dated the 20th: 'I am proud to see that my dear fellow citizens are worthy of liberty and are prepared to defend it without forgetting for a moment that to fall into excess is the most dangerous abuse of all. Continue to eschew all violence, but make sure that your rights are respected. If you think it necessary for your safety, maintain and improve your militia: every town is eager to form a national troop in its midst; and who would not be proud to be a soldier of his country? . . . If your country needs you, you can be ready at the first call. Dangers of every kind still threaten. . . . There are traitors in our midst. . . . Keep on writing to other towns in the province; it is through your union, it is through your mutual assistance that you will keep all calamities at bay.' If one ignores the dates when these letters were written – especially those by Barnave – it is easy to see why the responsibility for the revolution in the provinces could be placed fair and square on the shoulders of patriotic deputies. But in the early days, they did no more than offer encouragement and they made no secret of this: on 18 July, Martineau proposed to the Assembly that every town should have its own militia, and shortly afterwards Mirabeau suggested that the municipalities should be 'regenerated'. Neither resolution was adopted, but a deputy for the Cambrésis, Mortier, wrote to his fellow citizens as though they had been: 'It has been decided that we shall establish national militia composed of honest citizens throughout the kingdom; there is no longer any question of disarming the country-folk, nor of disturbing them in any way; it is a liberty all people should enjoy. . . . All people who have taken up arms against the aristocracy are going to keep them and their courage for the nation and the king.'

In Alsace, the aristocratic deputies Baron de Turckheim and Baron de Flaxlanden declared that some of their colleagues had advised offensive action in fairly clear terms. Turckheim also claimed to have held in his own hands letters 'which called on the *syndics* of our province to fight the seigneurs and the priests with all their strength, otherwise all would be lost'. Later, the *commission intermédiaire* itself indicted the correspondence of Lavie and Guettard, the deputies for Belfort. When one remembers the famous comment of Barnave to the whole Assembly after the murder of Foulon and Bertier – 'Is this blood so pure that one should so regret to spill it?' – when one reads Mme Roland's letter to Bosc: 'If the National Assembly doesn't put two famous heads on trial, or if our patriotic Deciuses don't strike them down, you're all mad' – then it can be no surprise to read in the deputies' correspondence words far more inflammatory than those reported by Turckheim .Young for instance seems to have heard some very dangerous remarks about the conspiracy. In Colmar on 24 July, eating dinner at a local hotel, he heard someone say 'that the Queen had a plot, nearly on the point of execution, to blow up the National Assembly by a mine, and to march the army instantly to massacre all Paris'. And when an officer looked sceptical, 'he was immediately overpowered with numbers of tongues. A deputy had written it; they had seen the letter, and not a hesitation could be admitted.'

As in Paris, a variety of incidents kept feelings of anxiety high. The troop movements which brought soldiers back from the outskirts of Paris to their garrisons were watched with great misgivings; many towns shut their gates in their faces; they refused to supply them with provisions; they were stoned and insulted. The Royal Allemand was very ill-received in Châlons on the 23rd, and in Dun on the 26th the crowd thought it recognized Lambesc's luggage in the convoy and refused to let the soldiers leave until the Assembly had given permission. In Sedan there was a riot after the arrival of Maréchal de Broglie and he was forced to leave town. The provinces saw a considerable number of nobles and ecclesiastics in full flight from Paris, either changing their place of residence or trying to emigrate; deputies who had left Versailles were particularly suspect: the people thought they were deserting the Assembly to avoid the consequences of the amalgamation of the three orders so that they could later dispute the nullity decrees. The Abbé Maury was arrested in Péronne on 26 July; the Abbé Calonne in Nogent-sur-Seine on the 27th; the bishop of Noyon in Dôle on the 29th and the Duc de la Vauguyon, one of the 11 July ministers, in Le Havre on the 30th. Paris may have thrown the provinces into a state of alarm, but the latter made no small contribution towards confirming the capital in its fears. This remark applies in particular to the collusion of aristocrats and foreign powers. On 1 August, the *Patriote français* published a letter from Bordeaux dated 25 July saying: 'We are threatened with thirty thousand Spaniards but we are well prepared for them.' From Briançon, one of the commissioners wrote to the president of the National Assembly: 'We have learnt of the misfortunes and disturbances which have taken place in Versailles and Paris and of the obvious danger to which the National Assembly and the capital have been exposed. Our alarms and our fears have not yet been dispelled. I thought it my duty, My Lord, to make inquiries and inform myself as to the present state of things and I am convinced, if the reports I have received are true, that the twenty thousand Piedmontese required by the former ministers of his Majesty the King of Sardinia have been granted by the council summoned for this purpose, but that he shed tears about it, probably from sorrow. We live in a constant state of alarm; we have a major commanding this town whom we

fear will contribute to the disaster and the misfortunes which threaten.'
As mentioned previously, it seems very likely that reports of a conspiracy
to hand Brest over to the English started in Brittany; on 31 July, the
Correspondance de Nantes announced that a man called de Serrent had
been arrested in Vitré: 'He was the bearer of a plan for the burning of
Saint-Malo; letters between the governor of this town and our enemies
have been intercepted.'

The nobles protested indignantly about these accusations of treason,
especially in Brittany; very often they and the clergy openly repudiated
the court's attempts against the Assembly, attended the meetings where
loyal addresses of support for the Assembly's decrees were prepared, and
gladly joined their signatures to those of their colleagues from the
commons – d'Elbée signed willingly in Beaupréau. Some rejected all
solidarity with their class: typical of these were the *maréchal de camp*
Vicomte de La Bourdonnaye-Boishulin, who in consequence was
chosen shortly afterwards as colonel of the militia for Nantes, and du
Plessis de Grénédan, councillor in the Rennes *parlement*, whose letter
was published in the *Correspondance de Nantes*: 'I have never professed
those principles for which the nobility is now so justly blamed; I have
on the contrary resisted them with all my strength', at which the
communes eagerly forgave him and honoured him with 'a civic crown'.
In almost all the provinces, the urban riots and agrarian revolts made the
upper bourgeoisie decide to welcome their prodigal sons and allow
them to sit on permanent committees; very often, as in Nantes, they were
given command of the militia: the reconciliation that Caraman had been
so pleased to note in Provence during March was even more noticeable
at the end of July and the beginning of August. There was less conciliation in Brittany: the vows sworn by nobles and clergy in January and
April had to be formally repudiated: meanwhile, they were placed under
the protection of the authorities, but 'as not belonging to the nation' and
'holding them well apart', as for instance in Josselin and Machecoul.
Moreover, the lesser bourgeoisie, the working class and the lower orders
in no way approved the condescension of the wealthier bourgeoisie.
In Nantes on 18 July, several nobles were admitted to the committee but
had to be withdrawn from it later following protests from the communes;
shortly afterwards, this was repeated in Fougères. It was the same in
Bourg. During the months which followed, one of the noticeable features
of municipal life was the more or less sustained and more or less successful

efforts of the popular classes to eliminate the nobles from all positions of authority.

For all these reasons, then, after 14 July, many towns followed the example of those who had boldly declared their allegiance at the height of the crisis. In Angers on the 20th, the château was occupied and public funds seized; in Saumur and Caen on the 21st, the castles were taken over; men were sent from Lyons to garrison Pierre-Encize; in Brest and Lorient, the maritime authorities were closely watched and the arsenal carefully guarded; the communes of Foix rejected all allegiance to the provincial estates and acknowledged only 'the laws passed by the National Assembly'; everywhere the militia visited châteaux and disarmed them; Paris set the example for the surrounding districts. The king's representatives offered no serious resistance. None of this took place without some sort of incident and some people found themselves particularly vulnerable. In Le Mans on the 19th, a lieutenant of the *maréchaussée* who had forbidden the wearing of cockades was nearly murdered. In Aix on the 21st, a gang of Marseillais arrived, led by the Abbé de Beausset, a canon of Saint-Victor and a hero of the March disturbances: the *intendant* prudently fled.

The municipalities set up under the *ancien régime* were powerless once the higher authorities had been suppressed or reduced to total impotence. They would have preferred to retain their bourgeois militia and give arms only to better-class citizens, as Barnave had suggested, but they were obliged to enrol anyone who wanted to join. Their police powers became nominal: the militia and the mob itself took them over. France was covered by a tightly-linked network of committees, militia and self-appointed investigators who for a period of several weeks made it almost as difficult to travel about as it was to be in the year II under the stern gaze of the vigilance committees. This led to the arrests mentioned earlier. In Saint-Brieuc, they searched the homes of suspects and dissolved the Chambre littéraire, thought to be counter-revolutionary. A close class solidarity linked the members of the Third Estate. Wearing the cockade became compulsory; in Nantes, those commoners judged 'disloyal to the people's cause' were forbidden to wear it. Anyone they did not know was naïvely asked: 'Are you for the Third Estate?' This nearly brought disaster on an aristocratic family travelling to Le Mans on the 19th, for as they passed through Savigné, they were asked this routine question and a chambermaid who was looking through the carriage window thoughtlessly replied: 'No'; obviously the poor girl was not aware of recent events and had probably never even heard of the Third Estate. But Comparot de Longsols managed rather more successfully when he arrived in Nogent-sur-Seine on the 19th; hearing a great deal of noise, he asked the postilion what was happening and was told: 'The armed militia is going to shout at us: Who goes there? If you don't answer Third Estate they'll kick you in the river.' Comparot wisely took this friendly advice and so did Young a short time afterwards. Neither took the matter too seriously. In 1789, people were suspicious but did not care too deeply about marks of conformity and it was not too difficult to pass as a 'patriot'.

Although the municipalities did their best to be as accommodating as possible in these matters, the people could not forgive them for not being freely elected by the local citizens. For this reason, it was decided that the organization and management of the militia should lie in the hands of specially elected committees. There were very few towns like Béziers where the municipality managed to survive without both for a considerable length of time. In many places, the town council was swept away in the course of local riots – in Cherbourg on 21 July, Lille on the 22nd and Maubeuge on the 27th. When this happened, the 'permanent' committee inherited all its predecessor's powers. But this was an extreme case. It is not possible to make any accurately detailed estimate, but it seems that most municipalities stayed exactly as they were: some survived the disturbances, as in Valenciennes and Valence; most often, they managed to avoid open conflict, either by bowing to public demands as in Clermont and Bordeaux, or by preparing for trouble in advance by spontaneously lowering the price of bread, as in maritime Flanders. But sooner or later, they almost always had to share their authority with newly elected committees and then gradually disappear.

Most of the disturbances were caused by the high price of bread: grain riots were never so numerous as during the last two weeks in July. They occurred in almost every town in Flanders, Hainault and the Cambrésis; during the night of 22–23 July, an escort travelling with a convoy near Amiens had to fight a pitched battle; in Champagne there were riots in Nogent and Troyes on the 18th; in the Orléannais, trouble in Orléans and Beaugency on the 19th; in Burgundy, disturbances in Auxerre on the 17th, Auxonne on the 19th and Saint-Jean-de-Losne on the 20th. Sometimes there were murders: in Tours, a merchant called

Girard was killed on the 21st; another merchant, Pellicier, died in Bar-le-Duc on the 27th. The districts around Paris were especially disturbed: on the 17th, a miller from Poissy was taken to Saint-Germain and put to death; on the 18th, in the same town, a deputation from the Assembly had great difficulty in saving the life of a farmer from Puiseux. Riots broke out in Chevreuse on the 17th; in Dreux and Crécy-en-Brie on the 20th; in Houdan on the 22nd; in Breteuil and Chartres on the 23rd; in Rambouillet on the 25th; in Meaux on the 26th and in Melun during the night of 28–29 July. The Midi was just as disturbed: similar riots led to the formation of a militia in Toulouse on 27 July. When the price of bread fell, people almost everywhere put forward yet another demand, one which had already appeared in Provence during the March disturbances: they wanted the abolition of tolls and they decided to stop paying the *gabelle*, excise duties on wine, stamp tax and internal customs duties. 'For the last two weeks,' wrote the director of customs dues for Rheims on 24 July, 'we have been in a state of constant alarm. They threaten to burn the tax offices; the collectors who live in them have taken steps to put their belongings in safety and no longer dare to sleep at home.'

It is easy to see the more or less direct relationship between this 'municipal revolution' and the Great Fear. On one side, the rising in Paris and the urban riots threw the countryside into a state of alarm; on the other, they encouraged the peasant to revolt and these agrarian riots became in their turn a direct cause for alarm.

4

The Reaction
to the 'Plot' in the Provinces
II: The Countryside

News of the 'aristocrats' plot' spread from town to countryside by the well-known paths but as the peasant never set pen to paper we shall never know what he thought or said about it. Certain comments made by village priests in their registers suggest that they shared the townspeople's opinions and it is very possible that their flock was of the same mind. In Maine, they were particularly explicit in their views. 'The aristocrats, upper clergy and upper nobility,' wrote the curé of Aillières, 'have used all sorts of means, some more outrageous than others, but have even so not been able to ruin the plans for reforming a vast number of flagrant and oppressive abuses'; the curé of Souligné-sous-Ballon attacked 'the many great lords and others occupying the highest places in the state who have planned secretly to collect all the corn in the kingdom and send it abroad so that they might starve the people, turn them against the Assembly of the Estates-General, disrupt the Assembly and prevent its successful outcome'. The curé of Brûlon who was later to refuse to take the oath for the civil constitution of the clergy, commenting on 2 January 1790 on the events of the year before and in particular on Necker's dismissal, wrote of 'a diabolical conspiracy to murder the deputies most ardently in favour of the new constitution and to imprison the others in order to restrain the provinces should there be a revolt. The queen, the Comte d'Artois and many other princes, together with the house of Polignac and other great persons who foresaw the changes that were to take place, . . . all these people, as I said, and a thousand others have sworn to destroy the National Assembly.' A manuscript preserved in the Ain archives relates that an inhabitant of Le Bugey claimed that he had heard it said that the queen sought to destroy the whole of the Third Estate: 'She has written a letter to her brother the Emperor in Vienna in Austria to get fifty thousand men to destroy the Third Estate which is our support and at the bottom of her letter she wrote that her brother should have her courier put to death. Luckily the poor courier was arrested in Grenoble by the Third Estate and his letter was confiscated.' The same annalist reproduces a letter which circulated in copy form in Valromey and which was supposed to have been found 'in the pocket of M. Fléchet, leader of the younger element in Paris, sent to him by the Comte d'Artois' on 14 July: 'I count on you for the execution of the project we have planned together and which must take place tonight between eleven and midnight. As leader of your party, you can lead their march to Versailles up to the hour indicated above, at which moment you can count on my arrival at the head of thirty thousand men totally sworn to my cause and who will rid you of the two hundred thousand people too many in Paris. And if, contrary to my expectations, the rest do not instantly obey us, they will be slaughtered on the spot.' This forgery gave substance to the rumours relating to the plot which had appeared in the newspapers and one can see a faint echo of Besenval's note to de Launay and the murder of Flesselles. We have no other examples of this kind, but we can be certain that many similar tales were passed around by word of mouth.

By taking up arms, the towns and villages officially confirmed the existence of a plot against the Third Estate. In Bourg on 18 July, they decided to send an appeal to the local parishes and many of these offered their contingent of men in the days that followed. In the *bailliage* of Bar-sur-Seine, the electors met on 24 July and set themselves up as a committee; they decided to establish a militia in each village and were instantly obeyed. In the Bayeux *bailliage* on 1 August, they tried to establish a committee in opposition to the one set up by the municipality of the *chef-lieu* on 25 July. In the Dauphiné, the initiative was taken by friends of Barnave who set up the Estates provisional committee; on 8 August the *procureur-général* to the *parlement* wrote with regard to the agrarian revolt: 'On the 19th of last month, we sent orders to the commons of villages, towns and communities of this province to take up arms. This lies at the root of all our problems: they took up arms everywhere and established a citizens' militia in every town.' In Aix, the committee members in the communes invited the *vigueries* to form militia of their own on 25 July, on the grounds that Provence was in a serious state of revolt.

But many incidents show clearly that the peasants did not always need appeals like these to encourage them to cooperate with the urban bourgeoisie. It was they who arrested the Duc de Coigny in Ver-sur-Mer in the Calvados on 24 July and Besenval at Villenauxe on the 26th. The frontier villages kept an equally sharp lookout. On the 18th, villagers in Savigné near Le Mans stopped the journey of MM. de Montesson and de Vassé, deputies for the nobility, and threw their carriage into the river. Many similar anecdotes show that the countryside was on the alert and lay in wait for any passing suspects. Young, for instance, was arrested twice near L'Isle-sur-le-Doubs on 26 July; then again in Royat on 13 August and in Thueys on the 19th. In the Isle area, he was ordered to wear a cockade. 'They said it was ordained by the *tiers*, and, if I was not a Seigneur, I ought to obey. *But suppose I am a seigneur, what then, my friends?*' – 'What then?' they replied sternly, 'why be hanged, for that most likely is what you deserve.' But this was only a manner of speaking, for they hanged no one.

It would be wrong to believe that people in the countryside accepted the 'aristocrats' plot' just because news of it came from Versailles and Paris. The peasants had had some dim forebodings of it as soon as they knew that the Estates-General had been called. They had seen some prospect of their own deliverance in the king's appeal and not for a moment did they believe that the seigneurs would submit without a fight: it would have been against nature. They may have known little about history, but they knew the legends well; they remembered the 'brigands' and they never forgot that every jacquerie, every peasant revolt, every ragamuffin rising aginst the seigneurs, had ended in a blood-bath. Just as the people of the Faubourg-Saint-Antoine trembled with fear and anger in the shadow of the Bastille, the peasant saw looming on the horizon the castle which from time immemorial had inspired more fear than hate in his ancestors' hearts. Time had sometimes softened its outlines; its cannons had long since disappeared, arms and armour grown rusty: no more soldiers, only servants. But it was still there and who knew what went on inside? Death and destruction might yet come from out its gates. The slightest thing made them fear plots and plans to crush the Third Estate. In the East, these fears found curious confirmation; in Lorraine, the Maréchal de Broglie issued orders for the disarming of the village communities; the *intendant* for Metz passed on these orders on 16 July and when the fleeing Maréchal reached Sedan on the 17th, he instantly put the order into execution in the neighbourhood. The project doubtless had its origin in the disturbed period when Necker was dismissed and though it is far from certain that it was inspired by the plan for a *coup d'état*, it was impossible to convince people otherwise. In the Franche-Comté, the business of the Château de Quincey was even more serious. On Sunday, 19 July, following general celebrations for the fall of the Bastille, some soldiers from the Vesoul garrison, in company with some local people, went in the evening to the château of M. de Mesmay, insisting that they had been invited to celebrate recent events. Whatever the truth of the matter, they were well received by the servants and were offered drinks. Towards midnight, they left. As they were going through the garden, a powder barrel exploded in a cellar: the entire building blew up. Five men were killed and many others were injured. It was an accident: it is quite probable that one of the visitors, possibly drunk or perhaps looking for hidden money, may have gone into the cellar with a torch. But there was one cry and one cry only: the Third Estate had been lured into a terrible trap. In Paris and even in the National Assembly, no one doubted this for a single moment. The affair had the most extraordinary effect all over France. In the Franche-Comté itself it was the signal for the agrarian revolt which gave birth to the Great Fear in the East and South-East. Though it has been little discussed by historians, the explosion at Quincey is one of the most important events of July 1789.

Convinced that the aristocrats had sworn to destroy the Third Estate, the peasants did not limit themselves merely to offering help to the urban bourgeoisie. There was one sure means of wreaking a splendid revenge on their enemies: to attack the feudal system the nobles were so anxious to maintain. The peasants refused to pay their dues and in many provinces rose and demanded their abolition, burning archives and even the châteaux themselves. They thought that by doing this they were responding to the wishes of the king and the Assembly. As we have seen, the very fact of calling the Estates-General had suggested to them that the king meant to improve their lot and that their demands had already been met. The conspiracy had obviously deferred the fulfilment of the wishes of the king and the Assembly; but the legal authorities announced on 15 July that the king had been reconciled with the deputies and that on the 17th he had given his approval to the revolution in Paris:

this, they thought, meant that he condemned the conspirators; to destroy their authority was to act in accordance with his wishes; he had even given orders that justice be done to his people; it was true that these orders had not been made public: this was because they were being kept secret and not even the curés themselves were allowed to read them from the pulpit: this concealment was all part of the plot. All the insurgents were absolutely convinced that this was so. In the Dauphiné from mid July onwards, there were complaints about the authorities who were 'concealing the king's orders' and they said that he was willing for them to burn down the châteaux. In Alsace, there was a rumour that he was allowing peasants to rob the Jews and take back the rights stolen from them by the aristocracy. In Laizé in the Mâconnais, 'the mob said that it was marching in good order and that it had only one week left to plunder all the châteaux seeing that they had unfortunately let pass the first two weeks of the three accorded them for that purpose'. Sometimes, their remarks show a delightful naïvety: in Saint-Oyen, the peasants complained to a bourgeois 'that they had a great deal to do' and in Saint-Jean-le-Priche, they were told that they must not hang about 'because there was still lots of work to be done plundering the châteaux from there to Lyons'. On the borders of Lorraine and the Franche-Comté, the Baron de Tricornot tried to enlighten a band he met: ' "Monsieur," these crazy creatures said to me, "we have the king's orders; they have been printed; but you have nothing to fear; you are not on our list and if you need our help, we are at your service." ' At the Château de Rânes in the Normandy Bocage, they apologized for being obliged to do violence to their master: 'They showed a great deal of regret at being forced to act in this way against so kind a master, but they had received information that his Majesty wished it so.'

It is quite logical that the peasants should have suspected the aristocrats of concealing royal commands when these were clearly against their interests. But how they moved from suspicion to total conviction is another matter. There is evidence that this may have been the work of some individuals who were rather bolder than their fellows, often invested with some official authority – *syndics*, tax collectors or rural policemen or even men with nothing more than a semi-official position such as deputies to the *bailliage* assembly: in any case, temperament or ambition pushed such men forward to take the lead. In the Mâconnais, many of the accused claimed to have obeyed the orders of *syndics* and tax collectors; a vinegrower from Lugny declared that one Dufour from Péronne had ordered him to march – waving a piece of printed paper, Dufour had said that he had received orders to that effect and that if he was not obeyed he would have them all arrested. In Revigny in the Barrois, the riots on 29 July were the work of two police sergeants who, according to the judgement of the magistrates' court, 'abused their functions' and proclaimed in the king's name and on his orders that they were to sell grain requisitioned from various landlords at the regulated price. In Saint-Maurice in the Moselle valley, one of the condemned rebels was convicted of having 'spread publicly that he had received letters announcing that he was allowed to do as he wanted'. In Alsace, a troop had as their leader a weaver wearing a blue ribbon: they passed him off as the king's brother. Even better, in Sarreguemines, a member of the Sarrelouis *maréchaussée* was accused by the mayor and various other witnesses of having said 'that during the next six weeks there would operate an ordinance allowing everyone to repossess their usurped properties'; that only the person of the farmer holding the common land stolen by the seigneur was to be respected; as for his goods, 'they could take the lot'. Was this purely auto-suggestion, or had these agitators misinterpreted some half-heard comment? Were they all acting dishonestly? It is impossible to say. Probably one or other of the explanations holds good in some cases, though more probably still, there is some truth in all of them.

The rebels were rather tempted to support their claims by showing printed or hand-written posters to peasants who could not read. The temptation was not to be resisted. . . . In the Mâconnais, a vinegrower from Blany, who was later hanged, was found to be carrying decrees issued by the Council in 1718 and 1719: he had stolen them from somewhere and he had apparently been using them to encourage the listening crowd. In Savigny-sur-Grosne, a vinegrower gave a farmer a book stolen from a château which he claimed 'contained the king's orders'. 'The witness had the curiosity to open it and saw that it was nothing more than a booklet relating to some legal matter in connexion with the house of La Baume-Montrevel, which led him to tell the aforesaid Sologny that if those were the best orders he had, then he was certainly not acting as he should.' In all the insurgent areas, it was said that forged posters in the name of the king were being distributed; these examples suggest many ways in which the rumours must have started. In the Mâconnais, the curé of Péronne stated that he had seen 'a paper written by hand in large letters stating that "in the King's name all people in the country are allowed to enter all the châteaux of the Mâconnais to demand their title deeds and if they are refused, they can loot, burn and plunder; they will not be punished" '. According to the notary in Lugny, the bearer of this document was one Mazillier, a salt and tobacco dealer from Saint-Gengoux-de-Scissé, later hanged in Cluny. The authorities in Cluny and Mâcon each claimed to have a copy of the offending poster. M. de Gouvernet, military commander for Burgundy, heard it discussed and the government itself was informed. But no one could find a copy. We do by chance have one written in similar terms and this is reproduced at the end of this book as an appendix. It had been posted – we do not know exactly when but probably during the agrarian revolts of July and August and possibly even before since it is dated 28 April 1789 – on the door of Beaurepaire church as well as in the neighbouring parishes of Bresse and around Louhans. The accused, one Gaillard, who worked in the Lons-le-Saulnier salt-pans, previously outlawed for stealing salt, refused to name the man who had written it, though the clumsiness of its execution and its dubious spelling show that it must have been the work of some village scribe, if not of Gaillard himself.

The rumours relating to these posters took their course and like all the others grew distorted as they travelled around. Before long, the Lugny notary was declaring that the poster seen by the curé in Péronne was printed, not handwritten. M. de Gouvernet seemed to think that a notary had passed it round: he was probably thinking of Giraud, the Clessé notary, whom the insurgents had made their leader. In this way, the aristocratic party related the agrarian revolts to the plot and soon afterwards the plot itself was attributed to the rebels by their opponents. The idea that the National Assembly and the urban bourgeoisie as a whole should have organized these jacqueries is totally untenable. Suffice to recall that the former were exceedingly reluctant to attack the feudal régime and that the latter, themselves often invested with seigneurial rights, were so actively engaged in repressive activities that they sometimes appeared especially ruthless. It is not impossible that some forlorn hope may have led the bourgeoisie to stir up the peasants. The attack on the Abbey of Cluny might well have been suggested by the inhabitants of Mâcon, and Chevrier, a specialist in the history of the revolution in the Ain *département*, gives the text of a small book which seems to have circulated after 14 July, calling the peasants to revolt: 'To the gentlemen of the Third Estate. You will be surprised by the nobility if you do not hasten to attack and burn their châteaux and put to the sword those traitors who will destroy us all.' In Montignac in Périgord, M. de La Bermondie later accused Dr Lacoste, soon to be a member of the Convention, of standing in the pulpit on 19 July and speaking in most inflammatory terms: 'I will now read you certain papers from the capital which announce a conspiracy on the part of the nobility which will bring shame on them forever, and now that we are all equal I can assure you in the name of the nation that the victims so justly sacrificed by the people of Paris are a sure guarantee that we can boldly imitate the authors of those enterprises which brought the deaths of the aristocrats Bertier, Foulon, de Launay, etc.' Others apparently read the people a false letter 'by which they libellously claim that the king has set a price of a hundred thousand francs on the head of his noble spouse'.

However, the accusation received its main support from the presence at the head of the rebels of a good number of country bourgeois – such as Johannot, director of the Wesserling factory in the Saint-Amarin valley, later president of the Directory of the Haut-Rhin; La Rochette, a former infantry officer, in Nanteuil near Ruffec, and Gibault, lord of Champeaux in Le Mesnil, near Briouze in the Normandy Bocage. Alongside them there were even nobles like Desars-Dorimont, seigneur of Verchain-Maugré in Hainault, who led his peasants in the attack on the Abbey of Vicoigne. All people so compromised claimed that they had been dragged along by force and this was certainly true for most of them. However, the attitude of some left room for doubt, though one can never be sure just how far they were consenting parties. At La Sauvagère in the Normandy Bocage, an ironmaster named La Rigaudière, member of the town council, and his son, a lawyer from La Ferté-Macé, seem to have played their parts as impromptu rebels with maximum enthusiasm. The curé accused the father of having said 'that they were going to burn the charter collection at La Coulonche and that if they did not find it then they would burn the château and the château of Vaugeois too and possibly the presbyteries also'. When La Rigaudière was arrested, his wife sounded the tocsin to arouse the peasants and rescue her husband.

It would not be surprising if a man like this had long harboured some deep animosity against the seigneur and this would by no means be unusual, for without going so far as La Rigaudière, there were many who were accused of creating a dangerous situation in order to satisfy some private hatred. In the same area – in Saint-Hilaire-le-Gérard – the two Davost brothers, one a priest, were reported by the curé as being responsible for the local disturbances: according to him, they were jealous of their first cousin, the lady of the manor, who though less rich than they, nevertheless enjoyed honorific privileges in the parish. In Lixheim in German Lorraine, an officer of the council indicted the lieutenant-general of the *bailliage* who had cried out on reading a letter relating to the recent murders in Paris 'that if the bourgeois of Lixheim had one vestige of courage, they would do the same'. In Alsace, the *bailliage* of Guebwiller reversed the roles and accused the magistracy and even the council with which it was then in official conflict. In the Franche-Comté, those who held the concessions for the Bétaucourt furnaces blamed the jealousy of various bourgeois from Jussey for the destruction of their mill. The curé of Vonnas in Bresse was implicated in the plundering of the château of Béost whose seigneur was engaged in a court case against him. At Châtillon-sur-Loing, the seigneur denounced a magistrate 'who had won popularity among the lower orders with the express purpose of damaging him'. The *directeur des fermes* in Baignes in Saintonge attributed the riot of which he had been the victim to the local tanners and the agent appointed by the Duc de La Vauguyon to exploit his forest of Saint-Mégrin: according to him, they had sought to have their revenge on him for taking legal action against their trickery.

But nothing here suggests conspiracy. Some people spoke out of turn and violently – what could be more likely in the days following the fall of the Bastille? In all the peasant uprisings – for instance, in the 1358 jacqueries in France, the 1381 Peasants' Revolt in England, and during the Peasants' War in Alsace, Swabia and Franconia in 1525 – the bourgeois, sometimes even the nobles, but most of all the priests came to set themselves on the side of the peasants for reasons whose very diversity instantly precludes all thought of planned cooperation. In the agrarian revolts of July 1789, such incitements to revolt were only of temporary importance. The peasants had their own reasons for joining the conflict and these reasons were more than sufficient.

5

The Peasant Revolts

There were no essential differences between these and their precursors in the spring: 14 July swelled the torrent, made it run faster, but was never the mainspring. Now more than ever, the uprisings found their *raison d'être* in the appalling poverty engendered by famine and unemployment. The most violent started in the mountains around Mâcon, the Normandy Bocage, the plateaux of the Franche-Comté and the grasslands around the Sambre, 'poor land' or at any rate land which grew little corn. As in the spring, the insurgents attacked either the taxes and the king's agents or the privileged orders, but most often they attacked both indiscriminately. Around the Eure, they wanted to bring the price of bread down to two sous or two and a half sous a pound and to suspend payment of excise duties; on the eastern slopes of the Perche, the forest dwellers, woodcutters and smiths who had been on the verge of revolt since the winter months gave the first indications of rebellion. There were riots in Laigle as early as 15 July; from here they moved eastwards: on the 19th, the tax offices at Verneuil were sacked; then there were riots in the markets in Verneuil on the 20th, moving to Nonancourt on the 22nd and 23rd. The same in Picardy – attacks on grain convoys and shops had never entirely stopped since the May disturbances; now they burst out afresh. Tax offices, salt-storehouses and tobacco warehouses were ransacked; no more dues were collected along the customs frontier between Artois and Picardy. It was the same in the Ardennes: the tiny towns in the Meuse valley were the first to strike. However, though like everywhere else tithes and feudal dues were no longer paid, in this area châteaux were not attacked. It was quite different in Maine where violent resistance to the salt tax and excise duties went hand in hand with attacks on the local seigneurs; in Hainault, famine turned men against the abbeys; in the Franche-Comté, Alsace and the Mâconnais, the entire movement was fundamentally anti-feudal.

The basic difference between these July revolts and the earlier ones lies in their distinct anti-seigneurial nature, itself enhanced by the influence of the aristocrats' plot and the Paris revolution. Even though the disturbances in the towns sometimes set things moving as they had done previously, there were now many villagers bold enough to preach revolt against the aristocracy and give the signal for action. So far, the Assembly had not even considered the tithes and feudal rights and the bourgeoisie had never talked of forcibly suppressing them, and even less of refusing compensation. The peasant population took its own cause in hand.

One must also remember that there was no distinct line of demarcation between the areas torn by jacqueries and those left in comparative peace. Everywhere there was strong hostility to the payment of dues; in areas where the country people did not rise in revolt, they offered passive resistance and brought the *ancien régime* to ruin by their stout refusal to pay. On 29 July, the bishop of Léon announced that his flock had agreed amongst themselves not to pay the tithe, at least not at the usual rate. The minister wrote back to him: 'Unfortunately this insurrection is not confined to your diocese; it has appeared in many other places.' Provence, the Dauphiné, Brittany, Picardy, Walloon Flanders and the Cambrésis persisted in the negative attitude they had adopted well before 14 July. In Artois, they rejected tithes of all kinds and set this out clearly in a decree of the Conseil d'Artois dated 1 August. It was the same in Champagne: 'They already consider themselves free from obligations,' wrote the officer commanding Thuisy on 23 July, 'several parishes have made a plan to come along and take forcible measures to ensure that they will not have to pay.' On the 21st and 22nd, the Marquis de Rennepont had been forced to sign a formal renunciation of all his rights for the seigneuries of Roches and Bethaincourt near Joinville; the Abbey of Saint-Urbain-lez-Saint Dizier was invaded at the end of the month, and in Hans, near Sainte-Menehould, the Comte de Dampierre who was later murdered by the peasants after the flight to Varennes was threatened with arson. In the Paris area, seigneurs and their agents had much to complain of. On the 19th, the *bailli* and the mayor of Brie-Comte-Robert came to the Assembly of Electors to ask for help; the next day, the *bailli* of Crécy-en-Brie had to flee; on the 27th, the seigneur of Juvisy came to protest against the harassments inflicted on him by the procurator-fiscal of Viry and Savigny-sur-Orge; on the 17th, the seigneur of Épinay-sur-Orge had been obliged to have his pigeons destroyed to calm down his excited tenants. In the Beauce, 'when the inhabitants heard that everything was going to be different,' wrote the curé of Moreille on the 28th, 'they began to refuse to pay both tithes and *champart*, considering themselves so permitted, they said, by the new law to come'.

But the events which are most significant in the history of the Great Fear are those relating to the armed revolts in the Normandy Bocage, the Franche-Comté, Alsace, Hainault and the Mâconnais. Their extent and their violence make them stand out above all the other disturbances. As always, the instigators were called 'brigands' and this contributed largely to the general feeling of alarm. Finally, the revolts in the Franche-Comté and the Mâconnais were the direct cause of local panics.

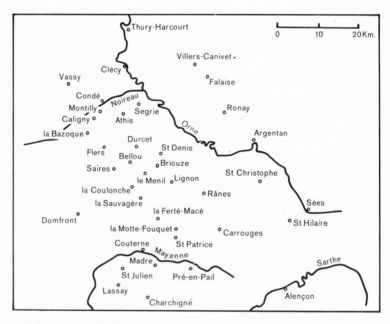

2. The Revolt in the Normandy Bocage

The ground for the rising in the Bocage was prepared by the urban disturbances which began to increase steadily throughout the western Perche and in the Normandy plain when the news of the Bastille reached the West. In Caen on the 20th, the price of corn had been fixed in the market and on the 21st, the château was seized and the returns for the *gabelle* and the *aides* were confiscated. There were similar scenes in Mortagne: in Mamers on the 21st and 22nd and in Argentan, fresh riots broke out. Falaise had acted before the other towns on the 17th and 18th and the impetus for the rising in the Bocage seems to have come from here. On the 19th, the Comte de Vassy, back from Versailles at the news that his property was threatened, was attacked and the entire region figuratively burst into flames. To the east of the Orne, however, there was no really serious incident: the abbey of Villers-Canivet was threatened with looting but the Falaise militia saved it; in Ronay on the 27th and 28th the château was visited by the local peasants; a few papers were burnt and the dovecote closed, but there was no looting. It was to the west of the Orne that events took a more serious turn. The Marquis de Segrie had to flee to Falaise in the face of his vassals and was able to save his château only by signing a renunciation of all his rights on 22 July; the Comte de Vassy, who had moved to Clécy, was attacked there on the 22nd and 23rd; his archives were destroyed and he too had to renounce his rights on the 27th. In Thury, the château of the Duc d'Harcourt was partially sacked. The Marquis d'Oillamson saw his château looted and his archives burnt at Caligny in the Noireau valley. This was the western-most point of the revolt. In the South, however, it spread further. Between 23 and 25 July, most of the châteaux between the Orne, Flers and La Ferté-Macé were attacked: Durcet, Saint-Denis, Briouze, Serres, Lignon, Rânes; usually all they wanted was the charter collections: there was little actual damage. The disturbances were worst to the west and south of La Ferté-Macé. At La Coulonche on the 24th and 25th, woodcutters and smiths from the Andaine forest came to demand the charters and made an unsuccessful visit to the château. On Sunday the 26th, the Comte de Montreuil had an announcement made by the curés of La Coulonche and La Sauvagère to the effect that he was willing to waive all his prerogatives. It was in vain. The charters relating to La Coulonche had to be given up: the best he could do was to insist they they should remain undamaged but under seals; on the 27th at La Sauvagère, the Château de Vaugeois was ransacked, the count held to ransom and his papers burnt. Then the next day, the two villages went along to Couterne where they were joined by everybody else in the area: the Marquis le Frotté had to hand over his title deeds and sign a formal renunciation.

It was even worse at La Motte-Fouquet on the 27th and 28th; the Marquis de Falconer who had bought the land a few years before had made himself generally detested by appropriating common land and keeping his tenants out of the forests. Not satisfied with burning his papers and forcing him to sign the usual renunciation, the peasants set themselves to torment the helpless old man and his guests; they pushed him so near the flames that he was actually slightly burnt.

The contagion spread towards Sées: at Carrouges and Sainte-Marie-la-Robert, Leveneur saved himself by abandoning all his rights; but on the 29th at Saint-Christophe-le-Jajolet and again on 2 August at Saint-Hilaire-la-Gérard, there was another outbreak of burning title deeds. The contagion moved across the Mayenne and went through the Maine Bocage as far as Coévrons: on the 28th, Couterne's rebels repeated their exploits in Madré and Saint-Julien-du-Terroux; on the 30th, several villages marched to the château d'Hauteville at Charchigné to force the seigneur to refund the fines they had paid and to seize the archives: it was claimed later that this was the ninth charter collection to be destroyed in the *mouvance* of Lassay, but the eight other acts of destruction do not seem to have been recorded. The last incident seems to date from 3 August: on that day, the *prévôt* of Mayenne, La Raitrie, arrived just in time to save the Château de Bois-Thibault near Lassay. The salt warehouses were still in danger: on 3 August, woodcutters from Fontaine-Daniel ransacked the Mayenne storehouse and in the night of 5–6 August peasants from the Lassay area came into town and tried to take the salt by force. Even outside the general area of revolt there were disturbing incidents. Correspondence sent from Domfront to a Paris newspaper announced that 'all the peasants in this area are armed' and commented at the same time that at Mortain and Tinchebray they had authorized the collection of dues owed to the Duc d'Orléans; towards the East, Mme de Grieu d'Enneval had to grant the parish of Sap, under threat of pillage, a complete discharge from the three thousand *livres* it owed her for a court case she had won in connexion with her right to a pew in church; around Caen itself on 26 July, the Sieur Avenel, who had taken over the Ranville marshlands, saw his house partially destroyed and afterwards had the common land he had seized taken away from him. In addition, the villages where there had been no acts of violence confirmed their decision to pay no more rents or at any rate only to pay them as they saw fit. 'Some parishes,' said the curé of Sainte-Marie-la-

Robert who had helped Leveneur save his château on the 27th, 'have met together and decided to pay their tithes only up to a fixed amount and have even signed their resolutions. Others have made up their minds to pay no sort of tithe whatsoever.' It was the same theme in Haut-Maine: in the suburbs around Le Mans, the farmers agreed to refuse the seigneurial rights; on the 22nd at Téloché, there was an outbreak of panic during the evening, but earlier in the day a mob had appeared at the château with every intention of creating havoc. In spite of everything, however, the jacquerie in the Bocage was much less serious than its counterpart in the East, for there was no burning of châteaux.

As we have seen, there had been very violent disturbances in the Franche-Comté ever since the end of 1788. There were various reasons for this: both nobility and members of the *parlement* had protested both loudly and obstinately against the claims of the Third Estate and the double voting granted to them by the king. In addition, the feudal régime was particularly strong in this area: there were over a hundred mainmortable villages in the Amont *bailliage* and this was the centre of the uprising; the *parlement* in Besançon had given every possible support to the aristocracy's activities in connexion with the enclosure of common lands and forests. The famine in La Vôge soon led to serious riots and the first movements southwards may possibly have been prior to 14 July; in any case, on the 19th, woodcutters from Fougerolles went to Luxeuil and sacked the tax offices; the people called on the mayor to turn out the nobles who were taking the waters there and he was obliged to give them twenty-four hours' notice. In Vesoul, there was no less excitement than in Besançon: on the 16th, when the *gentilshommes* arrived to attend the assembly summoned for the following day for the granting of new powers to the deputies, the crowd heaped insults on them; at the entrance to the town, M. de Mesmay, seigneur of Quincey, councillor in the *parlement* and a noted 'protestant', came in for considerable personal abuse and there was talk of attacking his château: he thought all was lost and fled during the evening of the 17th. The situation was indeed dangerous but two days passed without serious incident and the feudal régime might possibly have crumbled to a quiet close as it did elsewhere in France if the inhabitants of Vesoul and the neighbouring villages had not been awakened at midnight on the 19th by the explosion at Quincey. An hour later, the château was in flames and during the 20th all M. de Mesmay's properties were looted and burned: he lost two hundred thousand *livres*. By the 21st, the whole area was in open revolt.

No systematic study has been made of the revolt in the Franche-Comté and it is possible that no truly satisfactory picture can ever be given, for no judiciary or administrative inquiry was ever held here, as it was in the Mâconnais and the Dauphiné. Our information is fragmentary and often undated. We cannot therefore follow the movement as it spread gradually through the area. It is quite certain however that it spread outwards in all directions from its centre at Vesoul. The most alarming incident took place in the East: it appears that the Château du Saulcy was burnt on the 21st – the only building to be set on fire apart from the Château de Quincey; the Abbey of Lure was sacked on the 21st and 22nd. The local inhabitants stood by and watched, taking no action till the 23rd when they thought their own safety was threatened. The Abbey of Bithaine was attacked too; the châteaux of Saulx, Montjustin, Mollans, Genevreuille, Francheville and Châtenois witnessed scenes of greater or lesser violence on 3 August. In this area, the movement did not go beyond the Oignon: it was stopped by the Belfort garrison whose commander, the Comte du Lau, arrived on the 23rd and subdued the villages with detachments of cavalry. Towards the North, the area was in turmoil as far as the Saône and the Coney. The Château de Charmoille was destroyed; on the 21st, the château of Vauvilliers where Mme de Clermont-Tonnerre lived, the châteaux of Sainte-Marie and Mailleroncourt were all sacked; the Abbeys of Clairefontaine and Faverney and the priory of Fontaine were damaged or held to ransom. At Fontenoy-le-Château, the record office was sacked. From La Vôge, the revolt loomed dangerously near to Lorraine: at Val d'Ajol on the 23rd, the record office was looted and the seigneur's sawmill destroyed; the priory at Hérival was invaded on the same day. The villages decided to go and ask the canonesses of Remiremont to abandon all their rights: this town chose to defend itself and sent to Épinal for troops; however, the peasants managed to breach the defences, but did no damage: on this side of the Franche-Comté, this was the final limit of the devastation. Beyond the Coney, at the source of the Saône, the Darney record office, the Abbeys of Flabécourt and Morizécourt escaped damage, thanks in part to the bourgeois of Lamarche: the acts of violence went no further. But to the west, it seems that the disturbances were more widespread. The Château de Scey-sur-Saône, owned by the Princesse de

Bauffremont, was devastated; between the Saône and the Oignon, the Abbey of La Charité and the Château de Frasnes had suffered damage. The violence reached the Abbey of Cherlieu and the Amance valley, where the monks of Beaulieu near Fayl-Billot had to abandon their current court cases and give up their claim to *vaine pâture*: by now the trouble had reached as far as the gates of Langres. A few brief comments indicate that there was no devastation in the direction of Dijon. But the militia and garrison from Gray had to patrol the countryside to prevent any violence: the Abbey of Corneux and the Dame de Rigny sent to them for help and Young, who had dined in Dijon with two seigneurs who had fled from their châteaux, described their conversation: 'Their description of the state of that part of the province they come from, in the road from Langres to Gray, is terrible; the number of châteaux burnt not considerable, but three in five plundered.' To the south, in the Oignon valley, the Château d'Avilley was damaged, and further away still, the villages in the dependency of the abbey des Trois Rois near L'Isle-sur-le-Doubs looted and plundered it. This took the rebellion into the Doubs and across the area between Lisle and Baume-les-Dames. Between the 26th and the 29th, the abbeys of Lieu-Croissant and Grâce-Dieu and the priories of Chaux and Lanthenans were visited by crowds of local peasants in search of their title deeds; in general, though, there was no serious damage. The uprising moved swiftly across the Ornans plateau towards the south-east, reaching its final limits in the upper valley of the Doubs, where Pontarlier, already violently opposed to the local tolls, became a hotbed of restless disturbance. There had been trouble in Vuillafans on the 23rd and on the 25th there was an outbreak of violence when the archives of the seigneurie of Valdahon were captured and burnt as they were being taken to safety in Besançon. Soon afterwards the Château de Mamirolle was sacked: these two properties belonged to Mme de Valdahon who had enjoyed a brief moment of fame some time earlier when she fell in love with a musketeer (whom she later married) and quarrelled with her father. On the 28th and 29th, the Abbey of Mouthier-Hautepierre was attacked and then, also on the 29th, six thousand rebels came down from the mountains and invaded Vuillafans and Chantrans where the notaries who held the local archives were taken prisoner. Meanwhile the priory of Mouthe at the head of the Doubs was attacked during the night of the 28th–29th; the Abbey of Sainte-Marie further to the north was seriously threatened; finally on the 31st, the vassals of the Abbey of Montbenoît went to Pontarlier to demand the restitution of the title deeds kept there.

The disturbances in the Franche-Comté were more varied than those in the Bocage: not only did they force the seigneurs and the notaries to hand over the charter collections, they went so far as to destroy the court records relating to cases in the lord's court. There were many attacks on the mills, forges and sawmills which had been authorized by the seigneurs, much to the detriment of the peasants' forest rights: the sawmill at Val d'Ajol, the Bétaucourt furnace and the reservoir for the forge at Conflandey were destroyed. More serious is the fact that violence was in general more pronounced and was directed mostly at people rather than objects. The nobles had the greatest difficulty in finding an escape route through a countryside up in arms. The Marquis de Courtivron, a relation of Clermont-Tonnerre, and Mme Gauthier, both of whom were taking the waters in Luxeuil, and Lally-Tollendal, who had received letters on the subject from friends and relations, have left descriptions of what they had to endure in terms which may sometimes be exaggerated, but which cannot fail to be moving.

Lally-Tollendal's account is packed with dramatic incident – Mme de Listenay fleeing from the burning Château du Saulcy with her daughters; the Chevalier d'Ambly dragged on to a dunghill, hair and eyebrows pulled out; M. and Mme de Montessu arrested at the very gates of Luxeuil and taken back into the town under threat of being thrown into a pond; M. de Montjustin left hanging over a well whilst the mob discussed exactly how long they should leave him there. Apart from the flight of Mme de Listenay, for which we have proper documentary evidence, no other material has survived to support these stories. Lally's veracity is hardly in question, but he was not an eyewitness and we cannot be sure that his informants were either. The fate of the Duchesse de Clermont-Tonnerre, surprised by the rising at Vauvilliers, was less tragic: she hid in a hay loft and was eventually rescued by a detachment of cavalry which killed or wounded twenty peasants. Courtivron maintains that the mob was after her blood, but this is far from certain: all in all, though attacks and harassments were many, there were no murders. One feels particularly sceptical about a very scandalous incident which is supposed to have taken place in Plombières, according to a contemporary pamphlet and an article in the *Journal de la Ville*: three ladies who were known to have rejoiced at Necker's dismissal are supposed to have been captured in their baths and forced to dance naked in the main square.

As we already know, the Belfort garrison restored order in the town and managed to bring the surrounding area from the Doubs to the Vosges under some sort of control; detachments appeared in Delle to the south and Giromagny in the north; they pushed as far as the Doller and restored calm to Massevaux whose abbess had fled to Belfort; the Château de Schweighausen in Morschwiller, property of M. de Walder, father of the Baronne d'Oberkirch, was occupied too. It was however Prince Frederick-Eugène, regent of Montbéliard for his brother the Duke of Württemberg, who had the most reason to be thankful to the Comte de Lau. He and his wife, Dorothée of Prussia, sat trembling in their château at Étupes – not without reason, for their villagers were very disposed to follow the example of the men of the Franche-Comté; on the 23rd, they destroyed the salt-pan at Saulnot; Montbéliard was in a continual state of alarm: a French garrison took up residence there. In spite of this, the revolutionary movement managed to gain admittance. The Château de Saint-Maurice at Pont-de-Roide was sacked: from here, the Ajoie could be reached along the frontier with Porrentruy. Across the mountains to the north, the Thur valley was threatened. On 26 July, the *directeur des fermes* in Thann was 'in a terrible state': 'he said that there was a gang of brigands from La Vôge nine hundred strong, all pillaging, stealing, setting on fire and attacking everything relating to monasteries and farm workers, killing them and so on'. What had happened in the Franche-Comté went a long way towards unleashing violence in Haute-Alsace in spite of the language difference. Alsace was in any case ripe for insurrection and since the disturbances started in Basse-Alsace and moved from the north to the south, it is quite possible that the news from the neighbouring province was a support rather than an inspiration.

There had been violent disturbances in the towns of Alsace ever since the 1787 edict establishing Provincial Assemblies and granting local communities the right to elect the town councils, which had hitherto been appointed by the seigneurs or by privileged minorities. The nobility and the municipal oligarchy had resisted this reform very vigorously and on 3 June 1789 the king had decided to maintain the administration of the imperial towns exactly as it was, and at the same time to preserve the existing situation in towns where the councils were appointed by election, however nominal this might be. Where a municipality was installed, it inevitably came into conflict with the *gericht* or *magistrat*, a body of seigneurial officers who claimed that they and the legal corpus were in possession of some elusive administrative powers defined somewhat vaguely by the *ancien régime*. After 14 July, the bourgeoisie, with the calculated support of the common people, turned this existing struggle to its own account. Open rioting broke out in Strasbourg on 21 July; there were demonstrations in Colmar on the 25th; the smaller towns followed suit: Saverne and Hagenau, Barr and Obernai, Kaysersberg, Munster where the magistrate took flight on the 25th, Brisach and Huningue. In the countryside, the famine was not so very terrible, but even so there were vigorous complaints about high prices and royal taxes. As elsewhere, the peasants refused to pay tithes and were very active against the seigneur and his officers; up in the mountains there were great disputes about the forest areas and the situation became very tense. Fear of open revolt had started with the first disturbances in the spring; the Maréchal de Stainville, the military commander, had forbidden all kinds of unlawful assemblies: but he died and his replacement, Rochambeau, did not arrive till July. The urban riots finally disorganized resistance completely and acted as an open signal.

On the 25th, Dietrich, leader of the revolutionary bourgeois party in Strasbourg but seigneur of Ban-de-la-Roche in the Bruche valley since 1771, was informed that his château at Rothau was threatened. On the same day, the people living in the Sainte-Marie-aux-Mines valley and the Val d'Orbey came down to Ribeauvillé where the *chancellerie* of the Duc de Deux-Ponts, Comte de Ribeaupierre was in session. On the 26th and 28th, near Saverne, the nuns of Saint-Jean-des-Choux were also attacked. Shortly afterwards, there were disturbances at Bouxwiller, La Petite-Pierre and around Hagenau where the Abbey of Neubourg had to be protected. Further south, the Abbeys of Andlau, Murbach and Marmoutiers also asked for assistance. There was no damage in any part of this area. On the 28th, Dietrich gave way to the demands of his vassals; the *bureau intermédiaire* in Colmar was very active in many places and arranged a number of agreements: the Duc de Deux-Ponts in particular was willing to grant anything he was asked. In the southern part of Haute-Alsace, things took quite a different turn. The Fecht valley was already much more disturbed and from the 25th to the 29th there were violent riots in Munster, all of which had local repercussions all along the valley, as for instance in Wihr-au-Val. The trouble in the

Saint-Amarin valley and in the Sundgau had all the marks of a real uprising. On Sunday the 26th in Malmerspach, a local man appeared in church after mass and explained to the congregation what had been happening in Paris; shortly afterwards, they went off to attack the Abbey of Murbach, the homes of the local *gardes* and the tax offices. On the 27th, the inhabitants of the upper Lauch valley attacked the Lautenbach chapter-house and riots broke out in Thann where the bourgeoisie, far from coming out in support of the civil authority, turned against it. Great bands of insurgents came down from the high valleys to Guebwiller: the monks fled and their agents signed the agreements imposed on them by the peasants. It was the Sundgau's turn next; the initiative seems to have come from the villages around Huningue. As archives belonging to various seigneurs were being taken into this town on the 27th and 28th, the villages of Hesingen and Ranspach tried to block their passage and during the night of 27-28 July Blotzheim sacked the homes of Jews living in the town. There were worse incidents during the 29th and 30th in the Ill valley to the south of Altkirch: the châteaux of Hirsingen (belonging to the Comte de Montjoie) and of Carspach and Hirzbach (the latter held by the Baron de Reinach) were completely destroyed; at Ferrette, the house of Gérard, the *bailli*, was burnt down. In the Saint-Amarin valley and the Sundgau, the privileged orders were not the only victims: Jews were attacked everywhere, their houses were destroyed and they were driven out of their villages - but not before the rebels had got them to cancel all their debts: this was a particular feature of the rising in Alsace. Rochambeau's troops and *justice prévôtale* soon put an end to this new 'peasants' war', but it was impossible to restore the old feudal system, to collect rents or to protect the forests.

The disturbances in Hainault are not so well known, but were no less serious. The Abbey of Le Château just outside Mortagne was attacked on all sides and was forced to accede to all demands. In the Scarpe valley, other abbeys were attacked - Marchiennes, Flines and Vicoigne. To the south of the Sambre, the Abbey of Maroilles was sacked on the 29th and those of Liessies and Hautmont only just escaped serious damage. But as the Cambrésis had been under military occupation since the month of May, there was no possibility of an uprising and the area of disturbance was strictly limited. It was even so impossible to collect either tithes or *champart*.

The Mâconnais went even further than the Franche-Comté in the violence of its revolt. Its case is complex, but the surviving legal documents are extremely informative. They reveal very clearly the influence of the elections to the Estates-General and the manoeuvres of the revolutionary bourgeois party. The region still had a vague kind of Provincial Estates presided over by a bishop and the Third was represented in it only by the deputies for Mâcon, Cluny and Saint-Gengoux-le-Royal. As early as January 1789, the bourgeoisie had begun to demand its reorganization on the model of the Dauphiné Estates. Some of its members opted for the defence of aristocratic interests and wanted to defer all demands until such time as the three orders, summoned by the usual methods, should come to some agreement. In this connexion, most of the Mâcon magistrates followed the royal procurator, Pollet, who was directly opposed to Merle, the recently appointed mayor who was seeking the deputy's mandate. The arguments were heated and once the parish elections were over the two parties each tried to secure a majority. The people of Mâcon took the mayor's side and after the *bailliage* elections on the 18th surrounded the Assembly and threatened to kill Pollet. Merle was eventually elected. There is no doubt that close relationships were thus established between the revolutionary bourgeoisie and the parish deputies. The peasants saw the perfect scapegoat in Pollet. When disturbances began to increase after the 14th, Mâcon was eagerly aware of what was happening. They sent up their own committee on the 19th and on the 20th a mob of people stopped grain convoys which were passing through; on the 23rd, they met again to destroy the home of Dangy, the former mayor, at Flacé. There was one riot after another in Pont-de-Vaux from the 19th to the 21st, as peasants came into the town to demand the abolition of local tolls. There were similar riots in Chalon on the 20th.

There was shortage throughout the region, in the hillside vineyards as well as on the mountain grass slopes. On the 26th, Dezoteux, seigneur of Cormatin, called a meeting of village mayors on the Huxelles estate and made plans for controls and restrictions on the movement of grain, especially outward movements; on the 27th, just outside Villefranche, between Mâcon and Lyons, the Château de Mongré was sacked, a requisitioning committee having discovered a store of spoiled corn. People's anger was directed against the tithes in the early days and the curé of Clessé declared himself 'convinced that the uprisings in all the neighbouring parishes were mainly due to the desire to be free of tithes';

a few days before the outbreak, one of his parishioners had refused to hand over his tithes and had declared in the presence of a witness 'that he did not intend to pay them any more; that people everywhere were rebelling against them and that if the curé insisted on forcing him to pay, then he would burn down his house with him inside it'. On the 21st, the Mâcon committee issued a proclamation reminding the peasants that they did not have the right to refuse tithes or feudal dues whilst waiting for the Assembly's decisions on the matter. Some curés who collected tithes were so disliked that a cooper from Azé went around during the riots saying 'that we don't need curés'. It was not a very usual remark and apparently 'several people in his gang seemed rather disturbed by it'. Feudal rights were also attacked. The packs of hounds owned by M. de Montrevel, a deputy for the nobility, had made him very unpopular; in many parishes, one of the main causes for complaint was the seizing of common land by the seigneurs: it was in fact a drama of this nature which started the uprising in this region.

It is quite possible that the Mâconnais peasants were encouraged into action by the example of their neighbours, possibly those in the Franche-Comté and almost certainly those in Bresse. By the 18th, peasants from Bourg and surrounding districts were threatening the Château de Challes which the Bourg militia came out to protect; on the 20th, the Bishop of Mâcon had to promise the parish of Romenay in Bresse, where he had a château, that he would remit the personal debts of any poor labourers, but this promise does not appear to have been adequate, for the agitation continued and on the 28th he had to make new concessions.

The Great Fear was by now well afoot in the south of the Franche-Comté and Bresse: on the 26th, panic spread from Bourg to Mâcon and crossed the Saône; on the evening of the 27th, all the parishes on the edge of the river mounted guard to stop the brigands crossing into the province; in Senozan in particular there was great activity when the steward for M. de Talleyrand, brother of the bishop of Autun, assembled the peasants and kept them on guard all night. In the morning, when they heard that great bands of people were coming down from the mountains, he rushed to Mâcon to ask for help, but the vassals went back home when they saw that only châteaux were likely to be attacked; it was not long before they joined forces with the new arrivals. On the 28th and 29th, there were demands on all sides for armed bands to man the banks of the Saône and stop the brigands coming over to invite or force reluctant peasants to join them. It was therefore in the Mâconnais that the agrarian disturbances which were to be a consequence of the Great Fear first broke out, though the rising preceded the panic and started on Sunday the 26th before people in Igé had even heard of it.

From the 21st, the peasants in this village had asked their seigneur to hand back to them a fountain he had enclosed. When he persisted in his refusal, they went from words to deeds and after mass on the 26th they knocked down some walls and an adjacent barn. They were reinforced by people from Verzé who had been sent for earlier. Subsequent inquiries revealed the names of several agitators: the *brandevinier* Pain, Protat the former *garde* and, most prominent, Courtois and his son-in-law. Courtois was a former quarryman from Berzé-le-Chatel; he was virtually uneducated and his spelling was purely phonetic, but he owned some land. Various comments suggest that he had been imprisoned after an altercation with a person of importance, which had doubtless embittered him considerably. During the afternoon, the mob went to the château to present new demands to the seigneur, but he had fled; the château was sacked and the château of the monks of Cluny met the same fate on the same day.

On the next day, the whole mountain area began to stir. People from Verzé, Igé and Azé attacked the châteaux of M. de La Forestille at Vaux-sur-Verzé and Vaux-sur-Aynes and the home of M. de Vallin at Saint-Maurice, then moved northwards; one party went down to Péronne, which now became a centre of rioting in its turn, whilst the main body went on to attack the monks' farm at Bassy and then went into Saint-Gengoux-de-Scissé. In the afternoon, mobs from all over the country-side hastened to Lugny where M. de Montrevel's château was burnt. They then carried on towards Viré, arriving at nine in the evening in pouring rain: charters deposited with the notary were burnt, the presbytery invaded, and the curé himself was beaten and held to ransom.

On the 28th, the men from the mountains went down towards the vineyards and the banks of the Saône, whilst the movement in general spread northwards. In the south, the men from Viré sacked the châteaux in their own parish and then moved on to Fleurville and Saint-Albain, looting and destroying as they went; before daybreak, a mob from Clessé appeared at La Salle where they manhandled the curé and sacked his house; the Igé contingent passed through Laizé where they laid waste the Château de Givry. Finally, they joined up at Senozan: the magnificent château of the Talleyrands was soon reduced to a great blazing mass visible from Mâcon itself. In the north, the mob from Lugny went to Montbellet, attacked the Château de Mercey and then burnt the Château de Malfontaine; some pushed on as far as Uchizy where the Château des Écuyers was also burnt; then they marched to Farges and set fire to the bishop's tower and to Villars where the *ferme* of Saint-Philibert-de-Tournus met the same fate. The town of Tournus was in a state of total terror, but was on the alert: the mob swerved west towards Ozenay where the château was sacked. At nightfall, the mob scattered all over the mountains, in the north as far as the Château de Balleure, in the south as far as Cruzille, in the centre right through Nobles, Prayes and Lys; there was much eating and drinking but no significant damage; finally, they reached Cormatin on the 29th.

On that day, the rising very nearly turned into something of much wider consequence, for those who had burnt down Senozan set out for Cluny, this abbey being the greatest landowner in the whole area. The idea for this enterprise seems to have originated in Viré and Saint-Albain. At the subsequent inquiry, each village blamed the other and each claimed that the other had forced it to set out for the attack. The most extraordinary rumours flew around: that the people of Mâcon were marching on Cluny to defend the Third Estate against foreign troops, that Cortambert, the *prévôt*, was on his way with cannons and had ordered all the surrounding villages to come and help; as the people from Viré claimed to have received their orders from Boirot, the Saint-Albain postmaster, it is quite possible that some rumours emanated from Mâcon. Naturally the peasants instantly thought that they would 'do their bit' and get rid of the monks; even the most moderate fancied 'eating an omelette in the refectory'. Several thousand men advanced in great confusion across the woods into the Grosne valley. By now, there was organized resistance. The Tournus militia had advanced as far as Ozenay. Towards evening, there was a confrontation at Cormatin: all day long, bands of peasants had straggled through the village and Dezoteux had been obliged to hand out wine and money after being threatened with arson; now as evening fell, he decided to use force, probably with the help of the bourgeois of Tournus, and ordered the militia to open fire on the peasants who fled in disorder before their shots. By now, the Cluny municipality had organized a militia who came out of the town, threw up road blocks and fired on the rebels. The mob broke up in terrible confusion and many prisoners were taken. In spite of this, the most determined rebels made a few more attacks during the night of the 29th–30th; some went from Cluny to the Château de Varrange and the Château de Boute-à-Vent; the Cormatin contingent went to Savigny where they crossed the Grosne and to Sercy where their sudden appearance cast terrible alarm among the citizens of Saint-Gengoux-le-Royal at one o' clock in the morning. They were pursued by the militia and gradually dispersed. Their plan had been to advance towards Sennecey and there is no doubt that if they had succeeded, the whole country as far as Chalon would have broken out in rebellion.

Meanwhile, the area of revolt spread to the southern Mâconnais and the Beaujolais. On the 26th, there were disturbing meetings held in secret during the *vogue* or local feast day for Crèches; on the same day, the old school in Leynes, held on lease by Denamps, the lieutenant-general of the *bailliage* was destroyed, an example quickly followed by Pierreclos on the 27th; on the 28th, the Verzé rebels took a decisive step and at eleven o'clock in the evening they attacked Pollet's house in Collonges; on the 29th, they moved further south, sweeping every peasant in the area along with them. The Château d'Essertaix was sacked; so was the domain of the bourgeois Reverchon in Vergisson. Things were now well under way: Solutré burnt its monastery buildings, Davayé laid waste its priory, Chasselas ravaged or burnt its château. Towards the West, the movement swept towards Berzé-le-Chatel and Pierreclos where the two châteaux of M. de Pierreclos were attacked. On the 30th, it moved in two different directions: châteaux were damaged in Saint-Point in one direction and at Pouilly and Fuissé in the other. Things were the same on the 31st: in the South, the châteaux of Jullié and Chassignole were damaged and that of Thil burnt down. In the Mâconnais, rumour had it that the brigands had reached Tramayes; there was an instant rush towards the town. This was surely a backwash from the Cormatin and Cluny rumours: the rebels by now were managing to scare each other. However, they took advantage of their presence in the town they had come to help and turned things upside down: they smashed up the offices of the Mâconnais 'crues', fined the curé and the local notabilities and knocked down the weathercocks. This was the very last incident. Militia and *maréchaussée* were hot on their trail.

In every province, large numbers of peasants were arrested either

⟨immediately or in the months that followed. Everywhere the upper bourgeoisie joined the nobility in committees and cooperated gladly in repressive action where they did not actually make themselves entirely responsible for it. In Hainault, Alsace and the Franche-Comté, it was mainly the army which took control; in the Normandy Bocage and the Mâconnais, things were left to the town militia. Judiciary processes varied from place to place. In Hainault, the Bocage and the Franche-Comté, there seem to have been very few sentences. Trials dragged on and finally the Assembly suspended the activities of the *justice prévôtale*. In Alsace, however, the *prévôt* hanged a large number of peasants immediately or sent them to the galleys: in the Mâconnais, the bourgeoisie itself decided to punish this 'fourth estate': they set up impromptu courts in Mâcon, Tournus and Cluny and, after a brief trial, hanged twenty-six peasants. In Chalon and Mâcon, the *prévôts* hanged seven more. In the towns, people were deeply resentful of these harsh measures: at the end of July, there occurred a most significant disturbance in La Guillotière when the national guard of Lyons passed through the town on their way back from their expedition against the Dauphiné insurgents: the archives in Mâcon have preserved the popular protests which though they did not go so far as outright rebellion were extremely strong and passionate. Revenge was not too far distant.

Each of these revolts had its individual characteristics, but they have more features in common than outright dissimilarities. The July rebels were supposed to be brigands, too, just as they had been in the springtime. But even if there were a few suspicious characters among the wanderers who were naturally drawn to the bands of rebels, very few were actual criminals. We know who the Mâconnais rebels were because their names have been recorded: they were servants, journeymen from the vineyards, share-croppers, craftsmen and shopkeepers; there were also plenty of *laboureurs*, farmers, millers and *brandeviniers*; many of them were landowners. Among the people implicated in the revolts were a school-master, some *huissiers*, some *gardes seigneuriaux*, two castle bailiffs, the Lugny registrar, the brother of the notary from Azé. Many of the most prominent officials in the *bailliage* were often in the forefront of those involved and this was not because they were forced into action by sheer fright: far from it. There were very few really genuine acts of brigandage: in the entire Mâconnais, there were only two instances of carriages being stopped and their passengers robbed. Obviously, when châteaux were sacked, there would be quite a few who could not resist helping themselves to something they fancied and which was often quite valueless; they often demanded money because they were after all under the impression that they were working for the king and they could not work for nothing or wear their shoes out for no return: you had to eat and, above all, you had to drink – you couldn't live on air. These peasants did not band together to go stealing: they came to destroy and they gave this one basic aim their best attention.

Although the peasants were convinced that orders had been given – we have already explained why – they were not involved in any plot. The revolts had a very clear anarchical character: there was neither advance plan nor leader. Obviously there were local agitators in some places, for without such men no collective enterprise is ever possible. Circumstances, however, strictly limited their powers. The statements taken during the judiciary inquiries in the Mâconnais reveal that the accused wandered very much at random over the countryside; there was a multitude of small bands moving here and there, cutting across each other's paths and meeting up only around the large châteaux whose size and wealth were obvious attractions. The march on Cluny offers the only exception but surely the idea of attacking this great and wealthy abbey would have occurred quite naturally as time went on. Some contemporaries who were acquainted with the tale of 'orders received' and who sought as best they could to penetrate the mystery made no mistake: 'Fortunately, in all that vast throng there was not one man sufficiently educated or intelligent to take over this hastily conceived project', concludes an account which must certainly stem from Dezoteux. Similar opinions were voiced by the *lieutenant-criminel* for the *bailliage* of Chalon who sentenced twenty-four prisoners: 'None of them was moved by any motive other than that of the pillage and the licence which the exaggeration of their so-called rights appeared to allow them: they seem to have gathered by common consent with the intention of laying waste châteaux and houses and freeing themselves from their rents by burning their charters; one could add too that they were still stirred by the hatred the poor always feel towards the rich, indeed this hatred was even increased by the general state of over-excitement; but none of them seemed to us to have been driven by that secret impulse which is at the moment the subject of inquiry in our worthy Assembly.' This judgement seems to us exceedingly sensible.

It was vital to get rid of their crushing burdens: indirect taxes, tithes, feudal dues. As the weight of these varied from province to province and from parish to parish and as the feudal régime existed in a state of infinite variety, the rebel demands were extremely varied. It is not possible to examine them in detail in this book, but one can conclude that their aim was the same everywhere. Some might think that they were naïve to believe that they had abolished the *gabelle* and the excise duties simply because they had burnt the *bureaux des fermes* and put excisemen and *gabelous* to flight – that they had got rid of tithes and feudal dues because they had forced formal disclaimers and burnt charters. Events were to show that the peasants were not so very wrong after all: it is not easy to restore what has been so effectively destroyed. Moreover, it is clear that the desire to avenge past injustices influenced them every bit as much, if not more, than sheer greed. This is why they demanded the repayment of fines, legal expenses, destroyed records of court proceedings and harried or ejected the seigneur's men. It is no less certain that they intended to punish the privileged orders for their resistance to the Third Estate and it was their homes in particular that they attacked: furniture was thrown out of windows, broken to bits and burnt; doors and windows were smashed in; roofs were methodically stripped off; fire was more effective and simpler, but the peasants were reluctant to use it because they naturally feared that it might get out of control and spread to the village. These are not acts of collective madness, as has so often been suggested. The people always has its own way of dealing with things. In 1792, for instance, a miner from Littry was killed by a *garde seigneurial* and his comrades went in most orderly manner to the seigneur's farms and place of residence, which they then proceeded to destroy and burn in a very methodical way, one after the other, carefully evacuating anything belonging to the farmers and the servants so as not to damage the property of those not involved. All the peasant revolts followed this pattern. Right up to the end of the middle ages, the bourgeois of Flanders enjoyed the right of arson: they were allowed to punish anyone who had injured them or attacked their privileges by burning down his house.

But it was not hate alone which inspired the peasants. The written evidence of the Mâconnais uprisings has a very strong popular flavour: the rebels showed a naïve enjoyment and a sly good-heartedness shines through their broad-humoured jokes. It is easy to see that they were delighted to down tools on the spot and go for a day's outing as though they were setting off to the market or the fair. Going to see what was happening somewhere else was a pleasant diversion, though in this case somewhat out of the ordinary. The whole village would be on foot, the *syndic* leading the way in front of the most important inhabitants, sometimes with drums beating; there would be few guns, but a good number of farming implements and sticks instead of firearms; there were more young people than old: they have always played a great part in revolutionary movements. There were deafening shouts of 'Long live the Third Estate!' When they arrived at a château or a presbytery, they always began by asking for something to eat and more especially something to drink; someone would bring up a barrel from the cellar and broach it so that everyone could help themselves. Sometimes they went down into the cellar where the best wine was kept, but most often they were not particularly finicky: bread and wine was enough. The most demanding might ask for an omelette or some ham, or else they would slaughter all the pigeons in the pigeon-cote and cook them. When the seigneur was actually present and was willing to renounce all his rights, he might escape without too much damage. But if he was away from home, the matter might not go so well, especially if it was getting late and a lot of wine had been drunk. But even then it was possible to ask for time and hurry off to get the master's signature. There was no shortage of laughter among the threats and the violence. At Collonge, the Mâconnais rebels on their way to Pollet's country house put themselves into a great good humour by saying that they were going to 'fricasser ce poulet', a play on words which gave them enormous pleasure; they sometimes dressed up – a belt tied around a sheet, a curtain cord or a bell pull; a cockade made out of a lotto card. There was no sort of viciousness, no attacks against women. No bloodshed either. Taine's 'lewd and blood-stained monkey' made no appearance here.

The especial importance of these agrarian revolts lies in their place in the history of the abolition of feudal dues and tithes, both essential elements in the framework of the *ancien régime*. But the revolts are also vital to our understanding of this moment of time in the history of the French Revolution. They are closely linked to the rumours of the 'aristocrats' plot' without which the Great Fear could hardly have been conceived. In some areas, they were its immediate cause: in the East, the South-East and part of the Massif Central, the Great Fear came from the Franche-Comté and the Mâconnais. It is important to set the revolts in their proper place in order to present the fear in its true form: to get the peasant to rise and revolt, there was no need of the Great Fear, as so many historians have suggested: when the panic came, he was already up and away.

6

The Fear of Brigands

The rumour of an aristocrats' plot had alarmed the public and so greatly did the people fear counter-revolution that their own personal victory did little to calm their anxiety. The Third Estate's reaction to the plot had caused disturbances in the towns and the countryside and these in their turn increased the general sense of insecurity. In the first place, they provided for ever-increasing outbreaks of panic as harvest-time drew near and the fear of vagrants reached its height. Secondly, they gave a definite form both to the fear of brigands and to the conviction already firmly established in Paris that these brigands were hand in glove with the aristocracy.

It is clear that the tragic incidents which had taken place in the capital as well as in many towns and provinces had deeply affected people's imagination and left their minds much more open to fear. Private letters, occasionally printed in local newspapers, exaggerated the horror of what had happened and oral descriptions must have made it seem even worse. 'There is a rage in people's hearts it is impossible to describe,' wrote a Paris merchant on the 15th in a letter which the *Correspondance de Nantes* published on the 18th. 'We want twenty heads and we shall have them. Friends in Nantes, we have sworn to take our vengeance, and more fortunate than you, take it we shall.' 'Over a hundred agents from that den of vice,' said another letter printed in the issue of the 23rd, 'have been sacrificed to the people's fury, some hanged from street lamps, others decapitated on the very steps of their homes: their corpses have been dragged through the streets, torn to bits, tossed into the river or the rubbish dump.' In Valromey, Bellod noted that 'on 14 July, the people of the Third Estate killed many nobles in Paris and carried their heads around all the streets and squares in Paris and Versailles'. Add to these murders the looting and burning of châteaux. In those parts of the country which had remained more or less peaceful, there was no one, however much they favoured the Revolution, who did not fear that sooner or later similar scenes of horror would come their way. During the period of the Great Fear, many local alarms had their origins in nothing more than sheer apprehension – everyone watched fearfully for rioters from the neighbouring town or rebels from the countryside around. In some places there were rumours that patriots from other provinces were coming to help slit the aristocrats' throats, as the Bretons had done in Rennes in 1788 and the Marseillais in Aix after 14 July: this news cheered some but disturbed even more. In Douai on 24 July, the town was in a state of terror: they said that the Bretons were coming! On the 17th, a letter came from Rouen to Gorsas's *Courrier*: 'They say that five or six thousand Picards are coming to our aid with iron-shod sticks and pikes.' On the 26th, a militia was formed at Montbard 'against the brigands called in by the state on the pretext of supporting the Third Estate'. In the Normandy Bocage, the peasant uprising had caused deep anxiety: the fear in the East and the South-East had been caused by the revolt in the Franche-Comté and the trouble in Forez by the risings in the Mâconnais. Fear engendered fear. The towns tried hard to maintain or restore order within their walls and in the countryside around; left to their own devices, they cooperated with each other and with the villages within their jurisdiction. But there was one area where agreement was difficult: how to cope with the problem of supplies, now more pressing than ever before. There was no superior authority to impose its will in these matters and there were clashes of interest so violent as to come dangerously near civil strife and this in turn caused widespread fear. The situation was particularly grave around Paris where there were very serious difficulties in organizing food supplies. The Electors sent commissioners to buy in the markets and get supplies moving: Nicolas de Bonneville was sent along the Rouen road on 16 July, two others went on the same day to Senlis, Saint-Denis, Creil and Pont-Sainte-Maxence; on the 21st, Santerre started operations in the Vexin; there was another expedition to Brie-Comte-Robert on the 25th. It was clear that there would be considerable hostility from local people and it was thought prudent to have the convoys escorted by the Paris militia. Other detachments were sent to inspect châteaux where there were supposed to be 'great piles' of corn and to protect mills and stores; on the 19th, they arrived at Corbeil and the châteaux de Choisy-le-Roi and Chamarande; on the 27th, they paid official visits to the Comtesse de Briche near

Arpajon and the Comtesse de Brienne near Limours. A secret report that there were large quantities of grain hidden in Pontoise was confirmed and on the 18th the commissioners arrived to requisition it; it was as well that they came with an escort, for the local people flew into a state of tense excitement and almost prevented the troops from entering the town. The commissioners had the greatest difficulty in proceeding with their requisitions. It was worse still in Étampes on the 21st. Three days previously, a commissioner had come from Paris to ask them to exchange corn for flour; suddenly, they heard from some travellers that a detachment of troops together with a considerable number of peasants was approaching the town. This started off a terrible panic. The tocsin rang; the inhabitants took up arms, determined 'to protect their hearth and home' as well as their corn. Calm was restored when it was learnt that the militia intended to do no more than escort the expected convoy. In fact, they did take matters a step further and made Étampes hand over two hundred sacks without any mention of the suggested exchange. When Étampes heard that a new band of troops was due to arrive on the 27th, the excitement broke out all over again.

The exploits of the inhabitants of Saint-Germain triggered off the first fear in Pontoise. Since there was no corn in the market, they started attacking and robbing corn convoys from Poissy on the 15th. On the 16th, they actually went into Poissy and stopped more than forty waggons. Others boldly went into merchants' and millers' storehouses and on the 17th a miller was executed in Saint-Germain; on the same day, a farmer from Puiseaux was kidnapped. Bands of men overran the southern part of the Vexin as far as Meulan and Pontoise. Panic broke out in the latter town on the 17th: there was a rumour that five or six hundred men were on their way to Pontoise 'asking for heads'. 'Terrified out of their wits, the local people stayed indoors.' On the 18th, the situation grew even worse when commissioners from Paris arrived. Fortunately, the appearance of the Salis regiment restored order. There was no region where the arrival of expeditions of this nature, whether they were organized or disorganized, did not start off some sort of panic. In Champagne, the Great Fear seems to have started in the villages to the south of Nogent, Pont and Romilly, where there had been riots in the market place round about the 20th. The towns in their turn were always alarmed when the peasants came into market. On the 26th, Chaource took safety measures which suggest that the Great Fear was not too far away – there was anxiety about 'threats from neighbouring villages because of the scarcity of corn'.

And now we come to the most important consequence of the urban revolts: immediately after 14 July, a rumour went around to the effect that because the municipalities had taken careful security measures, the brigands (who were blamed for every crime in the calendar) had decided to clear off and were now scattered all over the country. This rumour was not restricted to Paris: in the South-West, Bordeaux was supposed to be responsible for the dispersal of local brigands, but obviously things were worse in the capital than anywhere else. This rumour played a vital part in the development of the Great Fear. Those who announced that it was the result of a subtle plot made sure at the same time – though they offered no proofs – that people believed that the news of the brigands' dispersal had been broadcast deliberately.

The idea that there were 'brigands' in and around Paris was a fairly general one and indeed the king had lent it support in order to justify his calling in troops; the bourgeoisie too needed the threat of brigands as a legitimate excuse to form their militia. These brigands, whose existence was so desperately needed for political reasons, were in fact the floating population of Paris, mainly the local unemployed: their numbers were swollen by workers from the *ateliers de charité* in Montmartre, small-time smugglers from the suburbs around the capital and the usual wanderers who always hang about any great city, singly or in gangs. On 24 July, the Electors gave orders that troops were to be sent to examine the quarries where a large number of 'brigands' were supposed to have their headquarters; on the 30th, a detachment went to arrest a band of brigands in the Ménilmontant quarries; on the 31st, a gang of workers from Montmartre were hunted down on the Monceaux plain. 'Rumour has it,' noted the *Quinzaine mémorable*, 'that there are many potential criminals and even brigands in Paris and that several thieves have been arrested in the Faubourg Saint-Antoine.' The *Annales parisiennes* for 27–30 July wrote: 'At night, the large numbers of vagrants who had managed to get hold of arms when the revolution started set up gangs of smugglers and brigands all round the city walls and managed to get all sorts of prohibited goods into the capital.' Apart from the smuggling, what sort of common law crimes did they commit? The *procès-verbaux* of the *maréchaussée* note a few. On 14 July, Dufresne was robbed at ten o'clock in the morning at Basse-Courtille by some men who went on to empty the pockets of a few more people; on the 16th, a lawyer from Melun who was travelling to Paris by gig was stopped and robbed; on the evening of the 21st, a *vicaire* of Saint-Denis was attacked and robbed by four men who were hiding in some corn; the Electors also claimed in a letter to the municipality of Évreux (which will be discussed later) that a number of bogus patrols had been going around with very obvious intentions. There must have been many minor events of this nature which were never recorded. One must not exaggerate the general insecurity of life, but one must at least acknowledge that the disturbances in the streets of Paris and, more especially, in the suburbs, must inevitably have increased it. The royal troops were encamped there and the number of deserters was considerable. Farmers were alarmed by the market riots and by expeditions like those undertaken by the inhabitants of Saint-Germain. In any case, in the fortnight which followed 14 July, there was one cry and one cry only throughout every parish in the suburbs of Paris: that they were overrun by disreputable-looking characters who had left the capital. This was almost always the only reason they gave for wanting to carry arms: witness Sceaux on 14 July, Suresnes on the 16th, Gonesse and Santeny-en-Brie on the 19th, Chevilly and L'Hay on the 21st and Marcoussis on the evening of the 22nd. The resolution of the latter village is particularly interesting: 'Rumour says that since the bourgeois militia was set up in Paris to combat the gangs of unemployed which have gathered in the capital, a very considerable number of individuals with criminal intentions have left the town and have scattered around the countryside: with a view to opposing the disorders and acts of brigandage which these individuals might commit, the parishes, especially those on the main highway to Paris, as far as Montlhéry, have formed bourgeois militia to protect their inhabitants.' Marcoussis, which is over twenty kilometres from Paris, had not suffered from the attentions of the brigands who were supposed to have left Paris, but it is easy to see why it felt so disturbed on the evening of the 22nd; the villages in the Orge valley had been very agitated and that morning Foulon had been seized in his Viry home and a howling mob had taken him to Paris where he was summarily put to death.

In such places, these fears had already started genuine panics. In Bougival, one such was the work of the seigneur, the Marquis de Mesmes; his concièrge had sent word that his château was likely to be pillaged and that all the parishes in the district were afraid for their homes and their harvests 'because of the brigands who are said to be all over this region'; he rushed back from Versailles on the 15th and at about five o'clock in the afternoon asked the beadle to sound the tocsin to assemble the villagers. The curé, who was in a certain amount of dispute with his seigneur on a legal matter, refused outright, saying that 'for a lieutenant-general of the king's army to come disturbing peaceful folk was a very unworthy action'. De Mesmes, probably somewhat intimidated, contented himself with telling people who came to see what was happening that a variety of criminals might well have escaped from Paris and gone to ground in the country; it would be prudent to keep a careful eye on strangers. On the same day a man was arrested in Sceaux for 'having begged for a number of reasons which troubled and terrified the inhabitants'. He was a hosier from Marville in Lorraine, a former deserter carrying a passport dated 28 April. Hanging around his neck, he wore 'a piece of white serge which bore a cross rather like the ones worn by the Brothers of Mercy'. He was begging for alms saying that 'he and a few others had been deputed to get enough money to support seven or eight hundred Bretons who were scattered around the countryside . . . , that they had come from the park of Saint-Cloud where they had arrested the queen at about eight in the morning; that he had given a hand in this matter and that the queen was now in a safe place; he went on to add that he was carrying pistols and would be sure to come back the next day'. His excuse was that he only sought to arouse their pity, but in fact he managed to get the town in a terrible turmoil. On the 25th at Villers-le-Sec to the north of Paris, in the area where the Great Fear was to break out only two days later, there was a panic of unknown origin: a former grocer living in Paris in the Rue des Cinq Diamants rushed into the town hall to declare that the parish was 'threatened by brigands' and that the local inhabitants had sent him to ask for a guard of twenty men whom they would gladly maintain in food. The Electors were faced by a never-ending procession of people coming to ask either for assistance or for permission to take up arms, and tried on the morning of the 27th to reassure the suburbs that all was calm 'after making the most careful inquiries' – and this at the very time the Great Fear was beginning to make itself felt.

The rumour very quickly spread into the provinces bordering on the Île de France. On the 17th, it made a sudden appearance in Bar-sur-Seine; by the 20th, it was in Pont-sur-Seine; it reached Bar-sur-Aube on the 21st, Tonnerre on the 22nd, Pont-sur-Yonne, Ervy, Chaource and Saint-Florentin on the 26th. Evreux heard it as early as the 20th. It was the same here as in the area around Paris – the authorities were delighted to be able to shift the blame from the local people to persons unknown. This is exactly what happened in Paris; on the 21st, a deputation from the municipality of Saint-Germain visited the National Assembly in order to state that they were not responsible for the murder of Sauvage since this was the work of 'some armed strangers who had come into the town'. Chartres used the same explanation for its riot on the 23rd. The *intendants* accepted these versions of the truth without batting an eyelid and indeed helped the rumour on its way. In Orléans, the *intendant* wrote on the 26th when discussing the outbreak in Chartres: 'The local people were roused by a gang of bandits who had been turned out of Paris', adding that the election in Dourdan was 'thoroughly disturbed and thrown into total confusion by gangs of bandits driven out of the capital by fear of punishment'. On the 24th, the *intendant* for Amiens explained that people in Picardy 'were disturbed by brigands driven out of Paris' and the evening before, the director of the *gabelle* had also expressed the fear that 'the brigands you are turning out of Paris' would cause new disturbances. On the 27th, the mayor and the *bureau intermédiaire* of Troyes wrote to the *intendant* and *commission intermédiaire* in Châlons stating very firmly that there were brigands in the district. They had not sought to verify the rumours on the spot and did no more than ask the Electors in Paris for an explanation. They received a reply, but M. Chaudron, who has made a detailed study of the Great Fear in Champagne, has not been able to trace it and he suspects that it might well have revealed that there was indeed a plot: he believes that the brigand rumour was the work of the Paris municipality who, with the cooperation of the patriotic deputies, announced the 'brigands' departure' to encourage the provincial municipalities to take up arms – which indeed they did as soon as the news reached them. The people of Champagne were not the only ones to write to Paris for information: the municipality of Évreux did the same and M. Dubreuil has published the reply they received on 24 July. This letter from the Electors simply re-states the facts we know already and goes on to express the fears by then general in the area around Paris: 'This capital, as you already know, has always been filled with vagrants anxious to escape the attention of their neighbours in the provinces. These are the men who first took up arms, who have stopped at nothing to arm themselves further and who have made the general state of fear greater still. In the early days it was difficult to tell who were genuine local inhabitants and who were vagrants with neither employment nor domicile. It soon became clear that we should have to draw up proper lists showing those who were properly domiciled in each district so that we could carefully and with the utmost precautions remove arms from the hands of those who might be prompt to misuse them. This project has been carried out in so far as it is possible in a town as large as Paris, but indeed it must eventually be carried to proper completion. There are still bogus patrols in existence and the least excitement brings into our streets and market places great numbers of people who surely cannot all be local residents. Certainly, the vast numbers of vagrants who have left Paris will divide itself into smaller units in time and then, we hope, the provinces will find them somewhat less formidable.' The natural conclusion of all this was that it would be sensible if the towns formed a bourgeois militia, but not the villages, and it is clear from this that if the Electors had wanted to spread panic they would surely have written in a very different tone.

Outside the provinces bordering the Île de France, the news was probably carried by travellers or private and official correspondence and newspapers. In Champagne itself, the *procureur* of the municipality of Villeneuve-sur-Yonne described on the 18th the danger that might result from the presence of 'vagabonds'; his report was based on what he had actually seen in Paris a few days before. We have already seen how travellers were responsible for spreading the fear of brigands in Charlieu. On the 25th, the *Correspondance de Nantes* printed an extract from a letter which attributed the disturbances in Paris to the English and the wretches they had taken as allies 'in order to set fire to the finest buildings in the city. . . . These Englishmen and their innumerable accomplices have fled and taken their frightful devastations into our countryside. In Saint-Germain-en-Laye and Poissy, they have brought death to citizens of irreproachable merit by falsely accusing them of hoarding grain.' Here too the authorities were partly responsible for maintaining the rumour. According to the committee of Château-Gontier, the fear in Maine was caused by the mayors of Chartres and Le Mans: the former is supposed to have written to the latter 'that large numbers of brigands have left Paris and are spreading all over the provinces'; the latter hastened to pass the warning to all local curés. In some places, the news was confirmed by the appearance in the district of suspicious-looking characters. On the 22nd, five such were arrested in Évreux, one a roofer from Basse-Normandie travelling back from Paris. 'I understand that you have got rid of all the brigands in Montmartre', wrote a lady from the Gisors area on 5 August, 'a few have passed this way; some have been arrested and put into prison.' One of them had said to a certain Chevalier de Saint-Louis 'that he had been sent by M. de Mirabeau and that there were about five hundred of them scattered around the provinces to gather information on what was happening'. Something slightly more serious took place in Charolles: on the 26th, a coachman was arrested. He had been at the sacking of Saint-Lazare on the 13th and had run off with seven hundred *louis*.

There can be no doubt that the disturbances which now broke out practically everywhere produced in the provinces spontaneous panics exactly like those prevailing in Paris and caused them by a very similar process. As early as 9 July, the magistrates in Lyons were loudly proclaiming: 'We have seen our town attacked by brigands who, expelled from various parts of the kingdom for their attempts to spread sedition, have come to our city to put their criminal plans into operation.' That such a rumour could not be of revolutionary origin must surely be proved by its acceptance and propagation by Imbert-Colomès. Toul on the 29th and Forqualquier on the 30th were still talking about the brigands who had come from Paris, but it is worth noting that the further away from the capital, the less specific was the information as to where the brigands had actually come from. In Lons-le-Saulnier, for instance, they were said to have been 'expelled from the capital'; Saint-Germain-Laval in the Forez on the 20th thought that they were 'spreading all over the provinces'; Nevers on the 30th said that they 'were spreading everywhere'; in Toul itself, they were coming from Paris 'and other places'. Another proof: on the 22nd the inhabitants of Semur met together 'on hearing the news about the riots caused by bands of brigands all over the province'; there was no mention of Paris: this news had come from Dijon and Autun after disturbances in Auxonne and Saint-Jean de Losne on 19 and 20 July. They also said that 'the brigands' were being reinforced by escaped criminals. Indeed it is true that in some places the prisons had been seized: in Luxeuil, Pierre-Encize and Aix, as well as the Bastille itself. On the 29th, the municipality of Toul wrote to its counterpart in Blénod: 'You should know that a great many brigands have escaped from prison in Paris and other places.' This in turn led to the rumour current during the Great Fear that bands of galley slaves had escaped. Finally, there was some talk of foreign regiments passing through the provinces: they were in fact the ones the king had had stationed around Paris and which were now being sent back to their garrison towns. But the people imagined that they were following the same path as the brigands and it seemed to them that there was very little difference between them and the troops which the kings of Europe were supposed to be lending to the Comte d'Artois.

Now that the brigands had as it were been formally announced, they seemed to be appearing all over the place – all around Paris, for instance, and as a result various local panics broke out. At Verneuil on the 20th, after a riot in Laigle, rumour had it that six hundred armed mutineers were moving towards the town and were only a league away. At Gyé-sur-Seine on the 26th, the presence of a few strangers was enough to 'arouse terror'. A few hours before a wave of terror swept over the entire region, there was talk in Clamecy on the morning of the 29th of farms burnt to the ground by brigands in the Aillant valley; the fire seems however to have been accidental. At Château-Chinon on the 28th, the *syndic* revealed 'that a number of brigands and vagrants have fled either from the prisons or from some of the large towns in the kingdom; that several bands of them have been seen in the woods surrounding the town'. In Brive on the 22nd, the municipality brought the local citizens up to date with the events of 14 July and at the same time warned them 'that brigands have been seen near Saint-Céré and Beaulieu'; that is towards the south and not towards the north, as would have been the case if Paris had been the sole source of the rumour.

There is no need to assume that the revolutionaries had deliberately planned to spread the rumours, but one must accept that the orators in the towns who encouraged the arming of local populations for political reasons did much to propagate them. They genuinely believed in the brigands. At the same time, however, the news operated to their advantage and they were prepared to use it for their own ends: of all the accusations levelled at them in this matter of brigands and rumours, this seems to be the one we may accept as true. Some of them, being uncertain as to how things would turn out, skilfully used the danger to justify arming the populace. This was the explanation offered by the municipality of Bourg to M. de Gouvernet, the military commander for the province, when they sought to justify the measures forced upon them by the local inhabitants on the evening before (16 July). Similarly, on the 24th, the committee for Château-Gontier turned the Great Fear to good account by forcing official recognition of its no less radical decree of the 18th. There was another point of view: by proposing the formation of bourgeois militia, they were preparing not only to use troops against the aristocracy, they also had in mind the stricter control of the working classes. It was not really possible to make this particular point clear, for the lower orders were either present at the meetings or else had excellent sources of information; the 'brigands' appeared at a moment which was particularly opportune for advising security measures suitable for keeping the people in a proper state of order. Finally, it is very probable that all these excuses served as pretexts both in the face of superior authority and towards those undecided citizens who were not anxious to take up arms without the king's permission. In the resolutions pertaining to the establishment of militia, the leaders used these different considerations in very varying proportions, according to their own particular temperament. At Lons-le-Saulnier on the 19th, a member of the Assembly dismissed the brigands in a word: with considerable virulence he denounced the nobles who appeared to him far more guilty and dangerous. Autun, on the other hand, took quite a different attitude on the 23rd: there it was a popular revolt that was feared: 'Prudence demands the establishment of a militia so that we shall be ready to repel the common enemy and, even more important, to nip the rebellion in the bud, if rebellion there be, by showing the anti-patriotic and the disturbers of public order that we have arms and are prepared to use them.' At Saint-Denis-de-l'Hôtel, a village in the Val d'Orléans, the *syndic* considered the reasons for taking up arms of equal value, and his report seems to express the average opinion of the bourgeoisie, upper and lower, in both town and country. On the 31st, he declared that 'citizens have felt themselves threatened both in their persons and their goods ever since the revolution of the 13th of this month took place in the capital; that the reasons why they are so alarmed are: 1) the reports, true or false, but public ever since the occasion of the furious storm which would have destroyed the capital if the patriotism of the citizens of that great town had not taken the strongest measures to dispel it, a storm whose violence has shaken the whole of France to its very depths; 2) the escape from the capital of a vast number of brigands which has spread fear and agitation through many provinces, for they have held many people to ransom; 3) the still-existing corn shortage, now with us for far too long and occasioning rumours and popular emotions of great and constant danger when they are not stopped at source'.

One way or another, fear of brigands and fear of aristocrats always managed to occur simultaneously in the mind of the people; this naturally hastened the synthesis (already well established in Paris) of the aristocrats' plot and the fear of brigands. The similarity between 1789 and 1848 is very clear: everywhere, people feared the arrival of mobs of rioters who would attack property and disturb the life of the provinces; the slightest incident turned anxiety into outright fear and panic spread unhindered because everyone was expecting it. In 1789, however, the agitation was greater and more widespread. The whole Third Estate considered itself under attack because the rioters were in the service of the aristocratic plotters and were helped by foreign regiments in the service of the king and the troops of neighbouring rulers brought in by the *émigrés*; they would be attacked from all the main towns, not just from Paris. And again, the economic and social circumstances, the famine and the number of vagrants wandering around the country were far more conducive to the outbreak of local panics in 1789 than they ever were in 1848, and it was precisely these local panics which engendered the Great Fear. This is why a phenomenon of this nature was able to spread in the most extraordinary way until it was transformed into an event of national proportions.

Part III
The Great Fear

I

Characteristics of the Great Fear

The *fear of brigands* appeared for the first time at the end of the winter, reaching its culmination during the second fortnight in July; at its greatest extent, it covered more or less the whole of France. Though it gave rise to the Great Fear, it was not at all the same thing and one must make a careful distinction between the two. The Great Fear had its own special characteristics, and these are what they were: until this moment in time, the appearance of the brigands was possible and much dreaded: with the Great Fear, it became a total certainty; they were there in the flesh, they could be both seen and heard; generally, this precipitated a panic, but not always. Sometimes, the villagers were content to adopt defensive positions or send a warning to the local militia that had already been organized to ensure security or fight against the aristocracy. Such alarms were by no means new and we have already described several of them. It was characteristic of the Great Fear that these alarms spread far and wide with the most astonishing speed instead of staying purely local. As they travelled, they produced in their turn new proof of the existence of the elusive brigands as well as fresh disturbances which helped the fear on its way and kept it very much alive by sending it on in 'relays'. This speedy propagation can also be explained by the fear of brigands: people believed that they were coming because they were expecting them. The fear streamed across the kingdom in a limited number of currents, but most of France was affected: this suggests that the Great Fear was universal; the currents moved with great speed: hence the impression that the Great Fear broke out everywhere simultaneously 'almost at the same time'. Both these ideas are wrong. They represent contemporary opinion and have been passed on without question. Once it had been decided that the Great Fear must have broken out every-where at the same time, it followed logically that everyone should think it the work of secret agents working together in a general conspiracy.

The revolutionaries instantly interpreted it as proof of the aristocrats' plot: they were frightening the people deliberately so as to bring them back to the *ancien régime* or else thrust them into total disorder. 'The alarms which broke out all over the kingdom on practically the same day,' wrote Maupetit on the 31st, 'seem to be a sequel to the plot and a complement to the disastrous projects intended to set the whole of France aflame. For who can accept that on the same day and at the same instant the tocsin should sound almost everywhere, if the alarm had not been given deliberately by people sent out for that very purpose?' On the evening of 8 August, just as an announcement was being made to the National Assembly to the effect that they had (supposedly) arrested a courier who had travelled through Poitou, the Angoumois and Guyenne, announcing the arrival of the brigands, a deputy called out: 'This diabolical confederacy is not totally extinguished; its leaders have fled, but it may yet rise from the ashes. We know that a host of ecclesiastics as well as *gentilshommes* are all involved. France cannot be too much on its guard.' The commission of inquiry set up by the Assembly on 28 July started an investigation: on 18 September, they wrote to the *bailliage* of Saint-Flour about the panic that had broken out in Massiac and the subsequent disturbances: 'It seems that the same impulse was given on almost the same day in every province, which leads us to suppose a premeditated conspiracy whose source is unknown but which, for the safety of the state, one must endeavour to uncover.' The proclamation of 10 August had already given the following version official approval: 'The enemies of the nation, having lost all hope of preventing public regeneration and the establishment of liberty by the violence of despotism seem to have conceived a criminal plan for attaining the same end by means of disorder and anarchy: one of its endeavours has been to spread false alarms at the same time and almost on the same day in different parts of the kingdom, so that by announcing non-existent invasions and outbreaks of brigandage they might provoke violence and crime and thus attack both property and persons.' The revolutionaries never dreamt for a moment that by denouncing the aristocrats' plot they themselves made unknowing preparation for the Great Fear.

But in fact the event turned against the aristocracy: the Great Fear hastened general armament and produced new agrarian revolts. *Is fecit cui prodest*. The counter-revolutionaries threw the responsibility on to their adversaries. Dining in Turin on 25 September, Arthur Young heard a party of *émigrés* talking about their troubles and asked them 'by whom such enormities were committed; by the peasants or wandering *brigands*? they said by the peasants undoubtedly; but that the great and indisputable origin of most of those villainies was the settled plan and conduct of some leaders in the National Assembly, in union with, and by the money of *one other of great rank* [in other words, the Duc d'Orléans]; that when the assembly had rejected the proposal of the Count de Mirabeau to address the king to establish the *milice bourgeois*, couriers were soon after sent to all quarters of the kingdom to give a universal alarm of great troops of *brigands* being actually on the march, plundering and burning everywhere, at the instigation of aristocrats, and calling on the people to arm immediately in their defence; that by intelligence afterwards, received from different parts of the kingdom, it was found that these couriers must have been despatched from Paris at the same time [Young adds in a footnote that this was later confirmed to him in Paris]. Forged orders of the king in council were likewise sent, directing the people to burn the chateaux of the aristocratical party; and thus, as it were by magic, all France was armed at the same moment, and the peasants instigated to commit the enormities which have since disgraced the kingdom.' This version appeared in contemporary documents very early in the day. The curé of Tulette in the Drôme wrote in his parish register on 24 January 1790: 'The universal alarms which spread all over the kingdom at the very same moment on 29 July were caused by the paid servants of the Assembly who wanted to arm the people.' Lally-Tollendal accepted the same version in his *Seconde lettre à mes commettants*. It passed into the histories of the revolution prepared by such counter-revolutionaries as Beaulieu and Montgaillard as well as into various Mémoires: generation after generation has drawn its information from these sources without seeking to support it with any proper proof. Beugnot says in his memoirs that he tried 'to go right back to the prime cause', but having questioned the peasant from Colombey who brought the fear to Choiseul, he noted that this man had in fact got his news from a peasant in Montigny and supposing that the latter would almost certainly give him a similar answer, he abandoned this mode of inquiry and settled for the supposed plot. He should in fact have moved slowly backwards from village to village right to the Franche-Comté. Only the government could have cleared up the matter by means of a methodical inquiry, which indeed was the action taken in 1848.

This is not to say that they did not have their eye on the possible manoeuvres of their enemies. In May and June they were warned that there were indications of a plot and each time they tried to investigate the matter. On 8 May, for instance, a person from Paris was arrested in Meaux 'being very suspicious-looking and uttering words of scandalous and seditious import'. Puységur, the minister, drew the attention of the lieutenant of police to this man on the 21st: 'It is possible that this man is no more than a vagrant unworthy of attention, but on the other hand he could be the tool of some secret agents.' He asked them to send an experienced police officer to Meaux to interrogate him thoroughly. The prisoner was transferred to the Châtelet and on 10 June the minister admitted 'that we cannot draw from this prisoner's comments the inferences we had expected'. The government's lack of concern would seem to have been much exaggerated. At the time of the agrarian revolts and the Great Fear, there were inquiries about the purveyors of false information and the bearers of alleged orders, as we already know from earlier disturbances in the Mâconnais: all replies were negative. But it is quite possible that the inquiries were incomplete. Today, though it is naturally much more difficult for us to bring such investigations to a proper conclusion, we can at least achieve the end we seek; it is possible for us to collect and compare a considerable body of documents which contemporary authorities, operating in the very midst of overlapping and confusing events, were unable to gather into a proper dossier; it is also possible for us, at least in some areas, to go right back to the incident which started the panic, disentangle its ramifications and follow its trail.

They said in 1789 (and indeed have said it ever since) that the Great Fear was universal, because authorities have everywhere confused it with the fear of brigands. To admit that the brigands existed and might appear at any moment was one thing; to imagine that they were actually there was another. It was easy to pass from the first situation to the second: otherwise there is no explanation for the Great Fear; but the transfer was not absolutely obligatory and though the whole of France believed in brigands, the Great Fear did not appear in the whole of France. Almost all of Flanders, Hainault, the Cambrésis and the Ardennes were unaffected; the greater part of Normandy was undisturbed and there is scarcely a trace in Brittany; Médoc, the Landes and the Basque country, Basse-Languedoc and Roussillon were more or less unscathed;

in the regions where the agrarian revolts had been at their worst –
the Franche-Comté, Alsace, the Normandy Bocage and the Mâconnais –
there was no Great Fear whatsoever: at the most, a few minor scares of
purely local interest. Yet this traditional confusion is so deeply rooted in
everyone's mind that serious writers who have tried to study the phenomenon objectively have been unable to avoid it, so that their researches
have taken the wrong direction and their attempts at explanation have
served no useful purpose. Since the fear of brigands came for the most
part from the capital (though not uniquely, as we have already seen),
historians have decided that this must also hold good for the Great Fear
and have rarely sought to find the local incident which had in fact caused
it. M. Chaudron's study of the Great Fear in southern Champagne
reveals this mistaken focus: a simple comparison of dates would have
shown him that the centre of agitation was to be found in the province
itself and not in Paris. For the same reason, many writers have presented
the Great Fear as a huge wave spreading out concentrically from Paris,
whilst in fact it had a great many points of origin and its advance was
often capricious: sometimes it moved *towards* Paris, coming in from the
Clermontois and the Soissonnais in the north and from the Gâtinais
in the south, being an extension of the fear in Champagne.

It is even more difficult to understand why historians continue to
insist on the simultaneity of the outbreaks of the Great Fear. For contemporary writers to have done this is perfectly excusable: they lacked
proper information. Today, however, we have enough facts to be certain
that the fear did not break out everywhere on the same day. The Great
Fear of Les Mauges and Poitou started in Nantes on the 20th; that
of Maine, in the east of the province, on the 20th or the 21st; the fear
in the Franche-Comté set the entire East and South-East in a panic
on the 22nd; in southern Champagne it began on the 24th; in the
Clermontois and the Soissonnais on the 26th; it crossed the South-West
from a starting point in Ruffec on the 28th; it reached Barjols in Provence
on 4 August and Lourdes, at the foot of the Pyrenees, on the 6th of
the same month.

Nor does the conspiracy idea stand up when a proper examination
is made of the origins and the mechanism of the way the panics spread.
Many documents give the names of the people who brought the news
to the villages and towns: there is nothing mysterious about them and
their good faith cannot be questioned. Like Beugnot, one might claim

that they were sometimes tools in the matter and that the proof of the conspiracy must be sought at their starting point. However it is to this starting point that scholars have rarely troubled to go though there are less than a dozen such and they are scattered haphazardly about the country. In these circumstances, the legend which deliberately despatches couriers all over France does not survive a close examination either.

The basic argument which produced the idea of a conspiracy is that the Great Fear was intended to encourage the counter-revolution, according to some, and general armament and agrarian revolts according to others. It is clear that it did not operate to the advantage of the aristocracy, but although it certainly encouraged the spread of arms and stirred up new agrarian riots, it is not true that the fear was a vital factor for either. It must surely be obvious by now that the people began to take up arms as a direct consequence of the general fear of vagrants; the process was speeded up by the idea of the aristocrats' plot, long before the Great Fear; the bourgeoisie never had any intention of letting the peasants have arms. The agrarian revolts of the Normandy Bocage, Hainault, Franche-Comté, Alsace and even the Mâconnais preceded the Great Fear and only the outbreak in the Dauphiné can be put down to its influence. Between the agrarian revolts and the Great Fear, there is so little interdependence that the two do not coincide, except in the Dauphiné; on the contrary, it was the revolt in the Franche-Comté which started the panic in the East, whilst the uprisings in the Bocage, Hainault and Alsace caused no panic at all. Finally, to maintain traditional views, it would have to be proved that the revolutionary bourgeoisie was anxious to cause a peasant uprising: everything points firmly to the contrary.

The fear of brigands and aristocrats alike, the peasant revolt, the arming of bourgeois citizens and the Great Fear are therefore four separate entities, though there are very clear connexions between them and when one studies the last, one's method of inquiry must keep this basic fact firmly in mind.

2

The Original Panics

There were five currents of fear, though one of them (the Clermontois panic) ought possibly to be counted as two separate outbreaks. We are very well informed on the origin of three of them. For two others, we do not have sufficiently precise documentation, but we can make a very informed guess as to their cause. As for the Maine outbreak, documentation is so slight that we can do no more than fix its starting point very approximately.

Two of the original panics are very closely linked to the popular reactions to the aristocrats' plot and are therefore related to the political situation in France. In the East, the fear developed from the peasants' revolt in the Franche-Comté; there can be no doubt on that score and the basic interest here lies in the way the fear spread. The matter is more complex in Les Mauges and Poitou. We know already that there was a riot in Nantes when they heard that Necker had been dismissed: round about midday on 20 July there was a sudden rumour that a detachment of dragoons was arriving by the Montaigu road for the express purpose of restoring order to Nantes. No one knows where the rumour started, but it is not a particularly surprising one, bearing in mind that there had been alarms of a similar nature in Paris on 13 and 14 July. The citizens instantly took up arms and forced local gunsmiths to hand over their stocks; guards were set up on the Pirmil bridge; the bourgeois cavalry went out and scoured the countryside as far as the Grandlieu lake. These were the activities which started off the panic, as the *Correspondance de Nantes* clearly states on 25 July: 'We know that men with malicious intentions completely distorted the military preparations made in Nantes and spread a terrible panic in the neighbouring villages. They must take a cruel pleasure in the misfortunes of their country if they can so boldly misrepresent the actions of the inhabitants of a wealthy town which could only suffer most grievously if its surrounding country-side were laid to waste.' Unfortunately, the *Correspondance* imputes the peasants' mistake to the aristocrats and omits to tell us why they took the Nantais for brigands. Probably, they flew into a state of alarm at seeing troops moving in the distance: many local panics started in this way and we shall give examples of these further on. But it is not impossible that in any case the peasants were afraid that the Nantais would come out and seize their remaining stocks of corn; indeed on the 19th a detachment had gone to Paimbœuf to seize a grain ship as well as any meal that might be available; the booty was taken back to Nantes on the 20th. Shortages and the rivalry between town and country thus combined with the political crisis to produce the fear in the West.

In other areas, the economic situation and the fear of vagrants lay at the origin of the panics. In the Clermontois, what started it off was the anxiety about the harvest and a fight between poachers and game-keepers which looked so violent when seen from a distance that the villagers of Estrées-Saint-Denis were quite terrified. 'On Sunday even-ing,' the *intendant* wrote to the *prévôt* of the *maréchaussée* on 26 July, 'some poachers had a rather violent quarrel with the gamekeepers at Estrées-Saint-Denis, four leagues from here. The inhabitants of this parish who, like everyone else in the countryside, have got it firmly into their heads that people are going to come and cut down their corn, saw the disturbance from afar and thought a crowd of rogues was on its way to strip the fields. They sounded the tocsin and gathered everyone together. Neighbouring parishes did the same.' This current travelled down the Oise valley, possibly strengthened by another incident, for on the 28th the Electors in Paris received a report that there had been a disturbance in Beaumont caused by the looting of two boats loaded with corn: here too famine was a prime cause. The alarm got as far as Montmorency where a new misunderstanding made it worse. According to the *Journal de la Ville*, it was 'the measuring-out process which precedes the harvest. The land is divided up into sections by means of poles and each section is given to a different harvester.' Apparently the workmen engaged in this preliminary work were mistaken for thieves. The *Feuille politique* of La Scène-Desmaisons has a more likely version: 'A gang of workmen had offered their services to a farmer whose harvest was ready. When he refused to pay them the wages they asked for, the spirit of anarchy prompted them to use threats. They said that they would cut his corn without his permission and ruin his harvest. The terrified farmer ran to get help. The news got worse as it spread. The tocsin was sounded in all the parishes around.' A similar explanation is given for the Soissonnais fear which started in the Béthisy plain between Verberie and Crépy-en-Valois. This is probably a branch of the current which started in the Clermontois, and the Béthisy affair may constitute nothing more than a 'relay', but the Duc de Gesvres, writing on the evening of the 28th to the Duc de la Rochefoucauld-Liancourt, president of the National Assembly, suggests that it was independent of any other panic. Whatever the truth, it started for very similar reasons: 'These rumours, so far as we can make out, were based on nothing more serious than a conversation between five or six strangers who were slightly drunk and who settled down for a rest near the corn they were supposed to have threatened to cut down, the farmer having refused to pay them what they wanted.' The municipality of Crépy-en-Valois said the panic started with a dozen peasants squabbling in the middle of the corn still standing. The Meaux town council reported that some harvesters 'had cut some farmers' barley in spite of the said farmers' wishes because they refused to feed them'. At Roye, the poacher incident 'in the forest of Compiègne' and against the king's own gamekeepers got mixed up with the harvest incident, but the latter was now attributed to a farmer who had been turned out of his farm in favour of a rival who had accepted worse terms: this farmer was supposed to have avenged himself on his successor by making him cut two acres of green corn. These explanations are in perfect agreement with what we already know of the conflicts between farmers and harvesters which were so typical of this area and of the '*droit du marché*' so widespread in Picardy and so persistent in spite of edicts against it – a right which forbade anyone to take a lease on a farm or *marché* without the agreement of the departing farmer.

In southern Champagne, the fear appeared on 24 July to the south of Romilly, at Maizières-la-Grande-Paroisse, Origny and 'other places nearby', according to the *Journal de Troyes* for the 28th and confirmed by a letter from the *sub-délégué*. Rumour said that brigands had appeared in the canton; they had been seen going into the woods. 'The tocsin was sounded and three thousand men gathered to hunt down these alleged brigands . . . but the brigands were only a herd of cows.' It is a reasonable explanation, for there are plenty of other instances of someone starting a panic because they heard the mysterious rustles of grazing animals as they passed by the edge of a wood or else saw the dust raised by passing cattle hanging lazily in the distance. It seems as though the panic in Champagne had the most insignificant cause of all, though as in Nantes, past events might well have conditioned the local peasants to expect hordes of city dwellers to descend on them in search of corn. There had been a riot for this very reason in Nogent on the 18th and in Pont on the 20th; perhaps this is what happened in Romilly.

The Ruffec panic which was transmitted to Poitou, the central plateau and the whole of Aquitaine, is related to the general fear of vagrants and recalls the events in Sceaux mentioned earlier. We learn the cause from Lefebvre, secretary to the Limoges *intendance*, who had it from the *sub-délégué*: it was caused by 'the arrival of four or five men dressed as Brothers of Mercy and saying they were collecting money for captive Christians. They had gone to various houses but were not received everywhere with equal courtesy. Displeased with the smallness of their receipts, they had left the town threatening to return in greater numbers, but they had not been seen since; people knew only that they had gone deep into the forest nearby. As this minor incident travelled, it was told with ever-increasing exaggeration and undoubtedly started the fear.' We know that on the 28th, a man was arrested who had stated 'that there were bandits and hussars in the woods nearby'. Upset by what he had heard about beggars, he thought he saw them. His fear served as a 'relay' for the original alarm and it was his story which grew and spread. When it got as far as Angoulême, for instance, there was not a word about disguised beggars – it was definitely brigands hiding in the woods. According to the curé of Vançais, there was another relay to the west of Ruffec: 'a band of smugglers and thieves hidden in the forests of Aulnay, Chef-Boutonne and Chizé, desperate with hunger, had made incursions into neighbouring villages to get bread'. Together with fear of the vagrant, the essential element in this is the apprehension inspired by the forest. But one small detail – the mention of hussars – reveals yet again a belief in the aristocrats' plot.

As for the fear in Maine, it is not possible to say what particular incident caused it, but it must have taken place near La Ferté-Bernard: near here is Montmirail whose forest provided fuel for a glassworks which became a hotbed of trouble between 1789 and 1792 whenever there was a rise in the price of bread. It is likely that the panic originated in some workers' demonstration or, even more probable, in the same circumstances as in Ruffec.

It is clear then that the earliest or the original panics which started off the Great Fear had the same causes as previous alarms, and the most active causes of all were of a social and economic order, those which had always disturbed the countryside the most and which the crisis in 1789 had considerably aggravated. But why did the fear spread so far and wide instead of remaining purely local, as it had always done before? Why did the parish take up arms and hastily send for outside help? At the end of July, the general feeling of insecurity was so much more frightening than it had ever been before, and on the eve of the harvest there was a truly overwhelming sensation of fear and anxiety. This is why the aristocrats' plot and the news that the brigands had been driven out of Paris and other major cities gave a much more dreadful significance to the appearance of the merest vagabond. Finally, since the brigands had become the instruments of the enemies of the Third Estate, it seemed natural to appeal to national solidarity and to that half-formed federation between towns and cities. And for the same reasons, those who were asked for help never doubted for a moment that the news was true, so that they in their turn spread it further.

3

How the Panics Spread

Most often the panic was spread by people with no official status of any kind. Some thought they were doing their duty as citizens when they urged that help be sent; others wanted to alert relations and friends; travellers told what they had seen or heard; most talkative of all were the refugees whose eagerness to exaggerate the danger was matched by their fear of being considered cowardly for having run away. Their tales were packed with picturesque details. There was a miller travelling to Saint-Michel and as he went into the small town of Confolens through the Faubourg Saint-Barthelémy he encountered a certain Sauvage, a pit-sawyer, hurrying home with the information that the *maréchaussée* were in Saint-Georges only a kilometre away and were asking for help: he called to the miller to spur on his horse and warn the town. 'Have no fear,' replied the miller, 'I'll get some help.' Sauvage went home, got his gun and rushed to meet the brigands, whilst the miller rode through the streets noisily calling the citizens to arms. These worthy patriots got no reward for their pains: once the panic had died down, the local committee put the pair of them in prison. At Rochechouart during the morning of the 29th, the Sieur Longeau des Bruyères from Oradour-sur-Vayres rode into town along the Chabanais road: he shouted as he went that he was in full flight from Champagne-Mouton where with his own eyes he had seen the dreadful slaughter of women and children and old people – terrible – awful – blood everywhere – houses burning! 'I've got to save my family. Take care, get your guns! Goodbye, goodbye perhaps forever!' And off he galloped. Several people brought the fear to Limoges: first a monk of Sainte-Geneviève from the Abbey of Lesterp near Confolens, who had spent the night at Rochechouart and had been awakened at two in the morning by 'dreadful shrieks' – and had ridden off forthwith; next a former *garde du corps* who had been told about the brigands whilst he was out hunting and was now riding to warn the *intendant*; last, an architect returning from a journey who had picked up the news *en route* the evening before. At Castelnau-Montratier in the Quercy, the director of the Cahors *messagerie* suddenly appeared on a mule lent to him by the Capuchins, 'brought to a terrible state of excitement by the tocsin and the frightful disturbances in the town'. The panic in Samer in the Boulonnais was started by 'some travellers'; in Saulieu by the local doctor on his way back from Montsauche; it was taken all along the left bank of the Seine from Fontainebleau to Villeneuve-le-Roi by the Gaudon brothers, wine merchants from Boignes in the Gâtinais. A deputy for the nobility, whose letters to the Marquise de Créquy have survived, had confirmation of the ruined harvest in Montmorency from 'someone arriving by post-chaise who had actually seen the terrible damage this rabble gets up to'.

At the same time, the panic was spread – if not exactly deliberately, then at least with some apparent method – by people of some standing and by the authorities themselves. The curés thought it their duty to warn their colleagues and their friends in the nobility. In Maine, it was generally the local priests who seem to have spread the panic after they had received a letter on the subject from the mayor of Le Mans. In Vendôme, the town council was warned by the Mazangé curé; in Lubersac in Périgord, it was the curate of Saint-Cyr-le-Champagne who hastened to announce that his village was being attacked by brigands; in Sarlat, a curé ran at top speed to spread the news that Limeuil had been burnt to the ground during the night. In the Bourbonnais, the curé of Culant wrote to the curé of Verdun and he in turn sent a despatch to his counterpart in Maillet. The *gentilshommes* acted in the same way and their stewards followed their example. In the Dauphiné, the alarm in Aoste was given in the first place by the Abbé of Leyssens, the Dame d'Aoste, the Chevalier de Murinais and the steward of the Comtesse de Valin who rushed to take the news to La Tour-du-Pin. In Poitou, the steward of the Château de Maulevrier sent messengers everywhere asking the village priests to arm their parishioners as best they could and march to the assistance of Cholet. Around Neuvic in Périgord, the news was passed around by priests and nobles: Mme de Plaigne sent an urgent message to Baron de Bellinay asking him to warn Baron de Drouhet, who received many other warnings from nobles and churchmen, amongst them the Prior of Saint-Angel, and in his turn he wrote to the Baron de Bellinay and the curé of Chirac. Such incidents were common everywhere. Servants rode through the villages spreading alarm; sometimes the peasants did not recognize them, hence the tales of mysterious or unknown messengers.

The most curious part of all was played by the authorities. Today, they would of course make preliminary inquiries by telephone before warning the population. It is true that they did try to get accurate information first if they could, or else they sent the cavalry or the *maréchaussée* to scour the countryside. But they knew only too well that it would always take time to get to the truth of the matter and it therefore seemed prudent to take precautions immediately, put the parishes in the picture and ask them for help. To this end, the town councils and the committees sent messengers and even prepared circular letters – as for instance in Confolens, Uzerche and Lons-le-Saulnier. The Évreux committee warned the surrounding towns on the 22nd and 23rd, then on the 24th sent a printed circular to a hundred and ten country parishes. The leaders of the militia took the same task on themselves. From Bellême, they sent word to Mortagne; in Colmar, the colonel of the militia, one of the presidents of the *conseil souverain*, suggested that the rural communities should arm themselves on 28 July. The authorities of the *ancien régime* were also quick to respond, especially the royal judges and the *sub-délégués*. Uzerche was warned by a letter from the judge in Lubersac; letters written by the *procureur de la justice* in Villefranche-de-Belvez did much to pass the panic from Périgord to Quercy. The *sub-délégué* of La Châtaignerie spread it all through his *arrondissement* and especially in Secondigny. The *sub-délégué* for Moissac did even better: he told the village priests to sound the tocsin. The *commissions intermédiaires* of the Provincial Assemblies were less involved, but the body sitting in Soissons, or at least its *procureur-syndic*, was reasonably active, writing urgently to warn the town of Guise; the committee for the district of Neufchâteau urged the villages around to take up arms and hold themselves ready 'the moment the tocsin sounds'. On 31 July, the commissioners for Provence advised the parishes once again to form their own militia to repel the brigands. On 1 August, the very first breath of panic caused the *parlement* in Toulouse to issue a decree authorizing all villages to take up arms and sound the tocsin.

It was however the conduct of the military authorities which was particularly typical. The Bar-sur-Seine *maréchaussée* transported the fear to Landreville and its counterpart in Dun passed the news to Guéret; the Marquis de Bains, *inspecteur* of the *maréchaussée*, did the same in Roye in Picardy. As soon as the Comte de Lau arrived to take up his command in Belfort, he warned the parishes all around that brigands were coming and that each village would have to look to its own defence. The Marquis de Langeron probably did more than any other single person to send the fear sweeping through the Franche-Comté where he was in command. In a circular which was already travelling around Morez and Saint-Claude and which must therefore have been written before the 14th, he warned the local villages that a gang of over two hundred people from La Vôge had come into the province; we have no other details on this alleged incursion and possibly only one local panic can bear out its actually having taken place. When the peasants started their attacks on the châteaux, the Marquis hastened to blame the brigands in a circular dated 23 July; a third letter dated the 24th announced that another band had come in from Burgundy and was making its way across the province. For this reason, Vernier de Bians, a lieutenant in Salins who wrote an account of the disturbances in the Franche-Comté, had no hesitation in blaming Langeron for these rumours and makes it clear that he suspected him of acting in a deliberately provocative way. The annalists for the Clamecy area impute a similar course of action to Delarue, the local *sub-délégué*, judge for the *châtellenie* and later president for the *département*; in fact, Delarue had done nothing very sinister – he had learnt that the brigands were on their way *via* a letter that the *bailli* of Coulanges had entrusted to a dancing teacher from Clamecy who had come to give a few lessons and was on his way back home; however, the letter had been read out loud in the market place and he had sent the news abroad through a member of the *maréchaussée*.

It has often been suggested that the couriers and the postilions working for the postal service played a suspiciously large part in the dissemination of the panics. There has been some exaggeration, but documents bear out the suggestion. A postal courier from Conchy-les-Pots was partly responsible for the panic in Roye: the first news of the fear was taken to Limoges by the postmaster of Saint-Junien; in Clermont, the *prévôt* for the Soissonnais seized the letters sent by the Saint-Just postmaster announcing that the entire area had been put to fire and sword; a postilion from Churet carried the Ruffec fear into Angoulême: according to two judges, he had 'learnt from a peasant that there was a gang of robbers and bandits in the forest'. The dissemination of the panic by means of the postal service was particularly noticeable between Valence and Avignon; it travelled from one stage post to another with great speed. But this is perfectly natural – the travellers themselves passed on the news that the brigands were coming, so what could be more reasonable than that those who drove the stage-coaches and post-chaises should do the same? And when the authorities wanted to send official notification, surely the most expedient means was the postal service? On the 29th at five o'clock in the evening, a courier from Bordeaux arrived in Angoulême to ask the town council to send them information on the fear in Ruffec. This courier carried an unsealed letter and he had been told that if the news proved to be false, he should be sure to pass this information on to everyone he met. Probably he showed the letter all along the way as he travelled to Angoulême and it was probably this courier who was discussed in the National Assembly during the session of 8 August.

Not every important person showed himself lacking in common sense; there were quite a few who were very sceptical indeed about the rumours. At Gimont in the Lomagne, the Baron de Montesquieu refused to believe in the brigands; the Comte de Polastron refused (in vain, unfortunately) to sound the tocsin; an officer on leave in Saint-Clair was warned that four thousand brigands were at Lauzerte and wrote ironically: 'I hardly think they have actually counted them. . . .' According to the account of the fear in the Saint-Girons area which appears in the memoirs of the Comte de Terssac, he was equally incredulous. Lesser lights spoke out boldly against the dissemination of the fear: at Saint-Privat-des-Prés near Ribérac, a steward named Gouand stopped the tocsin in spite of the committee's instructions to the contrary, and when he was insulted and threatened he promptly got three villagers imprisoned. The curé of Castelnau-Montratier asked his parishioners 'if their enemies had landed in balloons'. The curé of Le Vers in the Agenais refused absolutely to let them sound the tocsin. In Frayssinet-le-Gélat, Delord the lawyer carefully read the gazettes and concluded that there was no basis for any fear 'because if the English or the Spanish had entered France, they could never have got into the heart of Aquitaine without our hearing about it earlier and that it was the firing practice in different parts of the province that has made people think there were enemies lurking all around'. The *sub-délégué* for Moissac expressed the same opinion, but this did not stop him taking every measure appropriate not only for the repelling of brigands but also likely to persuade everyone around him that these brigands did actually exist.

The reason was basically that the fear of brigands was so widespread (Bonald, future oracle of the counter-revolution and then mayor of Millau, offered no objection to the news of their approach) that an administrator who was properly aware of his responsibilities and totally deprived of any rapid means of information was obliged to take the rumour seriously, however unlikely it seemed. Dom Mauduit, the Prior of Saint-Angel, put the matter in a nutshell in his letter to Baron de Drouhet: 'All things considered, there is nothing certain in these tales of brigands. . . . But as they say, there is no smoke without fire, and after what has been happening in Paris it is quite possible that some such confederacy has been formed: as a result, we have met and made plans for mounting guard day and night. You would do well to follow our example.'

There was of course a certain risk in revealing one's scepticism. Those who made too obvious a play of it and refused to take defensive measures might perhaps be seeking to lull the people's suspicions. They must surely be hand in glove with the brigands and by association with the aristocrats too. This kind of reaction could cost the unbelievers dear. The Prior of Nueil-sous-les-Aubiers in Poitou reassured his own peasants by pointing out that it was quite impossible for twenty-five thousand brigands to fall suddenly on Nantes, as everyone was claiming, and that in any case a town of eighty thousand inhabitants would have easily been able to defend itself. But meanwhile some four or five thousand men gathered at Les Aubiers and were very angry to find that the prior had not brought a contingent from his parish with him: he had to attend the gathering in person and explain his ideas on the matter. The danger grew all the more rapidly because the people who brought the news felt their pride much damaged if they were not taken seriously and they were very likely to go off and spread alarming gossip about those who refused to believe them. This particular feature of the panic is well illustrated by an account of the fear in Limoges which was written by the secretary to the *intendance*. When the news first arrived, the *intendant*, d'Ablois, passed it on to the right quarter and thought no more about it. A monk of Sainte-Geneviève suddenly arrived in great haste from Roche-chouart with the news that eleven hundred men were on their way to Limoges. 'Monsieur le Prieur,' d'Ablois replied with a laugh, 'the brigands seem to have increased their numbers rather substantially, for there were supposed to be only five hundred this morning.' 'Monsieur,' said his informant, somewhat piqued, 'I can only tell you what I have seen and heard; you can do what you like, but I shall leave at once.' It was quite another matter when the *garde du corps* Malduit galloped up at noon, gun in hand. D'Ablois was eating his lunch. 'I did not think a *garde du corps* would so easily take fright,' he said. 'Now, do believe me, calm down, take a seat and eat a chop; the brigands will gladly spare you the time.' Malduit took this rather badly: 'Monsieur, I promise you that I am not in the least frightened; I am fulfilling a most important duty; if you don't believe me, then there are others who will pay proper attention to the warning I have given you.' Soon, the news was all over town that d'Ablois was taking steps to hand the town over to the tools of the aristocracy; his secretaries had to remind him of the dangers of imprudent speech and persuaded. him to take action. Even so, he spoke in a similar vein to an architect, M. Jacquet, when he called the next day with news of forty thousand Spaniards on the march: 'Monsieur Jacquet, I have always thought you a most reasonable man: today it seems to me that you have gone quite mad. How could you possibly believe such a tale? Forty thousand Spaniards! Go and take a rest and don't breathe a word of this to anyone, they will simply laugh at you.' On the contrary, the disgruntled Jacquet told everyone and no one laughed at all. They believed him and the matter might have turned out very badly for the *intendant* if more definite information had not arrived and allayed the growing panic.

The affair does however suggest that, where authorities were prepared to take the risk and refuse to spread the panic, they were able in many cases to stop it completely. Some areas had no trace of the Great Fear. Distance from major centres, the difficulty of communications, differences in local dialects, the small size of the population, all these factors contributed to their escaping the contagion. But the same factors also operated in areas where the Great Fear was very widespread and it therefore seems probable that some authorities were able to assert their control through their general calmness and the influence they exercised on the local population. This must certainly have been true of Brittany where ever since 1788 the local councils had constantly acted in a most confidence-inspiring way and where they had taken the most competent measures to restrain both the aristocracy and the lower orders. This is the opinion of the correspondent of the *Leyden Gazette* who wrote on 7 August: 'The greatest fears were entertained for Brittany and yet it is this province which is the most calm, thanks to the careful policing of the bourgeois who were quick to take up arms.' Far from bringing disorder, the municipal revolution and the arming of the people reassured the Third Estate and restored calm to troubled areas. This is what the revolutionaries maintained. But when the fear made its appearance, neither of these was properly established and for most of the time no one dared to block its path.

In spite of everything, the fear did not spread as quickly as we have been led to believe. To travel from Clermont in Beauvaisis to the Seine – a distance of about fifty kilometres – it took twelve hours of daylight; it travelled the five hundred kilometres from Ruffec to Lourdes in nine days; its speed here was lesser by a half, but it obviously moved more slowly at night. During the day, it seems to have gone at about four kilometres an hour. It moved from Livron to Arles – a hundred and fifty kilometres – in forty hours, which makes four kilometres an hour, night and day; but in this instance, it was carried by postilions; this speed is far slower than that attributed to the special couriers mentioned earlier. If we accept that the fear was spontaneously generated, then we must admit that it travelled quickly: however, if it was transmitted by couriers sent out especially for the purpose by conspirators, then on the contrary, its passage was slow indeed.

4

The Warning Panics

Usually, though not always, the news that the brigands were in sight started a panic, and in this connexion the circular letters sent around by the authorities seem to have roused less emotion than warnings by word of mouth or letters from private individuals. For instance, most of the parishes which read the circular from the Évreux committee seem to have paid no attention to it and Langeron's urgent missives do not seem to have provoked any startling response either. Where such apparent calm prevailed it is important not to confuse the fear of brigands with the Great Fear and one must remember too that such sang-froid can be considered exceptional. Each of the original panics, which we know were few in number, sparked off a train of countless further panics and these can be termed 'warning panics'.

They have been described many times and are the best known or possibly the only known characteristic of the Great Fear. First, the tocsin would sound and then for hours and hours the sound of bells would hang over the surrounding cantons. Mass hysteria would break out among the peasant women: in their imagination, it was already too late – they were raped, then murdered, their children slaughtered, their homes burnt to the ground; weeping and wailing, they fled into the woods and fields, a few provisions and bits of clothing clutched to their bosoms. Sometimes, the men followed close behind once they had buried anything of value and set the animals loose in the open country. Most often, though, whether through common decency, genuine bravery or fear of authority, they responded to the appeal of the *syndic*, the curé or the seigneur. Preparations would be made for the defence of the village under the direction of the seigneur himself or some old soldier. Everyone armed himself as best he could; sentries were posted; barricades were thrown up at the entrance to the village or at the bridge; scouting parties were sent out. At nightfall patrols were kept up and everyone stayed on the alert. In the towns, there was a sort of general mobilization: it was like being in a city under siege. Provisions were requisitioned, gunpowder and munitions collected, the ramparts repaired and the artillery placed in position. In the midst of this indescribable confusion, there were all sorts of moving incidents, some sad, some comic. In Vervins, a powder barrel exploded and killed several people. In Magnac-Laval, the pupils at the local school ran away and their head-teacher rushed around in all directions trying to get them back. Sometimes, the peasants started their preparations by setting their relations with God in proper order: the prior of Nueil-sous-les-Aubiers in Poitou and the curés of Capinghem and Ennetières in Flanders gave them general absolution. At Rochejean in the Jura, the official report (probably prepared by the curé himself) emphasizes these pious arrangements: the villagers, awakened in the middle of the night, 'began by begging for divine mercy through the intercession of the Holy Virgin and St John the Baptist, patron saint of the parish, and to this end they met for Holy Mass at four in the morning, with the exposition of the Blessed Sacrament, followed by the Blessing with the public prayers for special use in times of calamity; they promised God that they would mend their ways, cease from all strife, make good all damage if there were any and make a new and sincere profession of piety'. It must be admitted however that most scenes were not so edifying as this. Few accounts are as colourful as the one written by Jean-Louis Barge, the parish secretary of Lavalla near Saint-Étienne, a retired soldier who was given command of the local inhabitants when the alarm sounded. 'The number of men under my command was far smaller than the number of those who had lost their heads and run away. . . . Champallier who was one of those due to march said goodbye to his wife and children, saying "I shall never see you again!" ' At nightfall the cowards came creeping back, but the next day when the curé had given the village army absolution, Barge decided to avoid any further disappearances by giving marching orders 'otherwise, you will be shot dead where you stand'. Pathetic farewells followed. 'I said goodbye to my wife whose eyes were dry as tinder and to my mother who seemed half-dead, her eyes swimming with tears; she gave me a handful of small coins and said an eternal farewell and fell to praying.' They were just about to set off 'well-stocked with wine and food', fife and drum in the lead, when a man dashed in from the next village shouting that the enemy was approaching. They had to start all over again. 'Everybody flew into a dreadful panic and despair. Women, children and old men were screaming and wailing. You never saw anything so awful. Marie Pacher, Martin Matricou's wife, trembled so much she spilt all the soup she was carrying, shrieking and screaming "Oh, my poor little babies, they'll kill you, etc." Her husband, who was rather a big man but terrified for all that, wanted to comfort her and said: "Now, Marion, don't be frightened", but he said it in a very wobbly voice and was trembling all the time: we could see that he didn't want to set out with us in the least.' Part of the battalion had already disappeared; they started looking for the missing soldiers who had rushed off with the other fugitives. 'La Clémence, the pretty young lass who worked at the presbytery, and Chorel, Tardy's wife, were found half-suffocated, their heads deep in the hay and the rest of them sticking up in the air.' At last, Barge got them all together and they marched to Saint-Chamond: the panic was all over; they were complimented, feasted and sent back home again; 'When we got back to Lavalla, there wasn't a tear in sight: the cafés were crowded.'

According to this racy peasant account, the inhabitants of Lavalla did not find it too easy to overcome their fears, though in the event, they pulled themselves together and marched off to help their neighbours. This direct response to the panic occurred everywhere, though more quickly in some places than others. Fundamentally, though, it is not strictly correct to claim that the events represent the Great Fear. They are equally representative of the fierce enthusiasm which set the French face to face with any danger that threatened. They are even more typical of the passionate feelings which led them to hasten to each other's aid, immensely complex feelings in which pride of place was taken by the feeling of class solidarity which moved the Third Estate against the aristocracy, and which also offered proof of a national unity which was already well advanced since curés and seigneurs often marched in the fore-front of the impromptu armies. The towns found themselves invaded by great bands of men which they hastily dismissed since they could not feed them. On the banks of the Dordogne and the Lot, these bands looked more like armies in the field. On the 30th, the ports of Limeuil, Lunel and La Linde sent to Montpazier for assistance: the tocsin rang all over the area for twenty hours and more than six thousand men set off to help. Fourteen curés personally led their parishioners. They arrived at the riverbank in the middle of the night and the Montaigu notary wrote that 'they were very surprised to see over a thousand camp-fires burning on the other side'. It was an army of peasants who had also come to help and who had pitched camp to the north of the Dordogne. They began to fall back to await reinforcements. First light showed that there were forty thousand men. At the same time, thirty thousand men under the command of the local seigneurs had met up on the banks of the Lot at Libos and Fumel. Figures as high as these leave one somewhat sceptical and recall the exaggerations which appeared so regularly in the medieval chronicles.

Popular imagination, however, was deeply impressed and the memory of the panic lasted well into the nineteenth century. For the peasants of Aquitaine, 1789 was for a long time *l'anno de la paou*. But it was really the historians who put the expression 'la grande peur' into general use. In many areas, in Champagne in particular, people called it quite simply 'la peur', 'la terreur panique', 'l'alarme', 'l'effroi'.

As these events ran their course, many passing rumours revealed popular opinion and explain why the terror had such a shattering effect; the original panics were basically related to the economic and social circumstances which had made insecurity a regular feature of everyday life, but these rumours are closely allied to the current political circumstances, to the expulsion of the brigands from the towns and to the manoeuvres of the aristocrats. In Vendôme, Les Mauges and Poitou, there were supposed to be roving bands of Bretons, which can probably be explained by the fact that the disturbances in Brittany and the activities of the Breton deputies in the Estates-General had made a very deep impression on people's minds. In Baignes in Saintonge, and in Dozulé in the Auge region, the disturbances were blamed on the officials who had worked for the tax collectors, now unemployed. But everywhere else, it was brigands, robbers, galley slaves – all supposedly coming from Paris or some big town. Their number grew awesomely: at Champeniers in Périgord they were originally two thousand strong, then six, then fourteen, then eighteen and suddenly a hundred thousand. To the north of Paris, they attacked only the corn harvest which they cut down before it was ripe; it was the same in some parts of southern Aquitaine and at Montastruc-la-Conseillère: here they were also supposed to have poisoned wells and springs; at Gramat in Quercy, they said that a man had been arrested in Figeac carrying eight pounds of poison. But usually they were supposed to be looting, burning and killing simultaneously, and around Uzerche some were said to be equipped for starting illicit fires.

As well as brigands, there were royal and foreign troops. Hussars were said to be south of Paris and in Picardy. A German army was expected in Limagne and this rumour probably ties up with the presence of the Royal Allemand under the command of the Prince de Lambesc. The Emperor of Austria was seen in Forges in the Caux region; in Tulle, they said he was in Lyons or else in Caylus in Quercy: his intervention was explained by his relationship to the queen, for whilst Mme de La Tour-du-Pin Gouvernet was in Forges, she was taken for Marie Antoinette. In Aquitaine, Poitou and as far north as Cheverny near Blois, they said it was the English who had invaded; in Aquitaine and the Limousin there were supposed to be Spanish troops everywhere; in the Dauphiné it was the Piedmontese, and as the panic spread to Figeac, Mende and Millau, the Piedmontese were seen there too; at Malzieu in Lozère, they were supposed to have landed on the Languedoc coast, which might be an echo of the rumour that had gone round Montpellier in May. In Les Mauges and Poitou, there was some question of Polish troops who had landed from the sea. It is clear that geographical location had its effect on popular imagination and one notes that to the north of the Loire and around Paris there was hardly ever any mention of foreigners. But memories of books read in the past, old soldiers' tales and oral tradition all played their part in these rumours – in Aquitaine, for instance, they even talked of *pandours*, the Croatian troops who had served the Austrian Emperor in the eighteenth century – and, impossible as it may seem, the Moors; the Poles were doubtless involved because Louis XV had been the son-in-law of Stanislas of Poland and it was not illogical to find Genoese brigands to the north of Toulon. These explanations are not basic to the issues involved, however; what is essential is the fact that foreigners were supposed to be moving around the country and this comes from the notion of the aristocrats' plot and the supposed machinations of the *émigrés*.

In fact, the princes were often said to be leading the brigands and the invaders. The Prince de Condé was said to be marching across Artois at the head of forty thousand men, but most often the blame fell on the Comte d'Artois. In Uzerche, he was supposed to have come from Bordeaux with sixteen thousand men: 'his intention was to dissolve and dismiss the National Assembly, to expel all the members and reinstall his brother in all his rights and prerogatives.' Célarié, a labourer from Bégoux just outside Cahors, was more loquacious and interwove his memories of school-lessons most curiously with popular tales: 'M. le Comte d'Artois is coming with forty thousand men, all of them brigands he has brought from the kingdom of Sweden and other lands in the north, and they have seized all the convicts from the king's galleys in the ports of France and all the criminals who were in prison and he has made an army out of them; they say that the aforesaid count, the king's brother, is doing all he can to get together all the runaways and vagabonds in the kingdom of France just like the Vandals did in 406 and that with this fearsome army he wants to ravage the whole of France and conquer the Third Estate just as he wants to make the clergy and the nobility pay their share of the king's money.'

The entire aristocracy was associated with the activities of the princes. The committee for Le Mas-d'Azil wrote that 'several thousand brigands, hateful remnants of the murderers from the capital, of the loathsome instruments of tyranny and the devilish conspiracy were expected in the region'. In Puisaye, they said 'that several malicious individuals claimed that these brigands were sent by the nobility and the clergy to crush the Third Estate'. 'This troop,' they said in Saint-Girons, 'is in the pay of the priests and the nobles who have seen the failure of their plots in Paris and Versailles and now want to starve the provinces.' 'The assumption that the clergy and the nobility seek to crush the village populations, though clearly devoid of any appearance of probability, is even so extremely dangerous,' wrote the Comte de Puységur to the military commander for Languedoc, who had evidently warned him that the conviction was widespread in his area of administration. The curé of Touget in Armagnac also believed in 'this scandalous enterprise' and when he saw the local prior remain calm in the face of general panic, wrote: 'Either the aforesaid monk enjoys perpetual sang-froid or else he is involved in the nobles' plot.' The fact that many seigneurs showed considerable zeal in organizing local defences did nothing to alter public opinion: they were only trying to put us off the scent, said the peasants, and considered them as hostages; those who seemed disinterested were taken to task; and when it was finally established that the brigands did not exist, the peasants decided that it was all a deliberate ploy on the part of the nobles whose idea it was to avenge themselves by playing a trick on the poor workers so that they should lose a day's pay.

This led to new disturbances, often very serious, and these will be discussed later. The principal result of the Great Fear was therefore the deepening of the general hatred for the aristocracy and the strengthening of the revolutionary movement.

5

The Relays

Even though circumstances favoured its propagation, the Great Fear would not have travelled so far – from Ruffec to the Pyrenees, from the Franche-Comté to the Mediterranean – if its powers of expansion had not been constantly renewed by fresh panics which broke out in great profusion all along its route and acted as relays for its further dissemination. To distinguish these from the original panics and the warning panics, they will be termed secondary panics or relay panics.

Many of them were a more or less direct consequence of the warning panics. What happened was that the first messenger would appear with the news that the brigands were coming and he would then be followed by other messengers with the same news, but often coming from different directions. This is what happened at La Châtre, where the alarm was first raised by a notary from Aigurande who had himself been warned by the curé of Lourdouiex-Saint-Michel; on the following night at two o' clock in the morning a courier came from Châteauroux, unaware that La Châtre was already on the alert, and rode through the town calling the people to arms; this started a second panic. Again, the defensive measures taken often frightened more people than they reassured. More than once, peasants marching to the rescue were themselves taken for brigands. A mistake of this kind started off a second panic in Clermont en Beauvaisis and probably also in Loriol, south of Valence; the renewed alarm in Tallard to the north of Sisteron also seems to have had a similar cause. The citizens of Taulignan and Valréas caused a great panic in Montjoyer and La Touche when they were seen in the far distance marching towards Dieu-le-Fît: the gardener of the Trappist monastery at Aiguebelette rushed in great distress to Tulette; the news travelled to Pierrelatte on the Rhône, Bollène and, more particularly, Saint-Paul-Trois-Châteaux where it unleashed a terrible disturbance at six o'clock on the evening of the 30th. There was the same panic in Orange and this particular outbreak actually got as far as Arles by means of a message from Tarascon saying that Orange was aflame. At Saint-Jean-de-Gardonnenque in the Cévennes early on the morning of 1 August, detachments of local militia came hotfoot to defend the town and were mistaken for enemies: the news flashed all through the mountains and some three thousand men came in haste to lend support, which effectively carried the fear right into Millau. Such mistakes were naturally most common during the night. A first alarm came into Clamecy from the north at two in the afternoon of the 29th and a second one came slightly later, thanks to a mistaken report that Villiers to the south of the town was in flames; there was a third alarm at midnight: workers from the Nivernais canal alarmed the sentries as they left Tannay – there was a call to arms. On their way back, these same workers caused an outbreak of panic in Amazy. In the silence of the night, the watchers heard the sound of their marching feet: the news was sent to Clamecy where at two in the morning there occurred yet a fourth alarm, with all the inhabitants wide awake and in a fresh turmoil. The urban militia who had more guns than the peasants often caused fresh trouble by firing their guns without any special reason. At dawn on the 23rd, the Lons-le-Saulnier militia were on their way back from the Château de Visargent and decided to fire off all the ammunition in their rifles. 'There were some harvesters out early to cut the corn near the forest and when they heard the noise, clearly most unusual at that hour of the morning, they looked up and saw red uniforms and the glittering of light on rifle barrels.' They were overcome by fear and ran away shouting: 'Run for your life, the brigands are here!' This was all that was needed to put all the vineyards in a state of commotion. More often, the trouble was caused by sentries firing for the wrong reasons and in this connexion many of the alerts were very like army panics. It was said that the direct cause of the fear in the Agenais and western Quercy was the burst of gun-fire from the Château de Fumel where the commander for Guyenne had detailed fifty men to protect his property. In Viviers and Maurs, the trouble started with either patrols or guards firing at marauders. In Saint-Félix near Saint-Affrique, some young men fired off a few pistol shots during a wedding as part of the celebrations and started a fresh panic in the Vabrais.

However, the disturbances which followed the Great Fear formed a much more effective relay for the panic. It was through the revolt in the Mâconnais that the current originating in the Franche-Comté insurrection travelled to the Loire valley. And the subsequent rising in the Dauphiné gave the same current enough new strength to disturb the Forez and the Vivarais and eventually reach Provence and the area around Nîmes. In Saintonge, the riot in Baignes started the second alarm in Montendre and the current from Ruffec seems to have been maintained all along the borders of the Dordogne by incidents on which we have little information. There seems to have been a disturbance of some sort at the Château de La Roche-Chalais on the Dronne to the north of Coutras and this appears to have set off a chain of panics all along the road from the Dordogne to Toulouse: apparently – or so it was said – six hundred nobles had gathered to make a protest about wearing the cockade; the Third Estate sent a deputation to meet them, whereupon they cut the deputies' throats; the people set fire to the château and the nobles died in the flames. This far-fetched tale naturally made a deep impression but we know nothing of its origins apart from comments in two contemporary letters: one from the municipality of Sainte-Foy-la-Grande which said that 'this was nothing but a quarrel between some individuals from the nobility and the Third Estate'. The other letter comes from the municipality of Cahuzac which had been informed 'that there had been a disturbance the evening before [the 29th] in Sainte-Foy and La Roche-Chalais about the harvest'. If there had been a rising in Sainte-Foy, the municipality of that town would almost certainly have mentioned it in its letter; however the event might well have taken place only in La Roche-Chalais. In Domme, the disturbance was explained by the rising of four parishes in the Limeuil neighbourhood, 'who have destroyed the château of M. de Vassal between Limeuil and Le Bug'. This rumour travelled as far as Cahors, but was never confirmed and no one knows where it started. This also holds good for the rumour about the capture of the Château de Biron and the Château de Montségur in the Agenais and yet another one which was passed on by Durand, secretary to the Sénéchal de Castelmoron at Gensac: 'We have just heard that five hundred young men from Angoulême arrived quite calmly at the Château de Saint-Simon which they then burnt and, the operation completed, went away again just as calmly: this is the cause of our alarms.' A few instances of looting also lay at the origin of some local panics. At Tannay in the Nivernais, after a second alert of unknown cause at nine o'clock in the evening of the 30th, a whole crowd of people from Asnoy arrived, which started off a third panic: 'Over nine hundred men had escaped from the labour camp at the Châtillon canal and were attacking and looting the houses because, they said, they were hungry.'

Another series of events leads us back to the causes we have already attributed to the original panics. For instance, after Loches had heard from Tours on the 27th that brigands were moving in from Maine, yet before the current of panic based on Ruffec had travelled up from the south, a local fear broke out during the afternoon of the 29th; it moved up the Indre and apparently had started out from Azay-le-Rideau and Montbazon where there had been attacks on the harvest, though at the same time there was trouble in l'Isle-Bouchard where the militia were busy requisitioning corn from the farm-labourers. Similarly there was a belated outbreak in Clamecy at the beginning of August, apparently arising from a purely local quarrel – as already found in the Soissonnais and Montmorency: there was some argument about wages between a farmer and his workers and this led several villages to sound the tocsin. Even more often, the deep-seated fear of wanderers caused a serious disquiet, especially in the neighbourhood of forests. At La Châtre, the tocsin sounded for the third time because a patrol arrested an unemployed servant who was wandering around with neither money nor papers and who – obviously a feature bound to arouse suspicion – had a long beard. In Limoges, one of the many alarms must be attributed to the woodcutters in the Aixe forest who ran away because early one morning they saw some evil-looking strangers roaming around 'looking at the paths'. There was another panic in La Queuille, at the foot of the Dômes hills, because someone found six beggars hiding in a wood, and again in Forqualquier where three families were seen in the Volx woods. There was more drama in the Lourdes area on the evening of 8 August: a band of men came down from the mountains, apparently to help defend the town. Some shepherds saw them coming and sent them urgent messages that brigands were marching on their valleys (they had seen a few smugglers in the distance). Their villages, they said, were in flames. Back went the mountain men in great distress, whilst the shepherd-messenger went on to Lourdes to spread the news still further: it was the fourth alarm that day. The circular prepared by the Uzerche committee and dated 16 August informed the peasants of the inquiries into the causes of the fear and put them on their guard against unwarranted fears, quoting various instances. In Chavagnac, for example, 'a boy of sixteen who was ploughing a field saw the Comte de Saint-Marsault's gamekeeper and fisherman each with a gun in his hand' returning from buying tobacco and took them for brigands. On 12 August, as the commission of inquiry was proceeding to the same village, a woman saw them in the distance and ran away: when she was caught, she admitted that she was hurrying to give the alarm. On the same day in Saignes, some children started off a great panic when they saw the curé's nephew slipping into a barn with the curé's maidservant; on the 13th, a man living in Saint-Ybard was surprised by the rain as dusk was falling and knocked at a peasant's door in Sainte-Eulalie to ask for shelter: all he got was a cry for help.

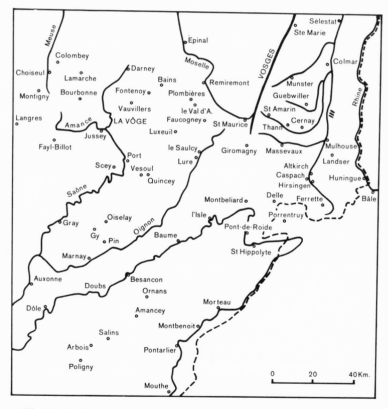

3. The Revolts in the Franche-Comté and Alsace

Finally, one last group of causes relates to the process of auto-suggestion. Flocks of sheep moving in the woods or raising dust-clouds along the road and in the fallow fields caused many a panic. It was a curate's fault in Châtillon-sur-Seine; a postilion brought the news to Rochechouart; in Limoges, the misinterpretation was due to a man from the Treasury who was riding towards Aixe on a voluntary brigand-search. The glow from lime-kilns, the smoke from burning weeds, the reflection of the setting sun in the windows of a château were enough to convince some that the brigands had started a fire – as for instance in Saint-Omer and also in Beaucaire on the 30th where they thought they saw the Château du Roy René in flames on the other side of the Rhône – and again in Saint-Félix in the Vabrais. Gradually, the smallest and least important incident was enough. A carriage travelling through the night put a sentry into a fit of terror in Villefranche-de-Rouergue. In Choiseuil, Beugnot saw a farm worker come dashing in with the news that he had seen brigands in the woods 'in the dim moonlight'. When M. de Terssac was travelling through the mist near Saint-Girons, he met a muleteer riding at top speed and shouting 'Enemies, enemies!' 'He said he could hear drums and trumpets, but I couldn't hear a thing.' M. de Terssac dismounted and tried to work out what could have frightened him. 'It turned out to be some harvesters working quite near the path and singing as they cut the corn. . . . That was all I could hear. And yet it was a still night and the weather was calm.'

Lastly, on 27 July a porter told the committee in Besançon that, when he was coming back from Vesoul the evening before, some brigands had dragged him into a wood 'where they had killed a gamekeeper, burnt a cord of wood and cooked two sides of bacon', discussing the while how they would attack an abbey and various châteaux. He offered to act as guide, but all in vain – there was nothing to be found. In the end he confessed that he had made up the whole story and was sentenced to wear an iron collar. Of all the distributors of false information – usually offered in all innocence – this is the only one yet found in contemporary documents.

6

The Currents of the Great Fear

If the Great Fear is seen as a series of concentric waves starting from Paris and spreading through the provinces, then it would be reasonable to suppose that it must have followed the natural paths imposed on France by the configurations of the terrain. For instance, it ought to have travelled from Paris to Bordeaux *via* the Loire valley and the Poitou gap, or from Paris to Marseilles down the Saône and the Rhône.

What happened was quite different. Only two currents affected the capital and instead of starting from Paris, they actually travelled towards it. The Loire valley did not act as a passage way for the fear, but was approached by it both from the Gâtinais above Orléans and from Maine, *via* Blois and Tours. It moved through the Poitou gap, but not directly along the natural line – i.e. it went from the South-West to the North-East, from Ruffec to Touraine. The panic did not reach the Franche-Comté by going along the Saône, but by moving along the Jura. The Garonne valley played no part at all in the dissemination of the fear.

The mountains themselves did not constitute forces of repulsion as one might imagine; in fact, the fear travelled from Ruffec over the Massif Central and right into the Auvergne. It went over mountain peaks and high valleys to reach the Limagne from the Mâconnais and the Lyonnais; from the banks of the Rhône, it passed deep into Lozère and the Causses. It went down the Rhône from the Dauphiné to Provence, though it could also have reached this part of the Midi by wending its way through the Alps. One might also expect to find some basic differences between the way it travelled in sparsely populated areas and in regions with small but well-populated villages; not at all – the fear travelled just as comfortably in Bas-Maine and Les Mauges as it did in Picardy and the barren regions of Champagne.

These anomalies can be explained by the origins of the panics and the way they spread. As they developed out of local incidents of chance occurrence and spread all around, they usually did not take the routes

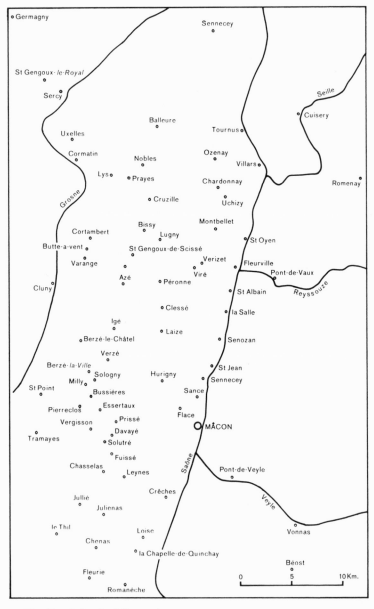

4. The Revolt in the Mâconnais

one might naturally expect. The population would send anxious demands for help to the nearest town, or else thought it their duty to warn the surrounding countryside: obstacles did not stop its progress easily, although a river with no bridge was always a more effective deterrent to their goodwill than a range of mountains. And again, the Great Fear spread somewhat spasmodically. It leapt from one municipality to another, from curé to curé, from seigneur to seigneur, and not in a logical unbroken sequence from house to house. Once the local authorities had sounded the tocsin, the inhabitants of a parish in Les Mauges were just as easily assembled as those in a Picardy village.

Of course, the Great Fear did not move with total impartiality across dales and hills: one must not exaggerate. Wherever possible, it moved along the valleys, using the traditional roads in Champagne, or the Rhône valley from Valence to Arles, or the old cross-country route from Poitou to Berry, along the Massif Central, or the well-trodden track from Limoges to Toulouse through Périgord and Quercy, or the road from Coutras to Béarn *via* the Agenais and Armagnac. And though the mountains did not normally stop the fear, it would be forced to come to a halt if they were too desolate or too steep. The fear skilfully worked its way round the Millevaches plateau, the high mass of the Alps and the Diois massif; the Haut Vivarais and the Cévennes were skirted rather than crossed. Sometimes it seemed as though the fear grew short of breath as it clambered up the hills – in Champagne it faded away quite noticeably as it moved up the slopes of the Côte d'Or. Regions which had little or no population were unaffected and this was quite natural since such areas could call on no one for help. This was typical of Sologne, the Landes and Dombes. The Double played an important part: the fear travelled from Angoulême towards Périgord and not towards the Gironde area and reached the Agenais by crossing the Dordogne above the point where it is joined by the Isle.

It would be tedious in the extreme to take the reader along every inch of the roads travelled by the main currents of the fear in that July of 1789 – if indeed we could do this. The maps show just how many gaps there are in our documentation of this event. It is however possible to convey in reasonably clear terms how these currents moved across the country and to indicate the extent and nature of the problems which still lie in wait for the local historian as he pursues his investigations.

.   .   .   .   .

The first fear relates to Les Mauges and the Poitou Bocage; it is the one on which we are least well documented and since most of the relevant documents were destroyed during the Vendée it is unlikely that we shall ever learn more. It was a backwash from the panic which swept through Nantes on the 20th. North of the Loire, there was no panic at all; it developed to the south, probably between the Sèvre and the lake at Grandlieu during the evening of the 20th or the morning of the 21st; the first mention concerns its passage through Clisson. From here, it went up the valleys of the Sèvre and the Moine. It was in Cholet by the afternoon of the 21st; the news reached Mortagne in the evening through a private message sent from Baissay and through the deputies for Cholet. From here, it spread through Les Mauges; it appeared in Saint-Lambert-de-Lattay on the 22nd, having come from Chemillé; on the evening of the 21st, all Maulevrier was in a state of fear and by the following day the rumours had travelled at top speed as far as Thouars, Airvault, Bressuire and Parthenay. It went south of the Sèvre: La Châtaignerie was affected on the 22nd. At this point, the fear was at its height and for a long time afterwards it was associated in people's minds with the feast of the Madeleine which took place on that day. On the 23rd, it continued to move south-east. Early in the morning, it reached Secondigny and caused disturbances which have been more than adequately recorded by Taine. Apparently the echo of this drama travelled from Parthenay to Poitiers and Saint-Maixent on that same day. It seems that the central area of the Bocage was also affected and at Les Herbiers it was claimed that the brigands had burned Légé and Montaigu. The news also arrived in Fontenay-le-Comte but it seems that in the maritime region of Bourgneuf-aux-Sables and Fontenay there was no actual panic, only a general fear of brigands. Towards the East, the fear did not pass beyond the Layon and the Thouet; the Poitou plain was untouched; it was the same in the South: the agitation in the Bocage caused great alarm in the plain, but this appeared quite reasonable – the natural opposition which existed between the two areas effectively prevented the 'contagion' from passing, as it were, over the border.

The fear in the Maine appeared almost at the same time, probably during the morning of the 21st, for it is mentioned for the first time as it swept through Bonnétable at three o'clock that day; it had come from La Ferté-Bernard and Nogent, apparently through Nogent-le-Bernard to the north-east of Bonnétable. We do not know where it started but its path had most certainly been prepared by news from the markets of the Eure and the Avre – Chartres, Dreux, Nonancourt and Verneuil, and also from Laigle where there had been continual riots. We have already spoken of the letter from the mayor of Chartres; in Mamers on the 24th, another letter announced that more than two thousand brigands had passed through Dreux and Verneuil, rioting and looting, 'and more than four thousand of them have been killed'. The panic passed through Bonnétable moving northwards and crossed the Perche via Bellême, Mortagne, Moulins-La-Marche and Laigle. By the 23rd, it was well installed in Évreux. Mostly it moved westwards. On the 22nd, it began to move towards the Sarthe: it appeared in Mamers and Ballon about nine in the evening and at some time later in the day in Le Mans. During the night of the 22nd–23rd, a messenger carried it from the latter town to La Flèche and at the same time the current crossed the Bas-Maine from the Sarthe to the Mayenne; the entire area was affected – Lassay, Mayenne, Laval and, by the end of the day, Château-Gontier: the curé of Brûlon has left us a description of what happened. It seems that the Haut-Maine was not particularly affected. During the 23rd, however, a very serious incident took place in Ballon: the peasants went in a mob and murdered Cureau, *lieutenant de maire* in Le Mans, and his son-in-law. These murders seem to have started a second wave of terror so that after this 'mad Thursday' there came a 'mad Friday'. The panic was particularly bad in Mortagne on the 24th. This time, all the Haut-Maine was disturbed and the Val du Loir was affected *via* Saint-Calais from Château-du-Loir to Vendôme during the night of 23–24 July.

To the west of the Mayenne, the panic in Maine ran as far as Château-Gontier *via* Craon; on the 24th, it took a variety of paths from Laval and Mayenne to the Port-Brillet ironworks and La Gravelle where the farm workers hastened to warn the Vitré committee. It crossed the Loir in the south. The fear reached Tours on the 24th through Neuvy-le-Roi, then arrived a second time on the 27th, moving from Vendôme *via* Châteaurenault; the same panic also went on to Blois from Vendôme. Tours seems to have been the starting point for a secondary current which went up the Loire valley on the left bank: it went through Amboise on the 25th; on the same day, it spread through the southern part of the Blésois (its effects in this area were described in M. de Cheverny's *Memoirs*), then reached the Cher valley near Saint-Aignan. It is possible that the news reached the people living in the Val de Loir between

Tours and Angers through Sablé and La Flèche, but so far we have no documentation on its effects; there is nothing to suggest that a current ever travelled down the Loire from Tours, as one might expect: on the 25th, Langeais asked for news, but there was no mention of any panic. But the fear went from Tours to the Indre valley and finished up in Loches on the 27th. Towards the north-east, the fear renewed its forces by travelling down the Iton valley *via* Breteuil and Damville. The Saint-André plain and the Ouches area heard of nothing but riots and disturbances all around. There was an insurrection in Rouen between 12 and 14 July which the Évreux committee attributed to brigands from Paris and this gave rise to great anxiety. There were similar events in Louviers and this town wrote to Évreux on the 22nd asking for cannons to protect their factories. All along the Seine, the grain convoys were constantly threatened and a few days later, between the 26th and 28th, the looting of a boat at the Poses barrage nearly started a civil war between the inhabitants of Louviers and those of Elbeuf who had tried to stop the boat. Between the 18th and the 23rd, there was perpetual rioting in Laigle, Verneuil, Nonancourt and Dreux. The conflict was even greater in Évreux and the surrounding area on the 24th. It travelled to Pont-Audemer by way of Le Neubourg and lasted longer than it should because of the circular warning sent round by the Évreux committee. From the source of the Rille, the alarm spread through the Lieuvin and through Orbec into Lisieux on the 24th, thence to Pont-l'Évêque. It also moved down the Avre valley; on the 27th, Nonancourt declared that the fear had been widespread in the town since the 23rd; rumour said that the town was to be burnt and that six or seven thousand men were coming to throw the prisons open and put the population to fire and sword. Panic ran like wildfire through the Thimerais and reached Dreux *via* Châteauneuf on the afternoon of the 24th.

But as far as we know, the fear did not cross the Eure and never penetrated the Mantes area. It is difficult to accept that the Perche Gouëy was spared, but the archives at La Ferté-Bernard, Nogent-le-Rotrou and Châteaudun mention nothing relevant for this period. The area around Orléans and Sologne was also left untouched and in the South, Loches seems to be its furthest point. Towards the West, it did not go beyond the Auge valley, entered neither the Normandy nor the Breton Bocage and stopped at Vitré; there was talk of it, but nothing more, in La Guerche and Châteaubriant.

The Great Fear, as we define it, did not touch Brittany or Basse-Normandy. Here as everywhere else, there was the usual fear of brigands. The outbreak in Vitré caused much concern in Brittany, as can be seen from the speech made by the *lieutenant de maire* to the assembled inhabitants of Lesneven on the 29th: 'Plots are being woven; there are conspiracies everywhere; under cover of these disturbances, there are gangs of scoundrels seeking to rob our small towns; letters have told us that this is what is happening in La Gravelle and Vitré.' The same source probably provided the remarks made on 3 August in the parish assembly in Baud, between Pontivy and Lorient, on 'the alarms spread all over the region by troops of brigands which are so large in size that in the last few days two hundred men have been forced to join together and pursue them. Once they have been driven away from the towns, it is all too likely that these desperate characters will do their worst in the countryside.' On 6 August, a similar tale was told in Paimpol – a gang of bandits had come from Paris to terrorize the provinces. Baud seems to have had wind of an alarm which disturbed Vannes, for there were rumours that bands of men had been seen round Sarzeau and Theix; on hearing this they demanded and obtained two thousand guns from Lorient. But this happened at the end of July and has no direct link with the panics in the west: it may possibly relate to the rumours circulating about the surrender of Brest to the English.

Though the Bocage was in general revolt, most of the disturbances were of local character, from La Ferté-Macé to Lassay. The agrarian revolt caused a great sensation in Basse-Normandy. In Cairon near Caen, patrols were organized 'in case brigands come out of the Bocage and attack us'; in Le Sap, a militia was set up on the 22nd; on the 24th, the nobility in Vire offered 'the alarms' as an excuse for not attending the assembly of their order in Caen; with the help of the director of the local coal mines, the inhabitants of Littry kept a close watch on the Cérisy forest where there were said to be brigands. The Bayeux bourgeoisie launched a panic by announcing in Caen on the 24th and Carentan on the 26th that bandits were prowling all around their town; this was a consequence either of the disturbing news from Littry or the riots which broke out in Bayeux when the Duc de Coigny was arrested after the *lieutenant du bailliage* had authorized him to leave the country. But there was no panic and in any case the trouble did not spread. On the 27th, there was a local alarm in Cherbourg, brigands having been 'seen' on the Valognes road; the panic was substantial but there were no consequences. As we have seen, the fact that Brittany remained comparatively calm has been attributed to the well-established and long-standing organization of the bourgeoisie which went back to the disturbances of 1788; it is however less easy to understand why the revolt in the Bocage did not send a swift stream of panic right across Basse-Normandy.

In the East and the South-East, the fear is allied to the revolt in the Franche-Comté, but the relationship varies in strength and the fear did not spread with equal swiftness in all directions. In the very heart of the most rebellious area, to the north of the Doubs, there was no panic. Towards the West, beyond the road from Gray to Langres, there was only one instance of a panic – in Chazeuil to the east of Is-sur-Tille; however, we have neither date nor precise details; there is no reason to think that it went any further. Only the fear of brigands was recorded: this apparently travelled as far as Dijon and it may be why a rumour circulated on the 26th to the effect that the privileged orders were to be massacred; there was some agitation on the Seine-facing slopes of the Côte d'Or and the Langres plateau: in Montbard on the 25th, there were some acts of brigandage blamed on 'those claiming to support the Third Estate'; further south, at Arnay-le-Duc, the news from the Franche-Comté joined with that from the Mâconnais: the local population formed a militia on the 26th on hearing that brigands in different provinces 'were attacking châteaux, burning them and forcing people of means to hand over their money'. The panic which broke out in Châtillon-sur-Seine on the 25th at three in the afternoon probably came from the Franche-Comté, but it spread no further. On this side, there were no real outbreaks of the Great Fear. It seems to have been the same in Bassigny; Langres was probably very disturbed, but the archives have disappeared and we do not know what happened between this town and Clermont, apart from the fact that the latter town heard of the brigands and nothing more.

Towards the North, only one alarm has been recorded, by Beugnot, in Choiseul in the upper valley of the Meuse; it was started by an inhabitant of Colombey who thought he saw some brigands in the moonlight as he was hurrying to Choiseul to warn the people there. Beugnot thinks that this took place in the early days of August: on the 2nd, there had been an alert in Sérécourt and Morizécourt: abbeys had been threatened and the Lamarche militia had gone to their assistance. This is possibly the source of the rumour which circulated in Colombey. According to Beugnot, the man is said to have had information from someone living in Montigny; this is probably either a printing mistake or a misunderstanding; Martigny, which is near Lamarche, would be more likely. But if the news really did come from Montigny-le-Roi, then the rumour must have developed from the disturbances in the Amance valley. In any case, Beugnot does not suggest that the Choiseul panic spread either towards Neufchâteau or Chaumont, so one can be reasonably sure that it expired exactly where it had started. Thanks to the firmness of the municipality of Remiremont – or so one must suppose – no panic was precipitated when the inhabitants of La Vôge came rushing into the town; Lorraine was indeed very restless: here and there, agrarian disturbances broke out and there were rumours that Remiremont and Plombières had been sacked: the municipality of Blénod-lès-Toul was warned of this by a letter from some person unknown to us. But there was no Great Fear in the proper sense. The Barrois was even more restless, thanks to the corn riots in Bar-le-Duc, Révigny and Ligny and the agrarian revolts in Waly to the north of Triaucourt and Tréveray on the upper Ornain, but here as in Lorraine, the general fear related basically to the brigands and only ordinary security measures were taken. According to the memoirs of Carré de Malberg, lieutenant for the *bailliage* of Varennes, there was considerable agitation in the Argonne and the Verdunois at the beginning of August: this was not related to the Franche-Comté. On the contrary, it was proclaimed that 'bands of brigands coming from abroad were moving across France towards the lower Meuse'; in fact, in Ivoy-Carignan, 'some malicious individuals' later reported that the municipality 'spread the rumour that there were gangs of brigands over four hundred in number threatening to overrun the frontier and the town. . . . The next news to be spread around was that all *employés des fermes* who had been dismissed planned to burn the harvest.' This is an echo of the revolts in the Ardennes area and one wonders therefore if such an echo does not indicate a panic. However, there are no written indications of this and it would indeed be surprising if there had been a panic without some sort of backwash being felt in Verdun and Metz; neither town has any record of such an occurrence.

From this, one may conclude that the panic from the Franche-Comté travelled northwards and died away when it met the slopes formed by

Lorraine and the Paris basin above the Saône plain, whilst in the South and towards Burgundy it expanded much more freely. In the East, the fear appeared in Belfort, Montbéliard and the Sundgau; on 24 July, the tocsin sounded from Belfort to Altkirch and the peasants rushed to defend Belfort where a new alarm was sounded on the morning of the 26th; there were several in Montbéliard. The outbreak of fear in the Sundgau probably prepared the ground for the revolt on the 28th, but it did not spread further into Haute-Alsace. The agrarian disturbances caused only local alerts – Colmar on the 24th and Mulhouse on the 31st. There appear to have been none in Basse-Alsace. The Sundgau sent warnings to the bishopric of Bâle. Safety measures were taken at Porrentruy and the frontier was closed; there was great anxiety in Bâle where the prince regent of Montbéliard had sent for help, especially since a letter from Pierre Ochs had said that the peasants in the Brisgau were joining in the revolt and threatening both to send no more recruits and to pay no more taxes.

The emotive power of the revolt in the Franche-Comté found its fullest expression towards the South, though the Great Fear does not seem to have been caused by any direct stimulus. It is true that there was a panic on 26 July in Marnay on the Oignon; according to the annalist Laviron, there was also one in Besançon, but he gives no date. The villages to the north of Marnay showed no sign of trouble. On the 26th, messengers were sent from Pin to inquire what was happening and we have the replies they received: Gy and Frétigney had taken up arms, but there was no mention of any alarm; all was calm in Oiselay. Indeed, they said most particularly in Gy and Frasnes that the brigands in question were only local peasants and that they were only interested in attacking their own seigneurs. To the south of Marnay, there was no trace of fear. It was quite different to the south-east of Besançon where an agrarian revolt was started on the Ornans plateau by a panic which brought the people down from the mountains.

The Great Fear mainly developed from warning letters sent by the authorities and from the local incidents which seemed to justify these warnings. One of the first steps was taken by the municipality of Vesoul who were alarmed by the Quincey affair and assumed that M. de Mesmay, the seigneur of the ruined château, had taken refuge with his mother-in-law at the Château de Visargent in Bresse, a little to the north of Louhans. They informed the municipality of Lons-le-Saulnier who hastened to despatch a strong force of men there on the 22nd. Their search revealed nothing and at dawn on the 23rd they started back home. And then as they were nearing Nance, the soldiers started off a panic by carelessly firing off spare rounds of ammunition as they passed by a wood. There was a terrible outbreak of panic throughout the entire area: five thousand men hurried to Bletterans, three thousand to Commenailles; the fear travelled up the Seille Valley and reached Lons-le-Saulnier where ten thousand men (or so they said) were assembled by nightfall – and then spread throughout the wine country. Its progress to the North-East is easy to follow: Mantry, Poligny, Arbois, which was reached at one o'clock in the afternoon of the 23rd, and Salins. It also moved towards Dôle where the seigneur of Le Deschaux had brought news of the revolt: as the news had come from Bresse, it was thought that the brigands must have come from Burgundy. This is what they told Langeron; Besançon sent a hundred and fifty men to Dôle and it is quite possible that this was the only incident responsible for the outbreak of panic. It is equally possible that the outbreak of fear on the Ornans plateau was no more than the extension of the fear from Visargent, travelling either through Salins – hence slowly and directly into the mountains – or else less directly through Besançon.

The circular warnings sent by Langeron discussed previously had even more positive effects. In the upper valley of the Doubs, the information they contained was confirmed by agrarian disturbances and this explains the alarms which broke out locally in Rochejean and Morez and which seem to be inextricably connected to them. The Swiss were also much alarmed by local events, especially since the regent of Montbéliard had sent to Berne for help and Saint-Claude had asked Geneva to send arms. They sent scouting parties up and down the frontier.

The municipality of Bourg blamed these same circulars from Langeron for the panic which broke out there on the morning of the 25th, 'coming from the frontier of Bresse on the eastern side', or more precisely from the Ain valley: 'at this warning, the parishes sounded the alarm; the fear came ever nearer'. The rumours which went around Bresse suggest that the parish of Pont-d'Ain was the starting point; here, the road from Savoy passes through the Ambérieu cross-valley and indeed there had been talk of an invasion of Savoyards ever since the beginning of the month. But the rumours could just as well have come from the North. It would be very unlikely for the fear in the wine-country to find no echo in the South. The communes thrown into disorder by the news included Toirette which is more to the north, near the confluence of the Bienne; the fear must have travelled from Lons-le-Saulnier, along the Reverment, through Orgelet and Arinthod, which does not exclude a local incident which could have made Pont-d'Ain or Ambérieu a dispersal point.

From Pont-d'Ain, the panic spread out fanwise towards the West: it reached Simandre in the North-East on the 25th at three in the morning, arriving in Treffort in the morning of the 26th; it was in Coligny that same day. Also on the 25th, it was taken to Bourg, Pont-de-Vaux and Mâcon and from here it went right into the Mâconnais; finally it travelled down the Ain and reached Meximieux, Montluel and Miribel. Meximieux appealed to Lyons for help and dragoons were sent. Moving eastwards, it reached the parish of Saint-Rambert and through here entered the Bugey: it reached Belley on 28 July; from here, the current went up the Rhône through Seyssel, as far as La Michaille where the Valserine enters the river, then through the Valromey and into Gex: as it retraced its path northwards, it seemed to grow weaker and turn into a simple fear of brigands. It must then have passed around the high ridges of the southern Jura, for Nantua makes no mention of it, and its last ripples died down in a series of anti-seigneurial riots.

On the 25th, it also moved south from Ambérieu and Saint-Rambert to the nearby village of Lagnieu; here it had crossed the Rhône and the Dauphiné was to act as a relay of vital importance.

At first there was no panic: during the 25th and 26th, news that brigands were approaching spread between the Rhône and the Bourbe; on the 25th, it reached the Guier valley on the Savoy frontier, a particularly sensitive spot. Here on the morning of the 27th took place an incident which was to give a new lease of life to the Great Fear. According to the *procureur-général* of the Grenoble *parlement*, 'there were only a few shots fired between eight or nine smugglers and some farm workers who fought them off'; the same version appeared in letters written by the municipality in Lyons. However, we do not know exactly where this incident took place. Some *gabelous* arrived in Morestel saying that Lagnieu had been sacked and the panic was carried from here to Aoste, then to Pont-de-Beauvoisin, which suggests that the source lay somewhere to the North. But it spread westwards from Pont-de-Beauvoisin and flowed back towards Morestel itself in a new and interesting shape –

the Savoyards (soon to reappear in the fear legends as the Piedmontese army) had crossed the border. La Tour-du-Pin got its warning on the 27th at three o'clock, Bourgoin at five o'clock, Virieu, the Bièvre plain and the Côte-Saint-André all at the same time. The fear rushed down all the valleys of the Bas-Dauphiné towards the Rhône valley, from Lyons to Saint-Vallier. Towards the South, it went by the Voiron road to reach the Isère at Moirans, and whilst it went up one side to reach Grenoble by eleven o' clock, it went down the other side to pass through Saint-Marcellin at midnight; it was in Romans at three in the morning on the 28th, moving from here to Tain, then Valence: it was now well established and on that same day the châteaux of the lower Dauphiné began to burn.

The revolt in the Mâconnais which, as we know, preceded the Great Fear but much encouraged it, and the uprising in the Dauphiné, its most serious consequence, were the most incomparable resonators. The first may not have spread the Great Fear itself, but it sent a tremendous feeling of anxiety and restlessness through the Chalonnais and consequently through the Burgundy vineyards (Nuits mentions 'the fright'); Dijon must also have been reached from the South. It was the same in the Charollais; there is no evidence of panic in the area further south, Charolles, Paray and Digoin, but the mountainous fringes of the Grosne valley were affected, as we can tell, by the trouble in Saint-Point and Tramayes: the inhabitants of these two villages said on the 31st that brigands were coming either from Germign, which was far to the North, or from Aigueperse to the South-East, half-way to La Clayette. More to the South, in the mountains of the Beaujolais, the fear came in from the southern Mâconnais, through Beaujeu and the Écharmaux pass, and probably also from Villefranche where the Château de Mongré had been sacked on the 27th. It spread everywhere on the 28th and was at its height in Chauffailles on the 29th, travelling from there to La Clayette at seven in the morning and to Charlieu where it was said that Thil and Cublize were going to burn their harvests, that thirteen hundred brigands were camping 'on the heights of the Beaujolais', that Beaujeu and Villefranche were in arms and that over forty thousand peasants were on the defensive between the Saône and the Loire. It does not seem that the panic crossed the Loire at this point, for it did not touch Roanne. It was not the same in the Forez, however. The panic which swept in from the Dauphiné through Lyons and Givors reached the Lyonnais uplands, Tarare and Saint-Symphorien on the 28th; on the 29th, Feurs fell into great disorder and the fear passed on through the Boën plain, Saint-Germain-Laval and Montbrison. From Boën, it crossed the mountains *via* the Noirétable pass, then went down to Limagne on the 30th and 31st and reached Thiers, Riom and Clermont. Further south, it crossed the Rhône between Tain and Tournon on the 28th, reached Annonay on the same day and crossed the Pilat to reach Lavalla *via* Bourg-Argentat at half-past four in the afternoon. The Saint-Étienne depression was thus approached from the North as well as the South, whilst another current coming from Vienne and Condrieu approached it on the afternoon of the 28th through Rive-de-Gier and Saint-Chamond. There was considerable violence in Saint-Étienne from half-past five onwards. On the 29th at ten o'clock in the morning, the panic was well established at Saint-Bonnet on the other side of the Loire; it crossed the mountains and reached Arlanc on the 30th and on the same day went as far as La Chaise-Dieu, whose abbot hastened to send for help to Brioude, which curiously enough did not grow alarmed at the request.

Meanwhile, the Great Fear went post-haste along the left bank of the Rhône, starting from Valence: it reached Livron and Loriol between four and five in the evening; by six o' clock it was in Montélimar; Pierrelatte was awakened at one in the morning on the 29th, Saint-Paul-Trois-Châteaux at four o' clock; it reached Orange at half-past eight and was soon afterwards in Avignon. Early on the 30th, it was racing through Tarascon and Arles and by evening had crossed the Crau and was well established in Saint-Chamas. This main current shot off a variety of secondary currents to the West and East. In the Alpine region, they carefully went around the main mountain masses. The strongest current started up the Drôme on the 28th; a branch broke away at Crest and moved southwards to Dieu-le-Fit; on the 29th, it reached Taulignan by five in the morning and during the day it got as far as Valréas and Nyons. Above Crest, it made its way through Saillans, Die, Châtillon and Luc, already somewhat disturbed by the rumours which had filtered through the Vercors: the Cabres pass led to Veynes which became a main centre on the 29th. There was a serious outbreak of panic in Gap on the 29th and 30th. Gap too is a major crossroads: towards the north, the Col de Bayard leads to Champsaur: the alarm came down the Drac via Saint-Bonnet and Corps on the 30th and La Mure on the 31st, and went back into Grenoble without affecting the Oisans; towards the east, it went up the Durance (through Embrun on the 30th and Briançon on

the 31st), then up the Ubaye at least as far as Barcelonnette: as far as we
know, there was no panic in any of these towns. The fear travelled southwards from Veynes *via* Serre and from Gap *via* Tallard as far as the
Durance and then beyond it in two currents parallel to the one travelling
from Dieu-le-Fit, channelled on one side by the massifs of Roche-Courbe,
Chabre and Lure, and on the other by that of the Cheval-Blanc, and in
the centre by those separating the Durance from the Bléone; Sisteron
was reached by way of the Durance on the evening of the 30th, Forqualquier on the 31st; also on the 31st, the panic from Tallard travelled
through Turriers to Seyne (Tallard was to have a second burst on
1 August) and from there to Digne through the Col de Maure. By the
evening of the 31st, warnings had been sent to Riez and Moustiers in the
South-West and Castellane on the Verdon through Barrême and Senez.
The trail of fear can be followed over the mountains from Castellane on
1 August, right up to Roquesteron, Bouyon and Vence: this was the edge
of the Var valley, on the frontier of France. In the South, the fear did
not cross the Verdon valley. The king of Sardinia set guards all along
his frontier from Savoy to the Var and published an official denial of all
the rumours circulating as to his intentions. A separate branch of panic
ran from Montélimar towards Grignan and Taulignan and a much
stronger stream broke away at Pierrelatte, moving towards Saint-Paul-
Trois-Châteaux and the Aygues valley; these joined up with the current
from Dieu-le-Fit and went around Mont Ventoux, passing through Vaison
on the 29th and Bédoin and Sault on the 30th. Yet another branch went
from Orange towards Carpentras, Apt and Cadenet on the Durance;
then up this river from Avignon. Between the mountains of Lure and
Lubéron, these separate currents clashed at some point between Manosque
and Banon with a wave coming down from Forqualquier, leaving a
backwash of small disturbances. The Durance was crossed at Cadenet
and Pertuis towards evening on the 30th and the fear now reached Aix
from this direction, apparently before the currents from Salon and
Saint-Chamas had arrived. During the next few days, it spread slowly
towards the East, across the plateaux which separate the Durance from
Brignoles and Draguignan, appearing in Trets and Saint-Maximin on
2 August, in Barjols on the 4th and finally in Salernes. There is not a
trace to the south of the Argens or on the coast of Provence, nor in the
southern Crau or the Camargue.

Towards the East, the lateral currents approached the right bank at

Le Pouzin, Rochemaure and Le Teil, Bourg-Saint-Andéol and Beaucaire, which received a great wave of fear from Loriol, Montélimar,
Pierrelatte and Tarascon; Arles should also be mentioned. As there were
two alerts in Loriol, there naturally were two in Le Pouzin in the afternoon of the 28th and at noon on the 29th; they spread to Privas, which
sent help. During the afternoon of the 29th, there was a tremendous
crowd of people in Le Pouzin and it was then that M. d'Arbalestrier was
murdered. The fear spread northwards from Privas towards the Haut-
Vivarais, reaching Le Cheylard on the 30th at five o'clock in the afternoon
and then Saint-Agrève (Yssingeaux and Le Puy must have been aware
of the fear but it did not actually cross the mountains) – then southwards
into Les Coirons: Aubenas was warned in the evening of the 29th.
This massif was approached in the South by Le Teil and Villeneuve-de-
Berg; on the 30th, Antraigues and Vals came down to Aubenas. Le
Tanargue to the west of the Ardèche was carried along by Aubenas and
by Villeneuve-de-Berg which sent a warning to Largentière during the
afternoon of the 29th, and by the current which started in Bourg-Saint-
Andéol before first light on the 29th: this travelled through Vallon as far
as Joyeuse and Les Vans. We are now on the threshold of the Villefort
gap through which the fear sped to Mende on the 30th. On that day, it
moved along the Rhône to the south of Bourg-Saint-Andéol as far as
Pont-Saint-Esprit; here, we lose all trace of it; it moved with greater
speed along the Cévennes, from Les Vans to Saint-Florent and Alais
during the night of 29–30 July, and reached Saint-Jean-de-Gardonnenque
where a second alarm gave the fear such a renewed burst of energy that
on 1 August it leapt over the mountains and appeared in Valleraugue
and Saint-André-de-Valborgne. From here, it rebounded on to Mende
and even as far as Millau *via* Meyrueis. Mende, attacked by two separate
waves, transmitted the fear northwards to Malzieu on 1 August, whence
the rumours reached Saint-Flour – and Laissac on the edge of the Rouergue, where it arrived on the evening of the 3rd and instantly rebounded
into Millau. Millau, Saint-Affrique and Vabre, which were already in
contact with the Great Fear travelling through the South-West, suffered
a series of violent local alarms till 3 August. The news was sent to Lodève
and on the 2nd it took the road to Montpellier. The fear prevailing in
Saint-Jean-de-Gardonnenque had also reached the *garrigues* in the region
of Lédignan and Sauve; Montpellier was warned of its progress. Finally,
on the 30th, it moved from Arles towards Saint-Gilles and Vauvert; on

the 31st, it went from Beaucaire to Nîmes. The capital of Bas-Languedoc also had proper warning of dramas to come. However, it remained calm and from here to the Pyrenees, no document contains a single word on the subject of the Great Fear. From its origins in the Franche-Comté, and with the help of its many relays, it had stretched as far as the Mediterranean and struck deep into the Massif Central.

The fear in the Clermontois had a much simpler history and its area of operations was smaller. As we know, it began on the evening of Sunday, 26 July, at Estrées-Saint-Denis and travelled during the night, arriving in Clermont at seven o'clock; by this time it had already reached Sacy-le-Grand and Nointel as well as Lieuvilliers on the Saint-Just road. It was an extremely strong current and spread in all directions with the same vigour. It arrived at Verberie in the Oise valley below Compiègne early in the morning and was in full swing at Pont-Sainte-Maxence, Creil and Beaumont at eleven o'clock. From Beaumont it was taken to Pontoise at half-past twelve and from there spread through the southern Vexin to reach Triel at eight in the evening and Meulan at ten: early on the morning of the 28th, crowds of peasants arrived in Meulan; however, the movement did not continue downstream to Mantes and Vernon, nor did it cross the Seine and, like the fear from the West, did not pass into the Mantois. It did however go beyond the Oise valley and it was from here that it caused the greatest commotion, for the fear now swung towards Paris and at this point was even discussed in the National Assembly. We know nothing of its progress from Beaumont, L'Isle-Adam and Pontoise, but it seems likely that things would follow the same pattern as in the Verberie area: it followed the roads which ran towards Saint-Denis and finally by the end of the afternoon arrived in Montmorency where it found the relay it needed. From here, it sent disturbing waves into the suburbs around Paris and the Electors despatched a small army with a cannon which advanced at least as far as Écouen. Meanwhile it spread from Verberie into the Béthisy plain where it soon found another relay which swiftly carried it into the Valois and the Soissonnais. It was in Crépy at half-past eight in the morning, in Soissons at half-past one and the municipality here wrote a letter which was read out to the Assembly on the 28th. News of it came to Laon from the Soissonnais, but there is no indication that it ever travelled up the Aisne nor crossed the desolate Sissonne area. Rheims must have had some news of it, but we have no record of its effects in this town. Its progress southwards is fairly well documented. On the 27th, it travelled from Crépy and Villers-Cotterets to Dammartin and Meaux and reached La Ferté-sous-Jouarre and Château-Thierry on the 28th. On the same day, it travelled up the Marne *via* Epernay and Châlons. More than this, we do not know. It is not likely that it reached Vitry because it did not affect the Barrois. There was an alarm at Saint-Dizier and Joinville, but it seems to have occurred on the 28th and was purely of local origin, relating only to disturbances in this area and the Barrois. Might it have crossed the Marne to move up the two Morins? It is possible, but there is no mention of it in Coulommiers nor in Ferté-Gaucher. It seems that the barren regions of Champagne were not favourable to its progress. Nor was Brie, and no trace of it is found here either.

To the North-East it went up the Thérain valley: Beauvais sent its militia to the assistance of Clermont. From Saint-Just it also reached the Grandvilliers area and left it in a state of chaos. Moving up the Thérain, it reached Forges on the 28th and from here affected the Bray region, though we do not know if it got as far as Dieppe; from Grandvilliers it went to Aumale and then down the Bresle valley through Blangy and Eu. As far as we know, Ponthieu in the North and, towards the West, the Normandy Vexin, the Caux region and the lower valley of the Seine were all untouched.

Up in the North, great waves of fear rolled towards the Picardy plain. At nine in the morning of the 27th, it was in Montdidier and from here it travelled on towards Amiens and up the Avre valley; at ten o' clock, it appeared in Roye and alarmed the entire countryside around, which effectively transferred it to Corbie, Bray, Ham and Péronne, all in the course of the same day. It also went up the Oise valley via Ribécourt and Noyon and indeed seems to have made good progress in this direction, for an inquiry into the attack on the Château de Frétoy notes that it was in Muirancourt to the north of Noyon at six o'clock in the morning of the 27th. It carried on through Chauny, La Fère, Ribemont and Guise and entered the Thiérache where it appeared in Marle and Rozoy, in the Serre valley and in Vervins. Its expansion was limited by the forests of La Capelle and Le Nouvion and the borders of the Ardennes. The Somme on the other hand proved no barrier and it swept across Artois. From Péronne it moved to Bapaume on the 27th, then burst into Arras on the night of the 27th–28th; it must have reached Béthune during the morning of the 28th for it appeared in Merville on the Lys in the course of the day; Aire and Saint-Omer were affected on the same day or else during the night of the 28th–29th, for on the 30th, the municipality of Watten sent warnings to the town councils of maritime Flanders. From Arras, it also moved north-west: we have evidence of it in Samer on the 29th and Boulogne on the 29th or 30th. From Saint-Omer, it moved towards Calais. From Béthune, it passed into Walloon Flanders, and disturbed villages to the west of Lille before it died down on the 29th in Frelinghien on the Lys below Armentières; it moved no further into Flanders and oddly enough did not penetrate the usually stormy provinces of Hainault and the Cambrésis. One should conclude perhaps that the panic was not particularly violent in Artois or perhaps that it never spread as far as the eastern borders of the province.

In southern Champagne, the fear first appeared to the south of Romilly on 24 July; it took one day only – the 25th – to cross the Sénonais from the North-East to the South-West: it was in Thorigny by six o'clock in the evening and soon afterwards reached Sens and Villeneuve-l'Archevêque. From Romilly and Nogent, it spread northwards from the Seine, along the Île-de-France bank of the river. Villegruis and Villenauxe took up arms on the 26th when they heard that brigands were in the area; it was probably on this day that the panic broke out in Provins at the news that there were bandits hiding in the forests nearby; on the 26th, Donnemarie formed a militia on the grounds that crowds of vagrants were leaving Paris and doubtless the fear in Romilly was responsible in some measure for this rumour. On the 26th, the fear was everywhere in the Sézanne *bailliage* and, according to Barentin, then travelled along the road from Sézanne to Châlons. On the 28th, it appeared in Vatry on the Soude and in Mairy and Gogny on the Marne above Châlons; in these villages it could possibly be an extension of the fear from the Soissonnais, but this could not be true for the Sézanne area as the dates do not fit. It also went up the Aube valley, but very slowly at first, for it did not arrive in Arcis till the 26th or the 27th; then with a quick burst of speed it travelled to Bar-sur-Aube during the morning of 27 July. In Troyes, they knew all about the fear in Romilly on the 25th, but the population seems to have been unmoved. The panic did not break out till the 28th and came from the West, for it made its first appearance in the *faubourg* of Sainte-Savine on the left bank of the Seine; then it went up the

Seine valley and along its tributaries on the right; by seven in the evening it was in Landreville, at the opening of the Ource valley, and at ten or eleven o'clock it appeared in Mussy on the Seine; from here it moved to Châtillon that same evening. On the 29th, it ran through the Barse valley and alarmed Bar-sur-Aube for the second time; the Ource valley also had a second visit. On the 28th, Bar-sur-Seine and Châtillon received a new thrust from lateral currents coming from the Armançon valley which as a result became a point of vital stimulus for the panic.

Its origins are not clearly defined. The fear of 23 July did not go up the Yonne from Sens and there is no reason to think that it crossed the Othe forest; in any case, the centres of panic are to be found on its southern fringes, at Saint-Florentin on the 26th and Auxon on the 27th or 28th; their position as well as their dates suggests that there must have been some link between the Senonais current and the Armançon; local incidents could of course have acted as relays; one is mentioned in Auxon by an annalist: it was started by a *vicaire* who was frightened by the sounds of a flock feeding in the forest; the panic spread to the neighbouring parishes of Chamoy and Saint-Phal and towards the forests of Aumont and Chaource; in the course of the afternoon it reached the Armance valley, Ervy and Chaource. It was probably this panic which reached the Seine valley at various points on the same day. It is sometimes thought to have come from Saint-Florentin and Brienon: in fact it appeared in Brienon and places to the south on the evening of the 28th; on the morning of that day it had been taken to Tonnerre by some travellers who had got as far as Germigny near Saint-Florentin and then had turned back when they heard the rumour that there were brigands on the move. So the Auxon fear must have run along the Othe valley as far as Saint-Florentin, or perhaps some unrecorded incident revived it in that town on the 28th. Possibly the fear went up the Armançon from Tonnerre, but this is not certain, for it reached Saulieu from the Morvan and not from Semur. On the 29th, Châtillon-sur-Seine sent to Dijon for help and a detachment of soldiers went as far as Saint-Seine on the 30th, but was sent back again since all was calm. In this way, the fear from southern Champagne came into contact with the fear from the East in the major city of Dijon; such meetings were to become more frequent in the days that followed: we have already mentioned one between Forqualquier and Pertuis. When such a meeting took place, the result was either a series of successive alarms or some complicated backwash of riots, or some zone of interference, for the different currents at this point would be very weak indeed. Dijon is a case in point: there was no panic when the contact came, even though they were affected by the last stages of the panics from the Gray region, the Mâconnais and finally from Champagne.

The disturbances in Champagne did not trouble the Seine valley only: they also found room to expand towards the West and the South. We have no special landmarks to guide us here, but it seems that the alarm on the 24th spread from Nogent and Provins to Montereau, Moret and Fontainebleau, along the left bank of the Seine, and that the fear in Nemours and Château Landon must have come from Sens. It must have travelled northwards from here, which would explain its arrival in Corbeil on the 28th and in Choisy and Villeneuve-le-Roi on the same day between six and seven o'clock in the evening; in addition, it was brought into these latter villages by two people from the Gâtinais who were travelling from Athis Mons and must have come down the river. They claimed that hussars were in Juvisy, burning and killing, and that they had already attacked Montlhéry, Longjumeau and Ris. Marmontel, who at that time was living in his country house in Grignon between Orly and Thiais, describes in his memoirs the general stampede that then took place and also refers to the rumour about the hussars. This provided the fear with an entry into the capital from the South, after it had already entered from the North on the previous evening. Hardy mentions it in his journal: they said that Longjumeau was being sacked and that help was being sent: this is how Longjumeau got its first taste of fear, for the town was in fact perfectly peaceful.

The panic passed along the Loing valley to reach Beauce: it was reported to be in Boynes and Boiscommun on the morning of the 29th and later that day was much further away in Toury; towards three in the afternoon it was in Châteauneuf-sur-Loire, Jargeau and Saint-Denis-de-l'Hôtel. The rumour arrived in Orléans where it was attributed to the presence of brigands in the nearby forests. There had already been an alarm in Chilleurs and Neuville-aux-Bois on the 27th: it is possible that there was an independent panic at this point. The rest of Beauce and Hurepoix was untouched so that between these two regions where the fear was prevalent (southern Champagne and the West) there was a great expanse of calm stretching from the Loire below Orléans to the Seine below Paris.

On the 28th, there was an outbreak of fear on both banks of the Yonne, then another one to the east around Seignelay at three in the afternoon and later still that day around Champvallon in the west. It moved from Champvallon into the southern Gâtinais, stopping at Châteaurenard and Châtillon-sur-Loing on the 29th and approaching Saint-Fargeau by Aillant and Villiers-sous-Benoît; it also moved towards the Puisaye where it appeared in Thury and Entrains on the 29th. Next it came down the Loire valley, appearing in Briaire and Sancerre on the 29th, spreading from there into the Sancerrois on the 30th; La Charité also was affected on the 29th, at five in the afternoon. It was probably from this town that the current moved towards Nevers, though to reach both La Charité and Nevers, it must also have come up the Yonne valley.

As it did so, it crossed through Auxerre and Champs. One part of it branched off down the Cure valley towards Avallon on one side and Vézelay on the other. Meanwhile, the main current raced on to Clamecy: there was a great commotion here and various detailed accounts have survived. It reached Lormes and Corbigny *via* Tannay and then moved to the West towards Montsauche and from here reached out to Saulieu on the 30th. Still following the Yonne, it appeared at nine o'clock on the morning of the 30th in Château-Chinon and was passed on from there to Autun on the same day, then further still to Moulins-Engilbert and Decize. It faded away between the Loire and the Arroux. Bourbon-Lancy and Digoin ignored it. The Charollais and the Creusot region provided a new zone of interference for this fear and the fear from the East.

Finally, the current moved up the Allier from Nevers and went deep into the Bourbonnais on the 30th and the 31st. It is not possible to define its area exactly in this region, for it became inextricably involved with the fear coming up from the South-West. However, there was excitement and panic in Sancoins, Bourbon-l'Archambault, Saint-Pierre-le-Moûtier, Moulins and Varennes-sur-Allier. Near Gannat and Vichy, its last small outbreaks came up against the current moving in from the West through southern Berry.

It was the last fear, the late-comer from the South-West, which travelled the furthest, but its propagation offers no difficult problems. Its emotive power, always strong, remained unchanged to the very end. It began in Ruffec on the 28th in circumstances already described. In the West, it apparently reached the forests of Chizé and Aulnay, though there might have been a centre of purely local panic here. It does not seem to have gone beyond Surgères. La Rochelle, Rochefort and Saint-Jean-d'Angély probably heard only distant echoes. In the North it appeared in Civray and Vançais on the 28th and the 29th found it in Lusignan and Vivonne: it travelled down the Clain but faded out in Poitiers. The rest of the Poitou plain was unaffected and therefore constitutes a sort of no-man's-land between this fear and the one from the Vendée which had in any case come to an end four or five days previously.

From Ruffec and Civray, it went into Vienne *via* Chabanais and Confolens at ten o'clock in the evening. From here, it travelled up the valley through Saint-Junien and reached Rochechouart during the night and was in Limoges by four o'clock in the morning on 29 July. According to George Sand who described it in *Nanon*, it then went on towards Saint-Léonard, but its expansion seems to have been hindered by the Ambazac hills and the plateaux of Gentioux and Millevaches. From the upper Vienne it moved only towards the South, where it joined up with currents from Mansle and Angoulême. It was the journey from Confolens to the Gartempe which was of capital importance. The fear went down this river through Montmorillon and Saint-Savin, probably moving towards the Vienne valley; it was apparently in Chauvigny and must have passed through Châtellerault; it also went up the Gartempe from Bellac at six o'clock in the morning on the 29th, going through Châteauponsac and Grand-Bourg, arriving in Guéret at about five in the afternoon; it spread fanwise from Le Dorat and Magnac-Laval, through the Basse-Marche to the Creuse valley which was affected throughout later in the day – at Le Blanc, Argenton, Dun-le-Palleteau and La Celle-Dunoise *via* La Souterraine. This was a fine jumping-off place for the Indre. The inhabitants of Argenton acted promptly and sent messages in haste to Châteauroux: the warning arrived at about seven in the evening on the 29th. News was also taken swiftly from Dun to La Châtre, arriving at nine o'clock in the evening. On the other hand, La Brenne and the Sainte-Maure plateau were crossed rather slowly. Tours, Loches and Châtillon were not warned till the 30th by La Haye-Descartes, Preuilly and Le Blanc; Châtillon and Loches had already been rudely awakened by the news from another source – Châteauroux – on the 29th. Loches was therefore the point where the fear from Maine met and joined up with the Ruffec fear.

The fear set off from Châteauroux and La Châtre to conquer eastern

Berry. Issoudun was on the alert at one in the morning on the 30th. During the day, it crossed the Cher at Châteauneuf and reached Bourges. There is no evidence that it travelled northwards: there seems to have been no union with the Blésois and the Sancerrois. In the South, the Cher was reached at Saint-Amand-Montrond and Vallon, *via* Château-meillant, and the Bourbonnais was affected on the 30th; the current ran to Saint-Bonnet-Tronçais and Cérilly, Maillet and Hérisson, ending as far away as Cosne and Bussière: this is on the threshold of Bourbon-l'Archam-bault and here they were to be shaken by the fear from Champagne.

Guéret alerted the Combrailles, the Auvergne and even the Haut Limousin. The alarm went up the Creuse, reaching Aubusson on the 29th at eleven o'clock at night, and Felletin at three in the morning on the 30th; from here it travelled round the edges of the Gentioux plateau and swept back to Meymac. It had far greater freedom of movement in the East. It moved from Guéret towards the upper Cher valley, to Montluçon *via* Boussac, to Évaux and to Auzances *via* Chénérailles; it seemed in a particular hurry to reach Montluçon, which was awakened during the night of 29–30 July; Néris was reached at two in the morning; Auzances was quiet till ten o'clock. Through Montaigu, Pionsat and Saint-Gervais, avoiding the Chaîne des Puys, the current ran into Limagne, reaching Riom and Clermont at about five in the afternoon. During the 31st, the entire Mont Dore region was encircled by the different branches of the panic. One of them took the mountain road which led to the Dordogne and got as far as Bort, moving from there to Riom-ès-Montagnes at eleven in the evening, then on to Vic-sur-Cère and Mur-de-Barrez on 1 August; the other went up the Allier by way of Saint-Amand-Tallende, Issoire and Saint-Germain-Lembron, as far as Brioude which was reached on the 31st at seven in the evening. The valley of the Alagnon which leads into the Cantal opens out between Issoire and Brioude: this was the way the current took to pass through Blesle and Massiac on its way to Saint-Flour, which it reached the same evening. In Riom, Clermont, Brioude and Saint-Flour, the fear from the West came into direct contact with the fear from the East. On 1 August, it made its way down to Murat and crossed the Lioran; it travelled gradually through the Luguet hills to Condat and Allanche; in this way, it eventually joined up with its northern branch at Vic-sur-Cère.

It was through its southwards sweep that the Ruffec fear had the greatest success for it rolled implacably through most of Aquitaine. First, it went down the Charente through Mansle and was in Angoulême by the 28th at three in the afternoon; then it followed the river through Jarnac and Cognac up to Saintes; we lose trace of it here and as far as we can tell maritime and southern Saintonge seem to have stayed undisturbed. From Angoulême, its influence stretched out to Barbezieux, Baignes and Montendre, but the Double stopped its progress on the road to Blaye. The main route moved south-westwards. It travelled from Mansle to La Rochefoucauld so that on the 29th it appeared in Champeniers between six and seven in the morning; it was in Piégut by eleven o'clock and in Nexon by the early afternoon; from here it jumped to Saint-Yrieix. Fresh news from Rochechouart and Limoges had given it greater strength. The valleys of the Dronne and the Isle lay open before it and it was now well on the way to Bas-Limousin. But at the same time, the fear flowed from Angoulême through Nontron, the woods of La Valette and Montmoreau, and on to the Dronne valley which was thrown into total confusion. It seems to have found a useful relay at La Roche-Chalais, arrived in Coutras at four in the afternoon and swept swiftly onwards to the edge of the Dordogne from Fronsac, Libourne and Saint-Émilion to Bergerac, all during the night of 29–30 July; it was in Sainte-Foy on the left bank by five in the morning. At the same time, it crossed the Dronne at various points and sped towards the Isle. Brantôme, Bourdeilles and Ribérac sent warnings to Périgueux which was duly alerted at one in the morning on the 29th; on the 30th, the entire valley was in a ferment from Thiviers to Mussidan. The wave rolled on towards the Vézère: on the 30th, at four in the morning, it was in Badefol-d'Ans, probably approaching from Périgueux through the Barade forest; an hour later, it was reported in Lubersac, coming from Saint-Yrieix, Thiviers, and Excideuil, moving onwards to Uzerche. The lower Vézère was affected everywhere on the morning of the 30th, at Terrasson, Montignac and Le Bug. The fear moved from the Vézère to the Dordogne but in two divergent currents: one swept from Uzerche towards the upper Dordogne and sank deep into the Massif Central; the other approached the central section of the river's course, reaching La Linde, Limeuil, where it joins the Vézère, and Domme, already alerted by Sarlat on the 30th, between two and three in the afternoon. The Dordogne was crossed at every point in the course of one day, the 30th, the fear appearing in the morning to the west of Bergerac and in the afternoon to the east. South of the river, three currents can be distinguished: all three naturally crossed each other's paths time and time again: the current from Sainte-Foy or from the Agennais; one from Libos or the eastern Agennais; one from Domme or eastern Quercy. The latter slanted towards Figeac and the Massif Central. The other two thrust southwards.

The Agenais current left Sainte-Foy and Gensac at daybreak on the 30th, disturbed the Dropt valley from Eymet to Duras and Monségur, then went up the Lot valley through Montflanquin and Tombebeuf, reaching Villeneuve and Castelmoron towards the end of the day and Agen by midnight. La Réole was affected and probably Marmande and Tonneins too. There is no evidence that it penetrated Entre-Deux-Mers or that it crossed the Garonne to enter Bazadais. It crossed on to the left bank at Agen and moved along the Gers and the Baïse through Armagnac. We know very little about this part of its journey. The fear was reported in Mézin to the west of the Baïse, so it must have gone through Nérac and Condom; it did not affect the Landes, but is found in the Adour, well to the south of Aire, at Maubourguet and Vic-de-Bigorre which it must have approached *via* Mirande. It was in Auch on 3 August, doubtless sent there by Lectoure.

The Limeuil current disturbed the Belvès plain, Montpazier and Ville-franche-de-Périgord at the source of the Dropt and here it split into two: one branch went towards the Lot at Fumel and Libos, another towards Cahors. The first crossed the valley to reach Tournon-d'Agenais on the 30th at eight in the evening; shortly afterwards it was in Montaigu and then during the night appeared in Lauzerte. Early on the 31st, it arrived in Lafrançaise where the Tarn and the Aveyron join forces, in Moissac and on the banks of the Garonne at Valence where it seems to have crossed the river. From Lafrançaise and Moissac it reached Mont-auban in the course of the day and on 1 August caused the first alarm in Toulouse. From Valence it crossed the Lomagne and we hear of it in Auvillars and Saint-Clair; from here it moved on 2 August through Touget, Gimont, Saint-André, Samatan and Lombez. It went up the Save through L'Île-en-Dodon and Blajan, up the Giome through Boulogne, joining the Sainte-Foy current near Castelnau, coming to an end on the slopes of the Lannemezan plateau: the fear was in Tuzaguet on 5 August. It had however already turned towards the West and reached Tarbes on the 4th, climbing the Pyrenees as far as Bagnères-de-Bigorre. From Tarbes, Maubourguet and Vic-de-Bigorre, the fear reached Ossun and Pontacq, then the Gave at Pau, Nay, Coarraze and finally Lourdes on 6 August. There is no trace of it on the Adour below Maubourguet, in the Chalosse, Béarn or the Basque country. Apart from a few incidents in the valleys around Lourdes and Argelès, there is no sign of it in the western Pyrenees.

Further north, it was in Cahors on the 31st at four in the morning and from here moved with great speed to Castelnau-de-Montratier, Montpezat, Caussade (arriving at nine o' clock) and then swept into the Aveyron at Saint-Antonin, Bruniquel, Montricoux and Négrepelisse. This stream too split into two lateral currents which went deep into the Causses. It moved obliquely from the Aveyron towards Gaillac on 1 August, then on the 2nd crossed the rye-fields through Graulhet, reaching as far as Castres. It probably found a relay in Gaillac, L'Isle-d'Albi or Rabastens; in any case, on the 2nd, it rolled around the bend of the Tarn to appear in Buzet and from here it passed through Montastruc-la-Conseillère to cause a second alarm in Toulouse on 3 August. On the same day at six in the morning, it also arrived in Villemur on the Tarn below Buzet and from here seems to have turned through Fronton and Bouloc towards Grenade and Verdun: from this direction came the alarm which spread along the lower Save to the north of L'Isle-Jourdain on the 3rd; it came from the North, though it might possibly have been a backwash from the Lomagne panic; in any case, it probably reached Toulouse through the West during the same day.

From Toulouse, the panic which swept the city on the 3rd went up the Garonne through Muret on the 3rd, then Capens and Carbonne on the 4th, at least as far as Martres. The earlier panic of 1 August had certainly gone before it, though this is not mentioned in any of these different places, and it must have progressed in a southerly direction through Montesquieu-Volvestre, for it appeared either in the evening of the 2nd or else at some time after midnight in the morning of the 3rd in Saint-Girons, Rimont and Castillon; on the 3rd it was in Le Mas-d'Azil, having come down from Daumazan in the North; at the same time, it had travelled up the Ariège, for during the night 2–3 August it appeared in Saverdun. Pamiers was warned only on the 4th, at seven in the evening, probably through the second wave from Toulouse. It is found in Vicdessos on 5 and 6 August and must surely have passed through Foix. From Pamiers and Foix it shot sideways towards the East through Mirepoix and Lavelanet, for we have reports of it in Chalabre, Ridel and Le Peyrat and on 5 and 6 August, in Bélesta. Gradually, it percolated through to

Quillan on the Aude and Bugarach in the Corbières, reaching Caudiés on the 5th; from here, it lost itself in the mountains, but we hear vague echoes from Saint-Paul-de-Fenouillet and Mosset slightly to the north of Prades.

The Massif Central received many small waves of panic after the main current had swept along. The first two derived from the Uzerche panic which left a state of extreme disorder in the Monédière massif between the Vézère and the Corrèze. The first travelled through Meymac and Ussel, Égletons, Neuvic and Bort, where it appeared late on the 30th; on the 31st, Felletin and Clermont heard that it was on its way and this town sent out warnings which we have already mentioned. This distant corner was racked by a series of alarms on the days following and on 1 August this led to the disturbance in Saint-Angel which will be discussed later. From Bort and Neuvic, the fear moved towards Riom-ès-Montagnes and Mauriac, then took the road to Aurillac. The second current reached Tulle and Brive during the morning of the 30th; in the evening, it got as far as Argentat and Beaulieu on the Dordogne on the 30th; on the 31st, it went up the Cère through La Roquebrou, again as far as Aurillac.

The Domme current travelled across the Gramat *causse*, moving slowly towards Gramat and Saint Céré, arriving as late as the 31st; its progress towards Figeac was more rapid and the news flashed around here on the 30th. On the 31st, it was passed on to Maurs, then to Aurillac yet again and to Mur de Barrez; Entraygues was soon informed and from here it went up the Truyère as far as Chaudesaigues, arriving in Saint-Flour in the night of 31 July–1 August. The currents from Guyenne and those from the Auvergne met and mingled on the western and southern slopes of the Cantal and the Planèze.

From Entraygues, the fear went up the Lot as far as Mende and here it crossed with the current from the Vivarais which was travelling down towards the Rouergue. This area had been alerted by southern Quercy. From Cahors, either by travelling up the Lot as far as Carjac or by a direct line, the panic crossed the Limogne *causse* and reached Villefranche on the 31st at ten o'clock in the evening. This town was also warned by a courier from Caylus which had in turn been warned by Caussade. Rodez, Laissac and Séverac were affected and news of the fear rushed down on Millau from the entire upper valley of the Aveyron on 2 and 3 August. Similar news from the Cévennes also came through to Millau, as did the rumour which had come up the Tarn from Gaillac and which appeared suddenly in Ambialet on the 3rd. So the fear from the East and the fear from the South-West joined up firmly along a line from Clermont to Millau, passing through Aurillac Saint-Flour and Mende: Millau is the town which formed the nexus for the greatest number of currents in all France.

This is how the Great Fear travelled through France and it represents the most complete description possible at the present time. It is clear that information is lacking on many aspects, but it is hoped that future researches will provide many of the details which are needed for a more complete picture.

7

The Later Fears

The fear of brigands which synthesized all the causes of insecurity and actually created the Great Fear did not automatically disappear once it was seen that the brigands were not actually coming. And in fact the reasons which made their appearance very possible continued to exist. The critical period of the harvest lasted right until the end of August; famine, unemployment, poverty and begging, the usual consequences, prevailed for even longer than usual and the first did not end till the corn was threshed in the autumn. In August 1789, the municipality of Paris closed the *ateliers de charité* and tried to send the workers back where they had come from: their reputation had made Montmartre a difficult place to live in. The aristocrats' plot was more than ever the question of the day: its existence was denied and the revolutionaries sharply taken to task for continuing to believe in it. We know today that these fears were increasingly justified: in July 1789 only the court dared to plan a *coup* against the Assembly, and towards the end of 1789 it set up countless counter-revolutionary leagues in the provinces, whilst at the same time the *émigrés* living abroad, and finally Louis XVI himself, sought the armed intervention of other European monarchs. Knowing as we do how people felt at the time, it is not surprising that there were many local alarms in the weeks that followed the Great Fear.

On 14 August, the committee for Senlis denied the rumour going around Paris that there were two thousand brigands in the forest. On the 15th, there was a panic at Montdidier; on the 22nd, it was claimed in Rambouillet that 'the countryside was swarming with brigands'. There was an alert in Asnan near Clamecy on the 5th and another in Orléans on the 16th, some harvesters having decided to hold to ransom the son of a merchant from Bacon near Coulmiers; on the 7th, there was an alarm in Caen and shortly afterwards another in the canton of Thorigny; at the beginning of the month, there was a violent panic to the south of Saint-Florentin around the Pontigny woods and several others at Issy-l'Évêque and Toulon-sur-Arroux; during the night of 3-4 August, a new current started off in Bresse, probably coming from Tournus, and was stopped in Bletterans only through the sang-froid of Lecourbe who refused to sound the tocsin; the same thing happened around Châtillon-de-Michaille to the east of the Bugey. During the night of 9-10 August, there was a great alert in the Auvergne around Champagnac and another on the 6th in La Queuille. On the 5th, some harvesters in Civray thought they saw a rifle butt and a gun-barrel sticking out of a loaded waggon and terrified everyone in the neighbourhood. The tocsin sounded afresh at Beaulieu in Périgord during the night of 10-11 August and there was a general alert in Castelnau-de-Montmirail to the north-west of Gaillac from the 10th onwards. The workers in the salt-pans of Pecquais started a new fear in Vauvert on the 22nd and on the 15th the municipality of Saint-Girons decided to seek information, 'the news that ten thousand fighting men had disembarked in Barcelona and were wending their way towards Spanish Catalonia on the border of French Catalonia having taken on some substance'. On the 21st, there was a fresh panic in Aix, a band of brigands from Marseille being on their way to the town. These fears were only local, possibly because what had happened in July had diminished general credulity, but also of course because the harvest was by now more or less over.

As far as we know from documents available at the moment, it seems that the alarms now stopped. But when the 1790 harvest drew near, they started up again, which shows the very important part played by this factor in the events leading up to the Great Fear. On 16 July 1790, it seems that a band of peasants went to an abbey near Guise where it was thought arms and ammunition were being hidden. Very soon, a rumour raced around the countryside to the effect that brigands were ravaging the harvest. The panic spread towards Ribemont and reached Laon at eight in the evening; it turned towards the North-West through the Thiérache, reached Rethel, spread through the Porcien and moved as far as Rimogne and Rocroy on the borders of the Ardennes. On the 12th, an incident of some unknown nature happened in Vézelise and caused great panic: its effects were felt as far away as Nancy and Lunéville. On the 17th, there was an outbreak of fear in Aboncourt in the Amont *bailliage*; there seems to be no connexion with the outbreak at Vézelise but it is not impossible that there was some link between them. Three weeks later, a violent panic brought into play yet again one of the essential factors in the Great Fear: the fear aroused by the machinations of the aristocracy. At the end of July, it was learned that Austrian troops were advancing towards the rebellious Low Countries; by virtue of the terms of the convention of 1769, Louis XVI had given them permission to cross French territory. The people living in the East of France were convinced that this revolt in the Low Countries was only a pretext and that the imperial army was in fact on its way to crush the revolutionary forces of France. On 3 August, one of its detachments was thought to be seen in Cheppy near Varennes – probably one of Bouillé's patrols was taken for Germans. Whatever the case, the news flashed through the countryside that the harvest was either burnt or destroyed either by brigands or the Austrians. The entire Argonne trembled and asked for help from all sides: the warning reached Bar-le-Duc on the 14th and the whole Barrois was called to arms; this took the news into Saint-Dizier on the 5th. It swept eastwards through Saint-Menehould to Châlons and Rheims; the panic was in Verdun and Saint-Mihiel to the west by the 4th, and from Verdun it moved to Metz on the 5th and then Thionville, setting the Woëvre on the alert as far as Longwy. It travelled down the Meuse at least as far as Stenay and up the Aisne, so that the entire Porcien was affected yet again from Vouziers to Rimogne, and the Thiérache from Rozoy to Montcornet. These alarms caused the same sort of disturbances as in 1789. The military commander in Stenay aroused suspicion and was threatened; at Méligny-le-Grand, the seigneur's house was raided and arms taken; the Château d'Aboncourt was sacked.

The fear of brigands appeared yet again in 1791 in Varennes and, after the king's flight, in Trappes in Seine-et-Oise, and again on 24 June in Dreux. It burst out again the following year in Gisors when the news of the destruction of the Tuileries was reported. Later still, on 20 April 1793, a violent panic broke out in the Caux region around Yvetot, the rumour being that the English had landed and that brigands in the pay of the aristocracy were ravaging the country to make the English advance easier. Finally, at the end of September 1793, a new alarm troubled the suburbs of Meaux; it is mentioned in a letter sent to Chabot by Vernon, the former *vicaire épiscopal* for Seine-et-Marne; he is not very explicit about what happened, but the events were so typical of the great fear in general that it is worth while reproducing what he wrote: 'We had a false alert last Monday [23 September]. In a trice, there was a mob of forty thousand *sans-culottes*: if the aristocrats sought to entertain themselves by this manoeuvre then it is the last time they will try it. They heard the tune we shall make them dance to.' As long as the Revolution was seen to be in danger, the fears continued. It is to be hoped that future researches will reveal others to add to those we have already described. They seem to us to confirm the explanations we have offered for the Great Fear of 1789.

8

The Consequences of
the Great Fear

During the period of the Great Fear, there occurred both in towns and countryside a great number of political events and disturbances for which it was automatically blamed, especially where the idea of a deliberate plot was accepted. It is in fact difficult to discern what was its true influence. One must not begin by taking as one solid unit of time the days which separate 20 July from 6 August, for the panic did not burst out everywhere at the same time; it must always be remembered that the Great Fear and the fear of brigands are two separate items; finally, coincidence does not necessarily imply the relation of cause to effect: this is true even for those regions which were in revolt before the panic. It is also true for those which bordered on the areas of rebellion. Bresse, for instance, was much disturbed during the Great Fear: on the 26th in Vonnas, the Château de Beost was sacked by the local peasants; charters were destroyed in Thoissey; others were burnt on the 27th in Pont-de-Veyle; on the 28th, the inhabitants of Arlay demanded their title deeds from the Duchesse de Brancas. But several days previously, the unrest had caused similar incidents just outside Bourg and in Rome-nay and when the Mâconnais rose in revolt all along the border, there is nothing to suggest that no one would have followed suit if the Great Fear had not come along. This observation is confirmed by the fact that the disturbances continued to spread even in areas which were less affected by the fear than others; one cannot for instance attribute to the Great Fear the riots which raged through Rouen on 3 and 4 August, nor the tumults which overthrew the municipalities of Fumay, Marien-bourg and Givet at the end of July and the beginning of August, any more than one can blame it for the growing independence often demon-strated in acts of violence – as for instance among the peasants of Lorraine, Hainault and the Cambrésis who took independent action against tithe-collectors and seigneurs. Finally, one must add that in the towns, the panic brought a strengthening of the communal defence system; it almost always suspended or diminished municipal disagreements instead of causing them. And yet again, one must stress that committees were formed and the people armed long before the fear made its appearance and it is a mistake to imagine that after it had died down, all the villages in the country had their own militia. Many waited for the proclamation of 10 August and there were quite a few who did not have a *garde nationale* till 1790.

Apart from these reservations, one must admit that the influence of the Great Fear is undeniable. In most cases, the committees and the town militia were still in embryo state or else existed only on paper; the fear forced the committees to organize themselves and gave them the opportunity to act; it obliged the militia to meet and obtain arms and ammunition. Thanks to the fear, the idea of taking up arms reached the country towns and villages. It tightened the bonds of solidarity which linked the town and the countryside around it as well as the towns themselves, so much so that in some provinces the origin of the local federations may be found to date from the last days of July. But there must be no exaggeration: when the brigands were announced, there were many whose first thought was to run away; arms were rare and the great majority of country folk was usually armed only with sticks and farming implements; they soon got tired of mounting guard and no one thought to start training these soldier-citizens properly. However, from a national point of view, the reaction aroused by the panic was far from negligible. It was by and large a rough attempt at a mass levy of able-bodied men and during this first general mobilization the warlike spirit of the Revolution was often displayed, especially by the popular slogans of the time which recall 1792 and the year II. In Uzerche, the militia wore a badge with the motto: 'Conquer or die', and in Besançon fifty children from the famous Battant *faubourg* formed a company whose flag bore the inscription:

Quand les vieux quitteront,
Les jeunes reprendront.
(When the old guard gives up,
Youth will take over.)

Now, these sentiments of national pride and unity cannot be separated from the fierce enthusiasm of the Revolution. If the people rose, it was to frustrate the conspirators, not the brigands or the foreign troops who were only the tools of the nobility: it was to complete the defeat of the aristocracy. In this way, the Great Fear had a very profound influence on the social struggle through the stormy reaction it engendered: class solidarity was startlingly obvious between members of the Third Estate – they reached a deeper realization of their own strength and power. The aristocracy made no mistake here. 'Madame,' wrote d'Arlay, the steward of the Duchesse de Brancas on 28 July, 'the people are the masters; they know too much. They know they are the strongest.'

The Great Fear rebounded quite frequently on to the nobles and the upper clergy, reputedly its instigators. Most often, people were content to do no more than grumble or threaten; this is what happened in Saint-Girons where M. de Terssac continued strolling through the crowd and took control merely by the assurance of his bearing; sometimes, however, things came close to violence: M. de Josses, president of the Pau *parlement*, was in great danger for a short time in Bagnères-de-Bigorre on 7 August, and the home of M. de Montcalm, a deputy for the nobility who had left the Assembly, was attacked on the 2nd in Saint-Affrique. Harassments were frequent. In Montdidier, the peasants harried the local nobles and forced them to wear the cockade and shout: 'Long live the Third Estate.' This is not the only example. More than ever, the châteaux were viewed with deep suspicion. They were visited ever more frequently. In Mauriac on 31 July, they suspected that the home of M. d'Espinchal was being used for harbouring important people: there were the same suspicions in Tannay in the Nivernais, Allemans in the Agenais and Asnan in the Toulousain. As usual, when the peasants arrived, they required food and drink and sometimes even money. They threatened to burn the châteaux – as in Chauffailles in the Forez; some of the houses were looted – the home of the bishop of Cahors in Mercueis and the house of the Chevalier de la Rouandière in Saint-Denis-d'Anjou on 24 July. The Château de Frétoy in Picardy was searched by the local peasants who hoped to find hidden corn: they were led by an old soldier who had arrived *via* Paris the previous evening *en route* for Berry where he had been a gamekeeper. Here and there, the peasants got back the guns that had been confiscated; they killed off the pigeons, they demanded the renunciation of all seigneurial rights as in La Clayette in the Forez, and in Baignes in Saintonge. There is a very evident link between these events and those which took place before the fear, but they have often been exaggerated. Taine for instance speaks of nine châteaux being burnt down in the Auvergne, yet there were none; in most provinces, the incidents which took place were not particularly serious, especially when one compares them with the very real strength of the movement as a whole, even though they continued the work of the agrarian revolts in terrorizing the aristocracy.

Taine has ensured the fame of events in Secondigny, a small town in Poitou to the south of Parthenay, but the report of the court proceedings shows that the plaintiff, Desprès-Montpezat, was basically the victim of his own clumsiness and imprudence. Early on the morning of 23 July, he received a letter from the *sub-délégué* of La Châtaignerie informing him that the brigands were on their way, so he sounded the tocsin and authorized an assistant to go and call together the wood-cutters who were working in the neighbouring forest; then he went back home and did not stir an inch. The workers appeared with their foreman and the Comte d'Artois's *garde*, all intending to join up with the local people. The morning passed and no one came to tell them what was happening. Finally, they went and found Desprès who was eating his lunch; he promised to go into town straight afterwards. He did nothing of the sort and tempers began to fray. They feared some act of treason, for Desprès, they knew already, had been chosen along with several others to act as official correspondent to the recently elected deputies for the nobility. In addition, 'there was a rumour that someone had tried to kill a worker'. At about half-past four, Desprès saw the crowd coming towards his house, all by now in a state of extreme rage. 'Ah, Monsieur the *syndic*, Monsieur the nobles' correspondent, we have you in our power.... Are you one of the Third Estate?... You are keeping us waiting rather a long time; you think you are making fools of us and wasting our time, but we want to be paid.' He was obliged to put on a cockade and they dragged him to Escot, the notary, and made him sign a renunciation of fiscal privileges. With much rhetoric he told the authorities that he had been manhandled and it was of course easy to believe him. According to his account, the workmen had assured him that Talbot the game-keeper had 'a letter' enjoining them 'to attack all the *gentilshommes* in the country and massacre without mercy all those who refuse to abdicate their privileges, to burn and pillage their châteaux, and promising them not only that they would not be punished for their crimes but also that they would actually be rewarded'. This detail gives the lie to the state of mind behind the jacqueries: the Great Fear did no more than provide the opportunity for its expression. Next, Desprès talked of a plot and charged Escot the notary and a tailor called Gigaut who said when they were arrested that they had had a quarrel with Desprès and that he was slandering them just to get even. What emerges from this report is that they had probably talked in such a way as to over-excite their listeners. Escot, who had just returned from Niort, seems to have said that the people there had killed a *gentilhomme* who had refused to sign a similar renunciation and Gigaut, who had just been to Nantes, said that they were looting and burning châteaux with the king's permission and that they must all do the same. The latter declared that he had been to Nantes 'to become a freemason' and M. de Roux in his *Histoire de la Révolution dans la Vienne* saw in this the proof that Gigaut was the agent of the leaders of the revolutionary party. He was by no means poor, but the tailor was not at all in the class of those who were usually admitted to a masons' lodge and his statement is most extraordinary: but the magistrate who interrogated him and who did not favour the Revolution did not pay any special attention to it. Desprès escaped the consequences of the fear and really had only himself to blame for what happened.

The Comtesse de Broglie also managed to avoid any real danger when the local peasants arrived at her château in Ruffec on 2 August: she was swift to hand back their confiscated guns. Paulian, the *directeur des fermes* at Baignes in Saintonge, was not so fortunate: the crowd rioted when the panic swept into the town and rushed to his offices where they looted and destroyed all records and his personal effects; the Comte de Montausier who tried to intervene was instantly taken to task and forced to renounce his rights. Even more unfortunate was the Baron de Drouhet, hero of the tragicomedy acted out at Saint-Angel in the Limousin and well known throughout most of France. On 1 August, after a local alarm, he set off at the head of his vassals to go to the assistance of the town where the brigands were supposed to be expected at any moment. Drouhet called a halt when he arrived with his men and waited for the local authorities to come out. They duly arrived and asked why he had come. He explained and was taken off to have lunch whilst his troops bivouacked where they were. However, the citizens of Saint-Angel did not trust Drouhet and very soon a riot broke out. His men fled, apart from a few who were taken prisoner, and their captors were very eager to execute Drouhet as well as the Baron de Belinay who by now had come to join him. They were saved only by being sent to Meymac, bound hand and foot; the danger was no less in Meymac so they were packed off to Limoges. The journey was extremely uncomfortable for them, since everywhere they went, the populace was convinced that they were the leaders of the brigands. When they got to Limoges, they were put into prison and even though the committee very soon proved their innocence, they dared not set them free. On 12 August, a booklet was published in Aurillac extolling 'the victory of the Auvergnats over the aristocrats'. Drouhet had to publish a manifesto of his own to clear his name and was not released till 7 September on the order of the National Assembly itself.

It is true that these particular disturbances were very unfortunate, but they did not lay waste entire provinces like the jacqueries in earlier times and they caused no deaths. Unfortunately this is not true of every province: the Great Fear was responsible for three murders and for the jacquerie in the Dauphiné.

The murders took place in Ballon, in Maine and in Le Pouzin in the Vivarais. On 23 July, Cureau and de Montesson were brought from Nouans and murdered by the crowd in Ballon: Cureau was the *lieutenant de maire* in Le Mans and had the reputation of being a food monopolist; de Montesson, a deputy for the nobility, had resigned from the Assembly and had barely escaped death by drowning at the hands of the mob in Savigné on the 18th. At Le Pouzin, it was d'Arbalestrier who was killed: he was an officer in the marines who had come from Loriol on the 29th to see a friend and had said that the alarm was not genuine. Unfortunately for him, there was a second alarm and the crowd decided that he had tried to deceive them so as to help the brigands. When threatened by the crowd, he apparently drew his sword and was promptly overpowered. The authorities tried to save him by putting him under arrest but he was dragged out of prison and murdered. These are the only murders recorded for the period of the Great Fear and the agrarian revolts. There is of course M. de Barras who was, according to various authors and Taine in particular, cut to pieces in the Languedoc. The accounts of his murder all derive from Lally's second letter to his constituents and this unfortunately does not indicate where the deed was done. We have not been able to find who this M. de Barras was, nor where he lived, nor even if the murder did actually take place. It is surprising that there should be no mention of the event in any contemporary document; so many offences were recorded that never actually took place that until further information is available it would be better to believe that Lally's unknown informant made a mistake, or at any rate that he exaggerated some minor and less fatal incident.

As to the jacquerie in the Dauphiné, this has been described in detail by M. Couard in his book *La Peur en Dauphiné* and we shall summarize this account very briefly. It began with a host of local peasants gathering at Bourgoin on 27 July when news had come through of a panic in Pont-de-Beauvoisin. They spent the night in the streets and then in a state of fury turned to attack the nobles who had spread news of the fear on purpose to harass them and make them lose a day's wages: they decided that since they were all gathered together they might as well make the most of it and attack their oppressors; they would indeed never have a better opportunity. At six o'clock in the morning on the 28th, they went off to burn the château of the Président de Vaulx to the west of the town, then split up and gradually aroused all the local villages. On the 28th and 29th, all along the Bourbe and to the west of it, château after château went up in flames. Militia came out from Lyons to intervene and managed to stop further damage, but the peasants went as far as the Rhône and burnt other châteaux on its south bank, the finest being the home of the Baron d'Anthon. On the 30th, they crossed to the east of the Bourbe and made their way gradually nearer Lagnieu where the men from Lyons, called out for a second time to help Crémieu, were able to save the La Salette monastery and put the rebels to flight. Meanwhile, the disturbances spread from Bourgoin to the Rhône and the Guier, though they were not of a very serious nature: no châteaux were burnt. The Lyonnais put an end to these attacks too, on the 31st, after a skirmish at Salignon and Saint-Chef. The revolt also travelled down to the South-West: on the 31st, the château of the Président d'Ornacieux was burnt in its turn; the mob moved into the neighbourhood of Péage-de-Roussillon where they made an unsuccessful attack on the Château de Terre-Basse on the 3rd; they had been more successful earlier on the night of 31 July–1 August, for the Château de la Saône was destroyed. In the South-East, the Grenoble militia had managed to stop the peasants' advance at Virieu, but on 1 August, the militia retired and the disturbances spread all around the town. No more châteaux were burnt but there were incidents of considerable violence right up to the 9th. The jacquerie in the Dauphiné was as bad, or possibly even worse, than its counterpart in the Mâconnais. The *procureur-général*, Reynaud, announced that eighty châteaux had suffered damage, nine of which had been destroyed by fire.

From this, it is clear that the Great Fear had much more serious consequences in the country than in the towns. It caused the downfall of the seigneurial régime and added a new jacquerie to those which had gone before. In the drama of peasant life, it is written in letters of fire.

Conclusion

The Great Fear arose from fear of the 'brigand', which can itself be explained by the economic, social and political circumstances prevailing in France in 1789.

Under the *ancien régime*, begging was one of the scourges of the countryside; from 1788 onwards, unemployment and rising prices made it worse. Famine brought countless disturbances which could only increase the general disorder. In all this, the political crisis played an important part, for the general excitement it provoked made the people restless and unruly. Every beggar, vagrant and rioter seemed to be a 'brigand'. There had always been great anxiety at harvest time: it was a moment the peasants dreaded; local alarms increased daily.

As the harvest started, a new factor came into play. The conflict which set in opposition the Third Estate and the aristocracy (supported by the royal authority) and which in several provinces had given a social character to the hunger riots, suddenly turned into civil war. The uprising in Paris and the security measures which sought to expel vagrants from the capital and other major cities spread the fear of brigands far and wide, and at the same time people anxiously waited for the defeated aristocrats to take their revenge on the Third Estate with the aid of foreign troops. No one doubted for a moment that they had taken the promised brigands into their pay and in this way the economic crisis and the political and social crisis combined their effects so that the same terror spread through everyone's mind and allowed alarms which began by being purely local to spread swiftly through the country. The fear of brigands was a universal phenomenon, but the Great Fear was not, and it is wrong to confuse the one with the other.

There is no trace of plot or conspiracy at the start of the Great Fear. It was far from foolish to fear the vagrant, but the aristocrat-brigand was a phantom figure. The revolutionaries helped to spread his image, but they acted in good faith. If they spread the rumour of the aristocrats' plot it was because they believed in it. They exaggerated its importance out of all proportion: only the court really considered a *coup de force* against the Third Estate and they showed themselves pathetically incompetent in its execution. The men of the Revolution did not make the mistake of despising their adversaries and as they credited them with their own energy and resolution, they were inclined to fear the worst. Furthermore, they did not need the Great Fear to bring the towns on to their side: the municipal revolution and the arming of the people had already taken place and this was a decisive point in their favour. As for the unfortunate poor who constantly moaned and murmured behind the bourgeoisie in both town and country, they gave great cause for concern; the bourgeoisie had everything to fear from their outbursts of despair and they left their mark deep on the revolution. It was natural for the enemies of the revolution to accuse its supporters of encouraging the poor to overthrow the *ancien régime* so that they could put in its place a new order where the new men would rule -- but it was equally natural for the revolutionaries to suspect the aristocracy of fomenting anarchy to keep them out of power. Clearly, the supposed appearance of brigands was an excellent excuse to arm the people against the royal power – and did not the king use the same excuse to mask his plans for attacking the Assembly? And as to the peasants in particular, it was not especially in the bourgeoisie's interest that they should overthrow the seigneurial régime by their jacqueries and the Constituent Assembly was not slow to show its concern in this direction. Even so, the Assembly did not need the Great Fear to help it on its way: the jacqueries had started long before.

But one must by no means conclude that the Great Fear exercised no influence on the course of events, or – to speak in philosophical terms – that it was an epiphenomenon. The panic was instantly followed by a vigorous reaction in which the warlike passion of the revolution was seen for the first time and which provided national unity with an opportunity to appear in its fullest vigour. Then, this reaction, especially in the countryside, turned against the aristocracy: by gathering the peasants together, it allowed them to achieve a full realization of their strength and reinforced the attack already launched against the seigneurial régime. It is not only the strange and picturesque nature of the Great Fear which should hold our attention: it played its part in the preparations for the night of 4 August and on these grounds alone must count as one of the most important episodes in the history of the French nation.

Appendix

Handwritten poster found in Beaurepaire in Bresse by one Gaillard*

[Archives Nationales, D^{XXIX} 90, dossier Oudin.]

Plaintes portées à Versailles par un homme inconnu de Bourgogne le 28ʳ avril 1789 au sujet de l'injustice qui se passe par les seigneurs justiciers envers le menu peuple et qui plus est trompé par actes, obligations, Billets et autres par erreurs en mal faits usurpateurs.

1° Que tous les Seigneurs qui ont exigés de leurs sujets des droits qui ne leur sont pas dû soient obligés de les rendre légitimement ainsi que les frais qui se sont faits à ce sujet.

2° Que touttes les procédures qui se sont intentées soient arrangées à l'amiable ou par experts des lieux qui en connaissent mieux que les avocats des villes.

3° Que tous les usuriers qui ont exigés des sommes qui ne leurs sont pas dûs plus que l'intérêt de leur argent soient obligés de le rendre.

4° Que tous les terreins incultes se dispercent aux pauvres qui n'en ont pas pour travailler, ou il y aura lieu de mettre des droits au profit de Sa Majesté et de la communauté.

5° Le Roi ne peut pas avoir connoissance de touttes les affaires qui se passent, ce n'est qu'entre nous que le Roi peut prendre connoissance de ces abus et en corriger les défauts.

6° Nous ordonnons à M. le Maire de l'endroit, Curés et Cavaliers des Maréchaussées Conformément à l'intention du Roi qu'ils auront soins de faire arranger les parties au plus juste pour éteindre touttes difficultés.

7° L'arrêt n'a pas eu lieu d'imprimer aiant trop presse à Versailles.

8° Vous le pouves transcrire dans tous les lieux ou l'on jugera à propos en peu de temps, tel est l'ordre du Ministre.

Approuvés par nous soussignés suivant que la ordonné Sa Majesté à Versailles le 28 avril 1789.

[signé]: Latouche.

[L'écrit est encadré d'un trait doublé d'un filet. Au-dessous du cadre, d'une autre écriture, est ajoutée la recommandation suivante:]

Lest Echevin auront soint de relevée Laret pour le faire pasé au paroisse voisine.

[A droite, l'autorité judiciaire et l'inculpé ont authentiqué la pièce:]

Cotté et paraphé *ne varietur* par nous assesseur en la marechaussée de Chalon soussigné le jourd'huy six septembre mil sept cent quatre vingt neuf nous etant soussignés avec le dit Gaillard.

[signé:] Charle Gaillard   Beaumée.

* See overleaf for translation.

The following placard was posted in Beaurepaire in Bresse by its author, a certain Gaillard. No translation can hope to convey the full flavour of this laboriously composed and touchingly misspelt document: one can only hope that the following version will give some idea of its air of earnest endeavour and its brave attempt to reproduce the legal language of the time.

(Archives Nationales, D^{XXIX} 90, dossier Oudin)

Complaints lodged at Versailles by an unknown man from Burgundy on 28 April 1789 about the unfairness of the lords' justice towards the poor and moreover how they be deceived by acts, obligations, documents and errors through false dealings.

1. That all Seigneurs who have obliged their subjects to render rights not properly due them be now obliged by law to hand them back as well as pay back any expenses incurred in this matter.

2. That all matters now afoot be settled out of court or else by local experts who know more about them than town lawyers.

3. That all moneylenders who have demanded moneys not due to them over and above the interest on their loans be obliged to pay them back.

4. That all land not being farmed be now shared out among the poor who have none of their own or else the rights be turned to the benefit of His Majesty and the people in general.

5. The King cannot be aware of every thing happening and it can only be from us that the King can find out the wrongs being done and set things to right.

6. We order the Mayor of every place, the curés and the members of the *maréchaussée*, as the King has desired, to have a care to settle all matters as fairly as they can so as to annul all difficulties.

7. This decree cannot be printed there being too much press of work in Versailles.

8. You can copy this down and set it up with all speed wherever seems right and proper such being the Minister's order.

Approved by us the undersigned as ordered by His Majesty in Versailles 28 April 1789.

(signed) Latouche

There is a hand-drawn line and a fillet all around this written document and below this ink frame another hand has written an extra injunction:

The Magistrates should take the decree and have it passed to the next parish.

On the right-hand side the judiciary and the accused (Gaillard) have authenticated the document:

Noted and certified *ne varietur* by us, assessor in the *maréchaussée* of Chalon undersigned today six September one thousand seven hundred and eighty nine being undersigned by the aforesaid Gaillard.

(signed) Charle Gaillard   Beaumée

Bibliographical Notes

I

1. Most of the unpublished documents used in this study come from sources in Paris. Those from the Archives Nationales, *Sous-série* D^{XXIX}, should be consulted first. This is particularly easy to use as the documents are arranged in alphabetical order, first by place names in boxes 16 to 84, then by names of persons in boxes 86 to 91; there is a manuscript list of contents. Unfortunately many items are scattered in different sections and it is not possible to give a complete list of them in this study: they are however to be found in BB^{30} 66 to 69, 79, 87, 159; C 83, 86 to 91, 134; D^{XXIX} *passim* (mainly in the first box); $D^{XLI}2$; F^{1a} 401, 404, 420, 446; F^7 3647, 3648, 3654, 3672, 3679, 3685, 3686, 3690; F^{11} 210, 1173–4; H 1274, 1438, 1440–2, 1444, 1446–7, 1452 to 1454, 1456, 1483–4; O^1 244–5, 354, 361, 434, 485–6, 500, 579; Y 18765–6, 18787, 18791, 18795–6. One should also mention the pamphlet AD^1 92: *Relation d'une partie des troubles de la France pendant les années 1789 et 1790.*

There are some items in the Archives de la Guerre (vol. V of the *Inventaire Fonds divers B*, boxes LIV, LV and LVI) and in the Archives des Affaires étrangères (*Mémoires et documents*, France, 1405 and 1406). In the Bibliothèque Nationale, I have consulted the diary of the bookseller Hardy (*Mes loisirs*, vol. VIII; Manuscripts, *Fonds français* 6687), newspapers, pamphlets and various works listed in the *Catalogue de l'histoire de France* Lc², Lb³⁹, La³², Lk⁷ (other pamphlets have been consulted in the valuable miscellany held at the university library in Strasbourg, catalogue no. D 120 513).

A certain number of documents and interesting pieces of information have been consulted in: *Procès-verbal des séances et délibérations de l'Assemblée générale des Électeurs de Paris* (26 April–30 July 1789), edited by Bailly and Duveyrier; *Recueil des procès-verbaux de l'Assemblée des représentants de la commune de Paris du 25 juillet au 18 septembre 1789*, vol. 1; *Actes de la Commune de Paris pendant la Révolution* published by S. Lacroix, vol. 1; Chassin, *Les Élections et les Cahiers de Paris en 1789*, vols. 3 and 4; Lally-Tollendal, *Deuxième lettre à ses commettants*; A. Young, *Journal*; Buchez and Roux, *Histoire parlementaire de la Rév.*, vol. 4, 166–70; the reprint of *Le Moniteur*, vol. 2 and the *Archives parlementaires*, vol. 8; G. Bord, *La prise de la Bastille*, 1882; Forestié, *La Grande Peur*, 1911; Funck-Brentano, *Le Roi*, 1912; P. de Vaissières, *Lettres d'aristocrates*, 1906; Vingtrinier, *Histoire de la Contre-Révolution*, vol. 1, 1924; Barruol,

La Contre-révolution en Provence et dans le Comtat Venaissin, 1928; Santhonax, *La grande peur* in *La Justice*, issue of 30 October 1887.

2. FOR THE WHOLE OF THE FIRST PART, see the following studies which contain numerous bibliographical references: H. Sée, *La France économique et sociale au XVIIIe siècle*, 1925 (no. 64 of the Collection A. Colin); *La vie économique et les classes sociales en France au XVIIIe siècle*, 1924; G. Lefebvre, *Les recherches relatives à la répartition de la propriété et de l'exploitation foncières à la fin de l'ancien régime* (*Revue d'histoire moderne*, 1928); *La place de la Rév. dans l'histoire agraire de la France* (*Annales d'histoire économique et sociale*, vol. 1, 1929); *Les paysans du Nord pendant la Rév. française*, 1924; Schmidt, *La crise industrielle de 1788 en France* (*Revue historique*, vol. 97, 1908).

3. FOR THE PROPAGATION OF NEWS: J. Letaconnoux, *Les transports en France au XVIIIe siècle* (*Revue d'histoire moderne*, vol. II, 1908–9); Rothschild, *Histoire de la poste aux lettres*, 1873; Belloc, *Les postes françaises*, 1886; Boyé, *Les postes, messageries et voitures publiques en Lorraine au XVIIIe siècle*, 1904; Bernard, *Essai historique sur la poste aux lettres en Bretagne depuis le XVe siècle jusqu'à la Rév.* (Mélanges Hayem, vol. 12, 1929); Dutens, *Itinéraire des routes les plus fréquentées ou journal de plusieurs voyages aux villes principales de l'Europe depuis 1768 jusqu'en 1791* (1791).

4. THE MAIN COLLECTIONS OF DEPUTIES' CORRESPONDENCE: The contemporary collections entitled *Correspondance d'Anjou, de Brest, de Rennes, de Nantes* (the Bibliothèque Nationale does not have the latter) are mainly useful for the local news and private letters they contain, for such letters as they include from deputies refer only to sessions of the National Assembly. Recent publications are more informative: Bord, *Correspondance inédite de Pellegrin, député de la sénéchaussée de Guérande*, 1883; Tempier, *La correspondance des députés des Côtes-du-Nord* (*Bulletin et mémoires de la Société d'émulation des Côtes-du-Nord*, vol. 26–30, 1888–92); *Corresp. de Boullé, député du Tiers état de Ploërmel* (*Revue de la Révolution*, vol. 15, 1889); Corre and Delourmel, *Corresp. de Legendre, député de la sénéchaussée de Brest* (*La Révolution française*, vol. 39, 1900); Esquieu and Delourmel, *Brest pendant la Rév.; corresp. de la municipalité avec les députés de la sénéchaussée* (*Bull. Soc. académique de Brest*, 2nd series, vol. 32–3, 1906–7); Quéruau-Lamerie, *Lettres de Maupetit* (*Bull. Comm. hist. de la Mayenne*, vol. 17–21, 1901–5); *Lettres de Lofficial* (*Nouvelle revue rétrospective*, vol. 7, 1897); Reuss, *Corresp. des députés de Strasbourg*, 1881–95; *Corresp. d'un député de la noblesse de la sénéchaussée de Marseille avec la marquise de Créquy* (*Revue de la Revolution*, vol. 2, 1883); see also G. Michon, *Adrien Duport*, p. 57 (Barnave's letter), and the works of Hoffman on Alsace, Denis on Toul, Poulet on Thiaucourt, Forot on Tulle, Jardin on Bresse, Sol on Quercy and Vidal on the eastern Pyrenees, quoted below.

2

Here are some references to works which cover the different regions of France.
5. THE AREA AROUND PARIS. Marmontel, *Mémoires*, vol. 3, p. 74 (1891);
de Rosières, *La Rév. dans une petite ville, Meulan*, 1888; Le Paire, *Histoire de la
ville de Corbeil*, 1902 and *Annales du pays de Lagny*, 1880; Domet, *Journal de
Fontainebleau*, vol. 2, 1890; Louis, *Huit années de la vie municipale de Rambouillet*
(*Mémoires Soc. archéologique de Rambouillet*, vol. 13, 1898); George, *Les débuts
de la Rév. à Meaux* (*Revue Brie et Gâtinais*, 1909); Bourquelot, *Histoire de Provins*,
vol. 2, 1840; M. Lecomte, *Histoire de Melun*, 1910. Provins Library, Michelin
Collection, vol. 1 (Donnemarie); Le Menestral, *Dreux pendant la Révolution*,
1929.
6. PICARDY. *Délibérations de l'adm. munic. d'Amiens*, 1910, vols. 2 and 3;
de Beauvillé, *Histoire de Montdidier*, 1857, vol. 1; Gonnard, *Essai historique sur
la ville de Ribemont*, 1869; Fleury, *Famines, misères et séditions*, 1849; *Épisodes
de l'histoire révolutionnaire à Saint-Quentin*, 1874; *La Thiérache en 1789* (*Revue La
Thiérache*, vol. 2, 1874); Abbé Pécheur, *Histoire de Guise*, vol. 2, 1851; Coët and
Lefèvre, *Histoire de la ville de Marle*, 1897.
7. ARTOIS. Le Bibliophile artésien, *La Rév. à Saint-Omer*, 1873. M. Jacob
of the Lycée Janson-de-Sailly is preparing a study of the fear in Artois.
8. FLANDERS, HAINAULT AND THE CAMBRÉSIS. G. Lefebvre, *Les paysans du Nord pendant la Rév. française*, 1924, pp. 359–61.
9. CHAMPAGNE. Chaudron, *La Grande Peur en Champagne méridionale*, 1923;
de Bontin and Cornille, *Les volontaires et le recrutement de l'armée pendant la
Rév. dans l'Yonne* (*Bull. de la Soc. des sciences historiques et naturelles de l'Yonne*,
vol. 66, 1912); Rouget, *Les origines de la garde nationale à Épernay* (*Annales
historiques de la Révolution*, vol. 6, 1930); abbé Poquet, *Histoire de Château-
Thierry*, vol. 2, 1839; Guillemin, *Saint-Dizier pendant la période révolutionnaire*
(*Mémoires de la Soc. de Saint-Dizier*, vol. 4, 1885–6); Bouffet, *La vie municipale
à Châlons-sur-Marne sous l'Assemblée Constituante*, manuscript memoir, 1922,
in the Châlons library; Porée, archivist for Yonne, *Rapport annuel*, 1907 (Thorigny); *Inventaire de la série B*, no. 901 (Champs).
10. ARDENNES. Picard, *Souvenirs d'un vieux Sedanais*, 1875; Collinet,
La g. p. à Sedan et la création de la garde nationale (*Revue de l'Ardenne et de
l'Argonne*, vol. 11, 1903–4); Vincent, *Histoire de Vouziers*, 1902.
11. LORRAINE. Parisot, *Histoire de Lorraine*, vol. 3, 1924; *Mémoires de Carré
de Malberg* (*La Révolution française*, vol. 61, 1911); Poulet, *Une petite ville de
Lorraine à la fin du XVIIIe siècle et pendant la Rév.: Thiaucourt*, 1904; Pierrot,
L'arrondissement de Montmédy sous la Rév. (*Memoires de la Soc. de Bar-le-Duc*,
vol. 33, 1904); Pionnier, *Histoire de la Rév. à Verdun*, 1905; Braye, *Bar-le-Duc*

à la veille du meurtre d'A. Pellicier (Bull. de la Soc. de Bar-le-Duc, vol. 42–3, 1922); Aimond, *Histoire de la ville de Varennes-en-Argonne*, 1928; Denis, *Toul pendant la Rév.*, 1890; Bouvier, *La Rév. dans les Vosges*, 1885; Bergerot, *Remiremont pendant la Rév. (Annales de la Soc. d'émulation des Vosges*, vol. 40, 1901); Beugnot, *Mémoires*, vol. 1, p. 160, 1866.

12. ALSACE. Hoffmann, *L'Alsace au XVIIIe siècle*, 1906; Fues, *Die Pfarrgemeinden des Cantons Hirsingen*, 1789; Ehret, *Kulturhistorische Skizze über das obere Sankt Amarienthal*, 1889; *Lettre de M. A. Moll sur les événements qui se sont passés à Ferrette*, 1879; d'Ochsenfeld, *Colmar pendant la Rév. (Revue de la Révolution*, vols. 3 and 4, 1884); Reuss, *Le sac de l'hôtel de ville de Strasbourg*, 1877; Schnerb, *Les débuts de la Rév. à Saverne (Revue d'Alsace*, vol. 73, 1926); Saehler, *Montbéliard, Belfort et la Haute-Alsace au début de la Rév. (Mémoires de la Soc. d'émulation de Montbéliard*, vol. 40, 1911); Mme Gauthier, *Voyage d'une Française en Suisse et en Franche-Comté depuis la Rév.*, London, 1790, 2 vols.

13. THE LOIRE REGION. Bouvier, *J.-F. Rozier fils et les débuts de la Rév. à Orléans*, 1930; *Vendôme pendant la Rév.* (anonymous), vol. 1, 1892; Dufort de Cheverny, *Mémoires*, vol. 2, pp. 85 sqq., 1886; Miss Pickford, *The panic of 1789 in Touraine (English Historical Review*, vol. 26, 1911); Desmé de Chavigny, *Histoire de Saumur pendant la Rév.*, 1892; Port, *La Vendée angevine*, vol. 1, 1888; Bruneau, *Les débuts de la Rév. dans les départements du Cher et de l'Indre*, 1902; Pierre, *Terreur panique au Blanc (Bull. Soc. Académique du Centre*, vol. 2, 1896); Courot, *Annales de Clamecy*, 1901; Charrier, *La Rév. à Clamecy et dans ses environs*, 1923; de Laguérenne, *Pourquoi Montluçon n'est pas chef-lieu de département*, 1919; Perot, *L'année de la g. p.* [en Bourbonnais], 1906: Mallat, *Histoire contemporaine de Vichy*, 1921; works by Denier, Grégoire and Viple on different cantons in the Allier; extracts from notes by Hérault, curé of Saint-Bonnet-Tronçais, sent to me by M. Mauve of the *école normale* in Moulins; Loiret archives, C 86 (Vendôme); L 767 (Saint-Denis-de-l'Hôtel); Bibliothèque d'Orléans, manuscrits Pataud, 565, f° 33.

14. NORMANDY. Borely, *Histoire de la ville du Havre*, 1880–1; Semichon, *Histoire de la ville d'Aumale*, vol. 2, 1862; Marquise de la Tour-du-Pin, *Journal d'une femme de cinquante ans*, vol. 1 1891; Moynier de Villepoix, *La correspondance d'un laboureur normand (Mém. Acad. Amiens*, vol. 55, 1908); Saint-Denis, *Histoire d'Elbeuf*, 1894; Dubreuil, *La g. p. à Évreux et dans les environs (Revue normande*, 1921); *Les débuts de la Rév. à Évreux (La Révolution française*, vol. 76, 1923); *Le comité permanent d'Évreux (Annales révolutionnaires*, vol. 12, 1920); Montier, *Le mouvement municipal à Pont-Audemer (Bull. Comité des Travaux hist.*, 1904); Du Bois, *Histoire . . . de Lisieux*, 1845; Mourlot, *La fin de l'ancien régime et les débuts de la Rév. dans la généralité de Caen*, 1913; Duval, *Éphémérides de la moyenne Normandie et du Perche en 1789*, 1890; Nicolle,

Histoire de Vire pendant la Rév., 1923; Jousset, La Rév. au Perche, 3rd part, 1878.

15. MAINE. Triger, L'année 1789 au Mans et dans le Haut-Maine, 1889; Duchemin et Triger, Les premiers troubles de la Rév. dans la Mayenne (Revue hist. du Maine, vol. 22, 1887); Gaugain, Hist. de la Rév. dans la Mayenne, vol. 1, 1921; Gauchet, Château-Gontier de janvier à juillet 1789 (Bull. Comm. hist. de la Mayenne, vol. 43, 1927); Fleury, Le district de Mamers pendant la Rév., vol. 1, 1909; Joubert, Les troubles de Craon du 12 juillet au 10 septembre 1789 (Bull. Comm. hist. de la Mayenne, vol. 1, 1888–9).

16. BRITTANY. Levot, Histoire de la ville et du port de Brest, 1864; Bernard, La municipalité de Brest de 1750 à 1790, 1915; Haize, Histoire de Saint-Servan, 1907, Pommeret, L'esprit public dans les Côtes-du-Nord pendant la Rev., 1921; Mellinet, La commune et la milice de Nantes, vol. 6, 1841.

17. POITOU. Marquis de Roux, La Rév. à Poitiers et dans la Vienne, 1912; Deniau, Hist. de la Vendée, vol. 1, 1878; Chassin, La préparation de la guerre de Vendée, 1912; Hérault, Hist. de la ville de Châtellerault, vol. 4, 1927; Favraud, La journée de la grande peur [à Nueil-sous-les-Aubiers] (Bull. Soc. archéologique de la Charente, 1915); Fillon, Recherches ... sur Fontenay-le-Comte, vol. 1, 1846.

18. PAYS CHARENTAIS. George, Notes sur la journée de la peur à Angoulême (Bull. Soc. arch. de la Charente, 7th series, vol. 6, 1905–6); Jeandel, La peur dans les cantons de Montbron et de Lavalette (ibid.); Livre-journal de F. et F. J. Gilbert, juges en l'élection d'Angoulême (Mémoires Soc. arch. de la Charente, 1900); B. C., La grande peur [à Ozillac] (Revue de Saintonge, vol. 21, 1901); Saint-Saud, La g. p. [à Coutras] (ibid.); Audiat, La journée de la g. p. [à Montendre] (ibid.); Vigen, La g. p. [à Saintes] (ibid.); Pellisson, Mouvement populaire à Angeduc (Bull. Soc. des archives hist. de la Saintonge et de l'Aunis, vol. 1, 1876–9); Delamain, Jarnac à travers les âges, 1925; Babaud-Lacroze, La g. p. dans le Confolentais and Lettre de Mme de Laperdoussie (Bull. et mém. de la Soc. de la Charente, 7th series, vol. 8, 1907–8 and 8th series, vol. 1, 1910).

19. LIMOUSIN. Many of the documents are in Leclerc, La g. p. en Limousin (Bull. Soc. arch. et hist. du Limousin, vol. 51, 1902); Sagnac, Lettre circulaire du Comité permanent de la ville d'Uzerche (Revue d'histoire moderne, vol. 2, 1900–1); Forot, L'année 1789 au Bas-Limousin, 1908.

20. AUVERGNE, FOREZ, GÉVAUDAN. Mège, La g. p., 1909; Boudet, La g. p. en Haute-Auvergne, 1909; Brossard, Hist. du dép. de la Loire pendant la Rév., 1905; Galley, Saint-Étienne et son district pendant la Rév., 1904; Gustave Lefebvre, Note de quelques événements arrivés dans la commune de Lavalla (Loire) pendant la période révolutionnaire, 1890; Charléty, La g. p. à Rive-de-Gier (La Révolution française, vol. 42, 1902); Cohas, Saint-Germain-Laval pendant la R., 1906; Delon, La R. en Lozère, 1922.

222

21. PÉRIGORD. Bussière, *Études historiques sur la R. en P.*, vol. 3, 1903; *Une panique à Brassac* (anonymous) *(Bull. Soc. du P.*, vol. 3, 1876); Hermann, *La g. p. à Reillac (La Révolution française*, vol. 29, 1895); Dubut, *La g. p. à Saint-Privat-des-Prés (ibid.*, vol. 75, 1922, p. 142).

22. AGENAIS, QUERCY, ROUERGUE, TOULOUSAIN, ARMAGNAC. Boudon de Saint-Amans, *Hist. ancienne et moderne du département de Lot-et-Garonne*, vol. 2, 1836; Proché, *Annales de la ville d'Agen (R. de l'Agenais*, vol. 8, 1881); Granat, *La Révolution municipale à Agen (ibid.*, vol. 32, 1905); de Mazet, *La Rév. à Villeneuve-sur-Lot*, 1895; Guilhamon, *La g. p. dans le Haut-Agenais (R. de l'Agenais*, vol. 38, 1911); Paumès, *La g. p. dans le Quercy et le Rouergue (Bull. Soc. des Études du Lot*, vol. 37, 1912), many documents; Latouche, *Essai sur la g. p. en 1789 dans le Quercy (Revue des Pyrénées*, vol. 26, 1914); Combarieu, *L'année de la peur à Castelnau (Bull. hist. et philologique du Com. des Travaux hist.*, 1896, p. 107); Sol, *La Rév. dans le Quercy*, n. d. (1929); Combes, *Hist. de la ville de Castres*, 1875; Rossignol, *Hist. de l'arrond. de Gaillac pendant la Rév.*, 1902; Baron de Rivières, *Trouble arrivé dans la ville de Montmiral (Bull. Soc. arch. du Midi de la France*, vol. 13, 1893); Pasquier, *Notes et réflexions d'un bourgeois de Toulouse au début de la Rév.*, 1917; *La panique à Villemur (Revue des Pyrénées*, vol. 10, 1898); *La panique à Seysses (ibid.*, vol. 26, 1914); Garrigues, *La terreur panique à Montastruc-la-Conseillère (Revue des Pyrénées*, vol. 25, 1913); Décap, *La g. p. à Muret (Revue de Comminges*, vol. 21, 1906); Lamarque, *La Rév. à Touget (Bull. Soc. arch. du Gers*, vol. 23, 1922).

23. THE PYRENEES. Arnaud, *Hist. de la Rév. dans le dép. de l'Ariège*, 1904; *Mémoires du comte Faydet de Terssac*, publ. par Pasquier et Durban *(Bull. de la Soc. ariégeoise*, vol. 8, 1901); Baudens, *Une petite ville pendant la Rév. (Castelanau-Magnac) (Revue des Pyrénées*, vol. 3, 1891); Note de Rosapelly d'après Sarreméjean, *Répercussions de la Rév. française à Villelongue et dans la haute vallée d'Argelès, 1914 (Rev. des Hautes-Pyrénées*, 1929); Duvrau, *Les épisodes hist. de la Rév. française à Lourdes*, 1911.

24. FRANCHE-COMTÉ. Estignard, *Le Parlement de Franche-Comté*, vol. 2, 1892; Huot-Marchand, *Le mouvement populaire contre les châteaux en Franche-Comté (Annales franc-comtoises*, vol. 16, 1904); Hyenne, *Documents littéraires relatifs au château de Quincey (R. littéraire de Franche-Cté*, 1864-5); Sommier, *Hist. de la Rév. dans le Jura*, 1846; Sauzay, *Hist. de la persecution révolut. dans le dép. du Doubs*, vol. 1, 1867; Gauthier, *Besançon de 1774 à 1791*, 1891; *Besançon de 1789 à 1815 : Journal de J.-E. Laviron (Revue rétrospective*, vol. 16, 1892)*: Girardot, *La ville de Lure pendant la Rév.*, 1925; Duhem, *La g. p. à Morez (Mém. Soc. d'émulation du Jura*, 11ᵉ série, vol. 5, 1927); Girard, *Chroniques arboisiennes*, 1906; Guillemaut, *Hist. de la Rév. dans le Louhannais*, vol. 1, 1899; Briffaut et Mulson, *Hist. de la vallée de l'Amance*, 1891; Gatin,

Besson et Godard, *Hist. de Gray*, 1892; Paget, *Monographie du bourg de Marnay*, 1927; Mathez, *Pontarlier dans la Rév.* (*La Révolution française*, vols. 9–11, 1885–6); H. and M. Baumont, *La Rév. à Luxeuil*, 1930; Vesoul archives (Deliberations of the municipal officers), of Haute-Saône (B 4187, 6486, 6886; C 134, 194, 229); Doubs archives (B 3923; E 141, 322; Motreau and Vuillafans archives); Besançon archives (Deliberations of the municipal officers); Dôle archives (n.1733).

25. BURGUNDY. Millot, *Le Comité permanent de Dijon*, 1925; Patoz, *Essai sur la Rév. dans le bailliage de Saulieu pendant l'année 1789* (*Bul. Soc. de Semur*, vol. 35, 1906–7); Durandeau, *Les châteaux brûlés*, 1899; Dumay, *P.-v. de l'adm. munic. d'Auxerre pendant la Rév.* (*Bull. Soc. de l'Yonne*, vols. 45–7, 1891–3); Giraud, *Analyse des délibérations municipales d'Avallon pendant la Rév.* (*Bull. Soc. d'Études d'Avallon*, 1910–11); Tynturié, *Notice hist. sur le village de Chazeuil*, 1851; Autun archives, BB 78.

26. MÂCONNAIS. Bernard, *Tournus en 1789* (*Annales Académie de Mâcon*, 3ᵉ série, vol. 13, 1908); H. George, *Hist. du village de Davayé*, 1906; Saône-et-Loire archives, B 705, 1322, 1716–7–8, 2056, 2276; L^{II-IV} (district of Bellevue-les-Bains); the Mâcon archives, BB 230, FF67.

27. SOUTHERN BRESSE, DOMBES, BUGEY. Jarrin, *Bourg et Belley pendant la Rév.*, 1881; Bourg archives, BB 227; Karmin, *La g. p. dans le pays de Gex* (*Revue hist. de la Rév. et de l'Empire*, vol. 7, 1915); E. Dubois, *Hist. de la Rév. dans l'Ain*, vol. 1, 1931; Documents provided by M. Morel, archivist for Ain, on Trévoux and Thézillieu; Mâcon archives, FF 67; *Lettre à Camus*, Lyon, 30 July 1789 (*Rev. de la Révolution*, vol. 6, 1885).

28. LYONNAIS. *P.-v. des séances du corps municipal de la ville de Lyon*, vol. 1, 1899; Wahl, *Les premières années de la Rév. à Lyon*, 1894; Besançon, *P.-v. des séances des administrations municipales de Villefranche-sur-Saône*, vol. 1, 1904; Missol, *Les derniers jours de la milice bourgeoise de Villefranche* (*La Révolution française*, vol. 32, 1897); Le Mau de Talancé, *Cahiers de mémoires inédits de la baronne Carra de Vaux* (*Bull. Soc. du Beaujolais*, vol. XI, 1910); Rhône archives, C 6 and fonds de la maréchaussée; Bibliothèque de Lyon, fonds Costes, 110, 910, 350 494, 350 499.

29. DAUPHINÉ. Conard, *La g. p. en Dauphiné*, 1902; Riollet, *La Tour-du-Pin pendant la Rév.*, 1912; Caudrillier, *La baronnie de Thodure en 1789* (*La Révolution française*, vol. 49, 1905).

30. VIVARAIS. Régné, *La g. p. en Vivarais* (*Revue hist. de la Rév.*, vol. 10, 1916); *Une relation inédite de la révolte des masques armés* (*ibid.*, vol. 8, 1915).

31. BAS-DAUPHINÉ AND PROVENCE. Miss Pickford, *The panic of 1789 in Lower Dauphiné and Provence* (*English Historical Review*, vol. 29, 1914); Destandau, *La g. p. aux Baux* (*Bull. Soc. des Amis du Vieil Arles*, 1913); Brun, *La g. p. à Saint-Michel* (Basses-Alpes), and Honoré, *La g. p. en Basse-Provence*

(*La Révolution française*, vol. 75, 1922, p. 141); *Aix en 1789* (*Nouvelle Revue rétrospective*, 10 October 1900); Viguier, *Les débuts de la Rév. en Provence*, 1894; A. Young, *Voyages en Italie*, trans. Soulès, 1796 (exemplaire de la Bibliothèque universitaire de Strasbourg, avec annotations manuscrites, D 126 400); *Un écho de la g. p.*, *à Montélimar* (*Provincia*, revue de la Société Historique de Marseille, vol. 9, 1929).

32. BAS-LANGUEDOC AND ROUSSILLON. Comte de Foulon, *Notice des principaux événements qui se sont passés à Beaucaire depuis l'assemblée des notables en 1788*, 1836; Chabaut, *La foire de Beaucaire de 1789 à 1796* (*Annales hist. de la Rév.*, vol. 4, 1929); Rouvière, *Hist. de la Rév. dans le dép. du Gard*, vol. 1, 1887; Falgairolle, *Vauvert pendant la Rév.*, 1897; Granier, *Lunel pendant la Rév.*, 1905; Duval-Jouve, *Montpellier pendant la Rév.*, vol. 1, 1879; Joucaille, *Béziers pendant la Rév.* (*Bull. Soc. de Béziers*, 2ᵉ série, vol. 16, 1893–4); Torreilles, *Hist. du clergé dans le dép. des Pyrénées-Orientales pendant la Rév.*, 1890; *Perpignan pendant la Rév.*, 1897; Vidal, *Hist. de la Rév. dans les P.-O.*, vol. 1, 1886; du Lac, *Le général comte de Précy*, 1908 (Collioure); Armagnac, *Les premières journées de la Rév. à Caudiès* (*Revue d'hist. et d'arch. du Roussillon*, vol. 1, 1900).

33. EARLIER AND LATER FEARS. Cabié, *Paniques survenues dans le Haut-Languedoc au XVIIIᵉ siècle* (*Revue du Tarn*, 2ᵉ serie, vol. 17, 1900); Chaudron, *op. cit.*, no. 9; Chiselle, *Une panique normande en 1848* (Revue: *Le Penseur*, April 1912); Macaulay, *History of England since the Accession of James II*, chapter X; letter from Vernon, former *vicaire épiscopal* for Seine-et-Marne, 25 September 1793 (*Annales hist. de la Rév.*, 1931, p. 171); *Le Menestrel*, *op. cit.*, no. 5, p. 102; Klipffel, *La g. p. à Metz* (*Le Pays lorrain*, 1925).

Index of Place Names